THE

DIVIDE

A 2700 MILE SEARCH
FOR ANSWERS

THE
DIVIDE
A 2700 MILE SEARCH
FOR ANSWERS

NATHAN DONEEN

ThoughtBed Publishing

The Divide
A 2700 Mile Search For Answers by Nathan Doneen

Cover by Rob Allen

ISBN-13: 978-1-948371-04-9
ASIN: B0OO0SGFNE (Kindle)

ThoughtBed Publishing

This is a work of narrative nonfiction. Dialogue and events herein have been recounted to the best of the author's memory. Some details have been changed to protect those therein.

Chapter 1

Beginnings

"WHAT THE HELL AM I DOING?"

My legs burned with a week's worth of laziness, and my lungs stung with the cold morning air. I sat next to my bike in the shadow of the mountains, gravel digging into my legs. Why had I ever considered this?

"You can still bail, Nathan. Megan can't be that far away yet. You have no idea what you're doing."

My first bike tour was off to a great start. Twenty minutes earlier, my friend Megan dropped me off at a trailhead at the south end of Banff, Alberta. I had assembled my bike and packed my gear. We asked two mountain bikers to snap a few photos before I set off. Locals. My gear gave away my intentions, and my chest swelled when they said neither of them had attempted the route and only knew one guy that had—he hadn't been able to finish. Riding high on my bike, my chin to the sky, I set off into the mountains where the sun had just touched their tops. I extended my arm and gave a final wave to Megan and the mountain bikers.

Now, 1.6 miles later, instead of riding my bike, I sat next to it trying to assess the damage. I had come around a blind corner and hit a trench carved into the trail by the rain. The impact, paired with my poor pannier-packing skills, caused each of the rear plastic pannier clips to snap. I was 1.6 miles in and not sure I could effectively carry my gear. That's a problem when you're riding the Great Divide Mountain Bike Route, the longest route in the world, following the Continental Divide through two Canadian provinces and five U.S. states, reaching as far south as the Mexican border.

"What the hell am I doing?"

* * *

I wasn't a mountain biker. So why was I even out there? It all started with a graduation card given to me a year earlier. I had been at home, skipping my own college graduation. It wasn't a big deal—I planned on going to graduate school anyway. Besides, I had gone to an award ceremony the night before that was ceremonious enough. In truth, graduation was another one of those events I feared would leave me empty.

I was in the living room when there was a knock on our front door. It was Amber, my ex-girlfriend. She didn't cross the threshold, but remained on our front steps, the hideous preformed concrete that had begun to crumble at the corners. She had stopped by on her way out of town for the summer to drop off a graduation card for me. This was unexpected, but not surprising. Before Amber and I started dating, she had started sending me letters and cards, homemade and hand-written, the kind of solid sentiment you tend to hold on to in the proverbial shoebox. But Amber and I had broken up more than a year before. "Friends" is too bold a word to describe what became of us, but we were more than just cordial and polite with each other. We hadn't ended in a bad way, but our closure hadn't been satisfactory. It had just been bad timing.

Now, after a year of friendly, impromptu conversations, here was Amber on the crumbling steps. Her freckles faded behind the rising burn in her cheeks, her hand holding the card extended. I fumbled it as she let go and turned to leave, uttering a quick goodbye. I watched her go, the card unopened, as the pale blue sky carried the sounds of graduation through the door, the source only a few blocks away on top of the red turf in our football stadium.

I closed the door and opened the card. The color in my own cheeks rose. I could always trust Amber to be honest. A second, then a third reading revealed the one word that was misplaced: "man." I was one of the "greatest men" she knew? I squinted at the word and closed the card, beads of sweat on my forehead.

I had never thought of myself as a man. The previous year had been difficult, but I didn't know if it qualified me as a man. I didn't feel like a man, but maybe I should have. Why didn't I?

Amber's card raised all kinds of questions. Questions without answers. And that word: "man"—it was the inciting incident of my journey, a journey that had begun several months before.

• • •

The previous September, I was home on my family's wheat farm, working with my dad and oldest brother. Harvest was always stressful, but even more so this year. It had taken longer than usual, and we were under pressure to finish before the weather turned. I also had to get back to school, which started the following week.

The day started like any other: me in a combine harvester in a field of peas. Meanwhile, my brother's combine suffered a serious breakdown that disabled him for the majority of the day. That afternoon, when it was running again, my dad and brother traded places.

Brandon, now in a grain truck, pulled out of our shop's driveway headed for the field. Running alongside him, our dog Axel. No dog has ever known freedom as Axel did. He never knew what a fence was, or a leash, or even a collar. He roamed free, played with coyotes, tailed us all day in the fields begging for the scraps from our lunch boxes, and as any free dog would, he chased cars. In fact, he became quite notorious for it. He would occupy the middle of our narrow country roads, waiting. Drivers that knew Axel did not flinch. He always waited until the last second, but he would always move. Despite his agility, he earned us more than one visit from the police. He never once got hit though. Cars, pick-ups, school buses, grain trucks, tractors, tractor-trailers; nothing. Until that day in September.

My brother, in the grain truck for the first time that harvest, pulled from our shop's drive—Axel chasing after him—when he got "that feeling." But his quick reflexes and evasive maneuver were not enough to spare Axel. Axel's body crumpled under the suspension. My brother locked up the brakes and jumped out. Behind him on the road, our dog of 15 years lifted his head through labored breathing to look at my brother, the gravel digging into his body.

"Tim, you copy?!"

"Yeah, I got you Brandon, go ahead."

"I need to know where your gun is right now!"

"… What… what do you need my gun for?"

"I got Axel. It's not good."

I sat alone in my combine and heard the fate of Axel sealed over a CB radio, the fate of a life-long companion I had known since he was a puppy. I stopped the combine, a farming sin, but I couldn't see through my tears. Axel was lying on that road alone and afraid. I wanted to be by his side, but there was no time to get there. Now he would never again follow me through the fields; he would never again bring me a dirt clod to play fetch with; he would never again chase a car. What a crappy friend to let my dog die alone, without the ones he loved most. My brother ended Axel's suffering. His body was buried with a wheel tractor.

The day only got worse.

• • •

A week later, I was back at EWU in Cheney, Washington, home in the Biology Department. That quarter, I took my Senior Capstone, an animal physiology lecture paired with experimental research of our own design. That one class may as well have been a full-time job. I was fortunate enough to work with two of my friends in a group of five, which was no surprise—groups were assigned according to shared interests. The majority of students in the class were biology majors of the "pre-" nature: pre-med, pre-vet, pre-dent. Of course the "outdoorsy" students interested in wildlife and ecology would be assigned to each other.

The experiment we designed focused on the effects a hormone had on freshwater crayfish. This was my first time doing physiological research, and it was fascinating trying to see pass the hard exterior and into the crayfishes' interior biochemistry. We decided to use a few measurements that would help us understand how outside stresses could change the internal processes of our critters. One involved provoking our crayfish—their response was then recorded.

This was a unique project compared to any research done in that class, in that quarter or previously and, in my opinion, had the most relevance. Why not perform an original study on an ecological problem common across the country? Our project was ambitious to say the least, but our group was looking for a challenge. Our experimental design had heads turning in the department, and we had to call in every favor our super-senior (5th-year senior) status could muster.

One favor came from Dr. Hancock, the man in charge of the aquatics lab, a basement level research lab that would make any plumber shit himself. The maze of water inlets, outlets, flow meters, valves, and drains was the perfect scientific backdrop to a cement room that smelled of seafood. Not only was the research of a graduate student taking place in this lab, but so was the research of Dr. Hancock himself. We persuaded him to give us a key to this lab. The paperwork he had to fill out to get a copy was justification enough to deny us the convenience of our own key, but we were convincing. When we got our key, the number of people who had access to that lab doubled.

Once our research proposal was approved by a review committee, we ordered our crayfish from a biological supply company. Our order was for 30, but orders of this nature always included extra specimens in case shipping was too much for some. We expected 35 crawdads would be shipped. Of those that survived, 24 would be part of the experiment.

The supply company shipped 50 crayfish.

They all survived.

* * *

"Please enter your password."

We had unpacked and found housing for all 50 crayfish, a number we were unprepared for. Once we reached that milestone, we called it quits. With the extra time at home, I ran our bins down to the recycling center a few blocks away. I was gone 15 minutes and found a new voicemail waiting for me when I got back.

"Hey Nathan, it's Jake. Listen man, I just got a call. We fucked up. Hancock is saying we need to get all of our stuff out of his lab…today. I just got home, but I'm headed back to campus now. Give me a call if you can't make it. If not, I'll see you soon."

My heart clenched, not rhythmically the way it was meant to though. For the first time in weeks, I had felt good. One missed call and one voicemail later, I was red in the face, my heartbeat was in my ears, and my head was buried in my hands to catch the groan that came out. I grabbed my bag and headed for campus.

We were moved from the lowest point of the building, the aquatics lab, to the highest, most removed part of the Biology Department: the greenhouse. The direction of this move in no way reflected the change in our status, but the magnitude did. We went from being the golden students with the highly original, ambitious, interesting experiment to those students that almost ruined actual research.

In our attempt to house our 25 extra crayfish, we turned on a water supply valve we shouldn't have. The opened valve caused a pressure drop elsewhere in the system, the in-flow to the hot tub-sized aquaria that housed Dr. Hancock's fish. The out-flow, regulated by a different system, remained the same and caused a slow, steady drop of the water level in his aquaria. Luckily, I had sent Dr. Hancock an email to give him an update of what we had been up to. When he stepped in to check on our work, he discovered his fish in too little water. We had almost killed his fish and wasted months of time he had invested into his study. He wasn't pleased. He wanted us out.

After we relocated, we went searching for Dr. Hancock. I expected him to be livid. When we found him he was anything but. He played the classic "not angry, just disappointed" card. I would have preferred him to yell and let out his frustration at us. But he was calm, collected. I couldn't say the same about me. Standing in the white, windowless hallway outside his office, I pulled the lab key from my keychain and held it out to him, as requested. The loss of the key was a big blow, but what it represented was even more devastating: the loss of Dr. Hancock's respect.

Chapter 2

June 2013

RESPECT.

Here I was losing it again, crouched over my bike at mile 1.6.

The air had lost its brisk edge, and my breath was once again invisible. Sweat glazed my palms and my heart raced as I tried to get moving again, not for the purpose of progress, but so I could leave behind the disdainful stares of the mountain peaks that looked down on me as the rising sun woke them.

My panniers lay on the ground while I adjusted the rear cargo rack when the cyclists from the parking lot came around that blind corner. They flew past without hesitation, not stopping to check on me. I sighed as they disappeared down the trail. I'm not sure I could have handled the embarrassment of admitting to these cyclists I had no idea what I was doing—cyclists that had had the slightest hint of reverence in their voices when we spoke just 30 minutes before. I could barely handle the chuckle I thought echoed back up the trail from their direction.

I adjusted the cargo rack and packing arrangement and used zip ties to secure what was left of the two broken pannier clips. They held, but how long would they last? The next bike shop was back in the States, some 300 miles away. Banff was right behind me, 1.6 miles backwards.

"This is crucial Nathan. This is going to set the tone of the whole trip."

Go back? Or press on?

Before I set out, I decided to avoid going backwards at all cost. It was the opposite of progress, but it was only 1.6 miles back to the trailhead. Maybe a total of 2.5 to the bike shop? I could solve the problem, or I could take my chances. I could go backwards or move forwards with a debilitated setup.

"This is a crucial decision."

The next 20 miles went much smoother than the first 1.6. I did stop and tighten every bolt of the cargo rack assembly after it was shook to pieces, but the sun filled valley made the day perfect for a ride. I cringed at my decision not to return to Banff, but only before I cracked a wide grin. The broken panniers might become a bigger problem, or they just might become a great story to tell my friends. No, a few pieces of broken plastic would not stop me. They would not force me to turn around. They would not weaken my resolve. Why should they? People have done greater things than this, in the face of adversity greater than any broken pannier clip. If anything, my resolve was strengthened.

Cycling along Spray Lake, I saw my first cyclist. Already? I guessed it would have taken longer to run into someone else riding the route, at least more than three hours on the first day. My pace was quicker than his, and it wasn't long before I caught him. His name was Freddie, and he was from Switzerland. Although he said he was impressed with my light load, he wasn't as thrilled about having me for company. He claimed he was stopping for a break after just a few minutes of riding with me. A break Freddie? Only three miles from where you camped the night before? I didn't want to be a nuisance, so I left Freddie sitting along the shade-less talus bank of the reservoir.

Several hundred yards farther, I crossed a bridge and glanced up a deep canyon to find the source of a thunder. I turned my bike around and left it on the side of the trail while I hiked up a small hill. This would have been a much better rest location, Freddie. The angular fractures of the canyon walls had been smoothed where the water flowed. Water that was robin's egg blue appeared from nowhere, fell five feet into a small pool, and continued down another 25-foot fall, the blues abandoned for the white spray that vanished into the shadows of the canyon below.

• • •

A smattering of rain began as I climbed away from the banks of

Spray Lake. The rain's light drumming on my waterproof material was joined by the rattle of my gear as another pannier clip broke as well as one of the repair zip-ties. I pushed up the remainder of the hill and stopped on level ground to assess the situation. Had I made the wrong decision to not return to Banff? Only 30 miles in and suffering from my gear situation was daunting. Knowing I still had more than 250 miles before I would have the chance to find replacements was unfathomable.

Zip-ties were not a viable solution to my pannier problem. I snacked on some Pop-Tarts and mulled things over while I decided on a course of action. In my gear, I had 50 feet of cord and a carabiner to suspend my food at night to prevent animals from snooping, especially bears. During the day though, these items had no purpose—until now. A variety of knots and friction hitches transformed the cordage and carabiner into the main support for the panniers. Was it pretty? Not a chance. Was it functional? I hoped.

As I arranged the cord on my panniers, a familiar face crept up over the crest of the hill. Freddie stopped, but still straddled his bike.

"Is everything all right?"

"Yeah, it's just my pannier clips are breaking. I think the panniers are too full for how hard some of these hits are, so I'm reinforcing them."

I was using the carabiner to tighten the cord when Freddie reached into his handlebar bag. I looked up at the click of his camera shutter. At least my panniers would make a good story for someone. What I would give for a copy of those pictures now. Freddie continued on as I finished securing my panniers. It was 5 minutes after that I was moving again, now with wobbly panniers, but without the fear of them falling off.

The light sprinkle continued as I emerged from the trail's tree cover onto a wide road. The sun was fully consumed by the clouds and the mountains began to disappear beneath the slate gray as well. I urged forward, trying to catch Freddie and trying to outrun the coming weather. I coasted down a hill and automatically applied the brakes as my next obstacle came into sight.

"You've got to be kidding me."

This was not the first time I had seen a moose. This was not the first time I had been this close to a moose. However, this was the first time a moose had been in my way. She was standing in the middle of a bridge only wide enough to accommodate one vehicle at a time on its wood planks. I wanted to appreciate my first wildlife encounter, but the long valley was disappearing in the waves of rain the wind carried towards me. This was not the ideal time to stop.

I pulled on my rain jacket as the first wave reached me. The rain, pushed sideways by the wind, raised the skin of my exposed legs; the wind circled me and whipped the fabric of my clothing; the moose didn't move. If she was bothered by the sudden weather change, she didn't show any sign of it. She remained where I found her, inhibiting my progress.

A pickup sat on the other side of the road. Where was the driver? It was apparent the driver, like the moose, was unperturbed by the rain. After a few minutes without any sign of the driver, I pushed my bike to the back end of the pickup where its orientation to the wind created a small rain shadow.

The moose milled around on the bridge for another fifteen minutes. My backside started to complain about the pointed gravel sapping the heat from my body; my joints whined about the cold air; water dripped from my helmet. Then a few things happened at once. My small section of sheltered road became inundated with runoff making its way down the road; a car approached the bridge opposite the side I was on; and the moose, jarred back to awareness by the car's horn, left the bridge and disappeared behind the tree line. I waved a shivering limb at the driver to offer my thanks and picked up my bike. Within seconds of leaving the rain shadow, I was drenched.

• • •

During the delay, I learned from my map that across the bridge was a turn that would take me to a lodge. It wouldn't hurt to stop in and see if I could wait out the rain, so I made the turn. I nestled my bike in a corner of the lodge, under an eve and found the door. I stepped inside and was greeted by Chris.

"Hi there. It looks wet out there."

"Just a little."

"Maybe more than a little. You must be a racer?"

"No, but I am doing a tour on the same route. I was just wondering if I could wait out the rain here?"

"Yeah, of course. Let me show you in."

Chris showed me where to hang my gear, still dripping with water, and led me to the lodge's dining room where I was offered coffee and tea. Chris knew all about the bike route and was a big fan of the race, which had been through only three days before me.

The race, the Tour Divide, was an annual collection of adventure cyclists that rode the whole route solo and unsupported. Racers could choose between an independent time trial or the Grand Depart, the official start. Racers carried GPS locators that were linked to the race's website. If you knew a racer's name, they could be located at any time.

Chris updated me on the racers and their locations, then returned to work leaving me with a mug of tea cupped in my soggy hands. Its warmth spread through my fingers while my eyes traced the red line that traversed the map laid out in front of me.

The 2,700-mile route was broken into seven maps and all were bisected by the red line that marked the official route. This was the line I would be following for the next several weeks. My goal was to average 80 miles a day. To reach that goal on day one meant crossing Elk Pass. I looked up from my map and through the large windows of the lodge. Rain blotted out the valley. Maybe Elk Pass would have to wait.

"Hi there. I just wanted to let you know that our guests will be served an afternoon snack in about an hour. You are more then welcome to join everyone if you would like."

"That sounds wonderful."

"Or, if you are hungry now, I can heat up some of the leftovers from last night's dinner for you."

"Really?! That would be amazing. What's your name?"

"I'm Shari-Lynn."

Shari-Lynn was Chris's wife and they managed the lodge together. I was taken aback by the kindness I received from Chris and Shari-Lynn. With the warmth returned to my hands, I pulled out my journal and wrote an entry about them.

"Here you are," Shari-Lynn said as she placed a bowl of steaming food in front of me. She leaned in with a lowered voice and said, "We don't serve our guests food outside of scheduled meals and snacks, so if anyone asks, you work here, ok?"

I held back a chuckle. "Of course. Again, thank you so much."

With a smile, she returned to her upright posture. "And don't forget to finish chopping that wood when the rain clears up," Shari-

Lynn said with a wink.

• • •

Two hours later, I returned to the bike with improved spirits. I pulled my bike from the corner, began to walk down the drive, and turned back for one last look. Would I remember this place? Would my feelings of gratitude for the lodge, Chris, and Shari-Lynn persist? They were immensely important to me today, but where would I be in four, five, six weeks? With the hope my memory was longer than the mountain's, I set out into a landscape lost to the fact it had just experienced a heavy rain. Blue hues dominated the sky, accented by the white wisps of clouds and sharp snowcaps. Had it just rained?

With my renewed vigor, I put Elk Pass in my sights, the first Continental Divide crossing of several. I found the parking lot where the climb began and started up what the map called a "virtual wall." There was no argument to be made about that. The hike alone made my legs throb and lungs burn while the sound of my breathing drowned out all other noise—forget riding up it. After a short descent and second steep climb, the trail emerged from the trees and into a clear-cut where a set of power lines crossed the range. The sun was warm still, but not warm enough to evaporate the rain that had fallen earlier. Riding through this mud was difficult. I walked most of this segment but fought my exhaustion long enough to find the top of Elk Pass.

There was no celebrating when I crossed through the gate that marked the top. The long day of riding paired with my pannier problems left me tired and unconcerned with my first crossing. Was it monumental? No, it was just another pedal stroke underfoot, a landmark on the map that could now be crossed off. What's next? What landmark would I use to track my progress tomorrow? That was what the route would become: goal after goal after goal. Always looking forward. Progress now, reflection later.

I removed my sunglasses and zipped my jacket as I rode into the mountain's shadow. Was it time to unpack my warm sleeping bag yet? The map showed a cabin available along the route, on a first come, first served basis. This was my goal for the night; if it wasn't available I would camp along the road.

It wasn't.

Clothes hung from the porch. My line-of-sight extended as I coasted past. Against the cabin was a bicycle, then a picnic table, then a stove, then the cyclist. It was none other than Freddie. I had caught him.

I remembered his early break and kept coasting, sure he didn't want my company. He turned at the sound of the gravel beneath my tires and we waved to each other.

I had never considered myself to be that competitive, but the sight of Freddie stirred something in me. With a new burst of energy, I kept going. Every mile I covered would be that much more I had done in my first day than Freddie had done in his first two.

Ten miles down the road was a campsite nestled alongside the Elk River. A fire ring was situated near a picnic table, the remnants of beer cans among the ashes, the brands unknown to me. There was also a small outhouse at the end of a short trail, its paint faded and peeling and its hinges in need of oil. The river water was fresh, icy, and fast flowing. The small bits of dry wood I gathered helped to warm my legs after a quick rinse in the water. The small flames were hypnotizing as they tasted the aluminum cans. The popping of the wood became less frequent and gave way to another sound: the crackle of gravel. A cyclist came down the road, passed my camp, and had crossed the bridge to the far side of the river before he saw me. When he turned around, I walked out to the road to greet him.

What a light load! A full suspension bike with a frame bag, a seat bag, and small handlebar bag. I was still inspecting his bike when the rider removed his hand from an insulated glove and extended it.

"Are you racing?" I said.

"Yup."

"Did you start today?"

"No."

"Did you start with the race?" This guy looked way too experienced to have started with the Grand Depart three days earlier. But he didn't start today?

"I actually started in May … down in Mexico. I headed out of Banff this morning and am heading back to Mexico."

Who was this cowboy? None other than Billy Rice, a veteran of the Tour Divide bike race. No one had ever attempted a yo-yo style ride of the route. Billy decided he would be the first.

"Are you a rookie?" Billy said, meaning if it was my first time on the route.

"Yeah, this is my first bike tour actually."

"What kind of pace are you aiming for?"

"I'm hoping to average about 80 miles a day."

"Yeah, that's a pretty moderate pace, you should be able to do that."

Moderate? Not for me, Billy. Thanks for the vote of confidence though, and the advice. Billy told me about places to rest, towns to resupply, sections of the route that were challenging. The guy had one foot on his bike pedal the whole time we were talking, yet he took the time to impart a bit of wisdom to me. I was grateful to listen.

"And be careful with your gear in camp," he said, pointing to my suspended bags. "I've seen a ton of bears this year. A couple today even."

With a final handshake, Billy remounted his bike and leaned on his aerobars, head ducked and hands gloved, the final light of the day failing. That would be my only encounter with Billy Rice, but not the last I would hear of him.

Chapter 3

I HATE RAIN.

I hate mud.

This sucks.

I battled with a mud-clogged drivetrain and front fork my second morning. In 30 minutes I had travelled 500 yards. If it weren't for the thick growth of evergreens, I would have still been able to see where I camped. I used sticks to dig the mud from my bike and left tracks that I'm sure were visible for weeks after. I cussed the mud and the rain and threw sticks at both. The day had started bad, even before the mud had stopped me in my tracks, literally.

In the several months that led up to my ride, I researched the route by reading books and blogs of people who had completed the route before. Based on that reading, I wanted to make my load as light as possible. To accommodate that goal, I gave up a tent for a smaller, lighter bivy sack. As far as bivies went, it was a spacious model—big enough to require two poles. Apart from the smaller volume, this particular type of shelter does away with some other comforts to cut weight, like ventilation.

My bivy had one door made of two panels: one mesh and the other a waterproof nylon. The inner mesh door was the only ventilation. That meant closing the outer door would prevent air from circulating. Despite the label that warned of such dangers, I didn't consider it a problem. All I had to do was not close the outer door all the way.

Of course, I didn't think of that when I woke up in the middle of my first night. I was dead tired from my first day of riding, which is why I was so confused when I woke with no trace of grogginess. I was very alert given the early hour. Why?

Something was wrong, but what? Was there an animal outside? Did I need to pee? Was I just thirsty? No, none of those were right. What was the deal? I laid there for almost a full minute before I heard it. Pounding. A rapid, rhythmic pounding. Well, what the hell was that? Now focused on the noise, I couldn't believe it had taken so long to notice it. Then there was another sound, almost as loud. Breathing. This breathing was not normal though. It was fast and shallow. How had I not heard that? Crap! That was my breathing. That was my heartbeat.

I reached to my neck to feel my pulse. It was insanely fast. And my breathing—hyperventilating. Why? I rolled over to look at the door. Closed. I reached to open it and felt my backpack beneath my arm. Wet. With the door open, I crawled up to the fresh air and breathed deep. Within 30 seconds, my heart rate began to slow.

Wide awake and physically strained, I felt like an idiot. Wow, Nathan. How had this happened? The cool air moved down the length of my bivy as I pieced together what had happened. My best guess, it started to rain while I slept, which caused me to zip the door completely closed. Not fully conscious, I gave it no thought. Until I woke.

That morning, I had a good chance to think about my first day in its entirety while I packed. Broken panniers rigged with cord, an inconsiderate moose and rainstorm, a suffocating bivy sack. I chuckled at the irony of it. I had told myself if I just pushed hard for the first few days of the ride—hard enough to make them difficult— the rest of the ride might be easier by comparison. Well, I was getting what I wanted. Challenge after challenge. These were not the kind of difficulties I had anticipated though.

Oh man, that would have been awful if I had suffocated.

Imagine the headlines.

Amateur bike tourist suffocates in his bivy, on his first night, of his first tour.

I could see Billy Rice reading the embarrassingly long headline, the paper spread out across his handlebars as he effortlessly pedaled his way across the Mexican border, and giving his head two slow shakes as if to say, "I knew it."

Like the water did the dirt, negative thoughts saturated my mind. Any amount of pressure squeezed them to the surface. Once I made it to more solid terrain, it began to rain harder. Not only that, but what I thought was going to be a descent into Elkford was more of a roller coaster ride.

I rolled into town on fumes, feeling like I had climbed back up Elk Pass. Not a good feeling when I had only covered 30 miles. I searched for a restaurant; a solid meal would make me feel better. One milkshake and half a burger later I felt like vomiting. Did not having enough oxygen through the night prevent my recovery? Today's first 30 miles felt like a continuation of yesterday's mileage. Being burnt out so early made me apprehensive. Not wanting to push too hard too soon, I took the rest of the day off. Because it was only midday with rain in the forecast, I skipped the campground and got a hotel room.

When my afternoon nap failed, I wandered over to a small mall and found a hardware store. Twenty minutes later I was back in my hotel room, the contents of my panniers scattered across the floor. I sat in the middle, my empty gear bags in my lap as I threaded them with 50 feet of brand new quarter inch rope. It took the rest of the night, but my bear hang cord was spared from its double duty. And the new rope was glow-in-the-dark.

● ● ●

"You're going to be riding your bike today?" The hotel clerk couldn't help but ask, her mouth slightly open and head cocked to the side. She was nine minutes late opening the front desk. Maybe she was one of the karaoke singers in the bar last night, the bar directly underneath my room. Lullabies hadn't yet made a comeback in the karaoke world, and I regretted that fact as I lay in bed the night before, staring at the ceiling, thinking about how much I needed to sleep.

The next morning, my bike was packed and propped against the wall next to the hotel door. I had already donned my rain gear, backpack, and helmet. I had paced, back and forth. Outside, the sky was a uniform gray. The pacing had continued while I waited for her to show up, glancing at the clock every few seconds. Nine minutes would normally not be an issue for me. Today was different though.

"That's the plan. I'm starting early so I can try to outrun the rain this afternoon," I said.

"This afternoon? I think it's going to start raining any second. That's how the clouds looked on my way in," she said, her head cocking farther and farther.

"Well, it's the afternoon rain I am most worried about."

"You mean the advisory?"

Yes, the advisory. When you spend a great deal of time outside, you have an inflated interest in the weather. Watching the news the night before, hoping to catch a forecast, I learned that Environment Canada had issued a Heavy Rainfall Advisory to southern Alberta and all of British Columbia for the afternoon of my third day.

"Yes, I mean the advisory," I said while I signed my name and turned over my room key.

"You plan to ride your bike through that? That's supposed to be a really big storm. You won't stop before then?"

"I don't know. I'm just going to see how things go, but I'd like to get ahead of it. I can't imagine being caught in it would be very fun."

"Well, good luck. I hope you make it through ok."

"Thanks, so do I."

I wheeled my bike through the door, eyelids heavy, and my ears still ringing with Bon Jovi, but I felt both poised and determined. The afternoon was a long way off, and I aimed to cover as much ground as I could until the rain started to fall.

It was amazing how the route had a mind of its own. Not just a mind, but a pretty selfish, borderline narcissistic, personality. I had been mentally preparing for that afternoon. A bit jealous, the morning slapped me across the face to bring my focus back to where I was. Climbing. Slowly. Up a 2-mile stretch. And just as the hotel front desk had forecasted, it started to rain. The moisture turned the pavement a glossy black, charcoals doused with water. The sky was dressed to match, the charcoal having rubbed off on the feathery white clouds I would have rather seen. The charcoal also rubbed off on my mood.

After the tediousness of the first 2 miles, I topped out and had an easier cruise on the flat pavement among a pine forest bisected by rail and dotted with evidence of mining. My map funneled water over the directions that kept me tracing the red line and took me onto a gravel road. Desperate for some help, I stopped at the turn and turned on my mp3 player for some motivation. I pedaled to the beat and began to sing. Soon the rain wasn't that bad, the loose gravel became fun, and—do I dare say?—I was having a good time.

My singing lasted to Sparwood, despite having to navigate my bike by foot through a rockslide and having to ride along a busy interstate. Music was the source of my smile, and I decided to leave my earphones in while on the interstate. If I was going to get hit by a semi, would the blaring of a horn in the seconds prior to collision make a huge difference? Doubtful … Crap! A semi passed me. Caught off guard, I had flinched and my handlebars took a dangerous wobble. My headphones came out when the shoulder narrowed.

I ate in Sparwood, and for the first time in days, I felt replenished. It was during that meal that I decided to follow an alternate route. It was a few miles shorter than the main route, but more importantly, it had virtually no climbing when compared to the main route that headed into the mountains. I was reluctant to leave behind the red line for the alternate route, marked in yellow, but with the afternoon rain advisory, I didn't want to be slowed down.

Leaving Sparwood, the clouds broke and the sun led the way out of town, all the way to a construction zone. There, the flagger told me I would get to lead the procession of cars through the site. On my gear laden bike? Uphill? A half-mile? At least it wasn't raining.

● ● ●

The rainless weather lasted almost 40 miles from Sparwood and had just started again in Elko. I pulled off to refuel at the 3&93 Dairy Bar, a roadside burger and shake stand.

"Can I please get a burger and chocolate shake?"

My bike did not go unnoticed and this would not be the last time it would serve as a conversation piece.

"Only if you tell us where you're headed."

"Well, I'm hoping to make it to Mexico."

"You too!? We just had a group of three here yesterday headed there too." He turned to pass the slip containing my order back to the grill. "Did you guys here that? He's headed to Mexico too."

The Dairy Bar made my stomach heavy with the food and my heart light with the conversation. I was ready to get back at it. The rain had continued the entire time I ate and it showed no sign of letting up. It was a light rain, though, that only caused problems when water from the road travelled the parabolic arc from my tire to my eyes. That would soon change.

Four miles later, it was torrential. Water poured off of me as though I stood in a shower: water flowed into my ears; I blinked water from my eyelashes; I blew water from the tip of my nose to keep from inhaling it.

But still I pedaled.

I wanted to get through the rain and out of Canada. I had liked Canada and all the friendly interactions I had there, but I was behind schedule. I had hoped to be back in the States already. Now I had the motivation: rain.

It came down in sheets. No, it came down in waves. Like a swimmer in the ocean, all I could do was hold my breath, lower my head, and let it wash over me. It wasn't long before I was soaked. But still I pedaled.

What the heck?

Why does my knee hurt?

At mile 80 of the day, my right knee began to throb. In my research, I found that old injuries sometimes surfaced in the first few days of the ride. These injuries would either make you or break you, with a tendency to either vanish at two weeks or become crippling. I had hyperextended my knee once, almost eight years before. I led a pretty active lifestyle through all of college and had had no problems from my knee. I didn't have any problem during my training for the route either. This pain was unexpected.

The pulse in my knee wouldn't be ignored though. After several miles the pain had increased in intensity and my heart apparently relocated to my knee. I gave in and stopped to dig the Ibuprofen from my backpack. As fast as I had unslung the pack from my shoulder and reached for the zipper, I started to have trouble opening it. My hand and arm shook uncontrollably.

Instant shivering? Not good.

I had been soaked through for a while, but being on the bike with the constant movement of my legs, I hadn't realized how cold I was. I threw a couple of pills in my mouth and swallowed; I forwent the wash down, sick of water. I had to shake my map off just to read it. The closest campground was a long way off. I scanned the area. I didn't care that the land was private; I just wanted something to shelter under. But the foliage was thin, the ground uneven, and the water came from every direction. To search for a suitable place to camp would have been to risk the loss of more body heat. If my whole body trembled after a few minutes of inactivity, setting up camp was no longer a luxury. I needed to generate some heat.

My legs were heavy and my bike swayed as my arms tried to help lift them. I pushed past the daily mileage I had trained for. My legs were overtaxed acting as both my engine and as my heater. The map became harder to read, harder to focus on and comprehend. I missed a turn. My mistake became apparent when the road I was on dead-ended. I pedaled right through a gate and onto an unfinished private driveway.

As I turned around, the saturated clay washed out from under both tires and I went down, hard. The clay bled water where I had landed. I pushed myself up to escape the puddle that grew in my imprint. The soil turned my left side tan. I walked back to the gate where the pavement ended and noticed the fall had bent one of the aluminum stays of my cargo rack.

The rain soon cleaned my gear and all traces of the fall were washed away. Almost a mile from where I fell, I found the missed turn. I smiled at the signpost, but shook my head at it too. It was good to be back on track, but these were not good riding conditions. I didn't want to ride any further than was necessary. My smile vanished; it was driven off by the crack of a whip.

Thunder?

Under normal circumstances, it might have been loud, but the rain was so heavy that every surface became a snare, a bongo, a tympani. The drumming and thrumming of this orchestra was constrained to a room meant for chamber music. Maybe I had imagined the thunder.

My doubt vanished when the clouds to my right flickered. I groaned.

The next few minutes were tense. Should I abandon the ride and set up shelter? Or ignore the lightning and press on? If I stopped to set up camp, I would have to take my chances with hypothermia. With the large volume of rain coming down, could I even keep dry? If I kept riding, I would have to take my chances with the lightning. There were tall trees along the road—they would be struck before me, right?

It came down to the math. I was sure the average person was more likely to become hypothermic than to be struck by lightning.

May as well choose the lesser of two evils. Now, I'm not a complete dunce. People are less likely to be struck by lightning because anyone with an iota of sense knows to take shelter during a lightning storm. This was of no comfort though, so I had to ignore that bit of logic.

All right Nathan. Let's keep going. You can do this.

Besides, death by lightning would be better than hypothermia. And it would sure be a hell of a lot cooler than suffocating, on my first night, of my first bike tour.

The cracking sky moved closer. The spot light was almost upon me. Time began to pass slowly as I counted the seconds between the white arc left by the hammer and the sound of its crash on an atmospheric anvil. I gave up my timing when the pungent sparks thrown from the anvil met my nose. Ozone. I was in the thick of it. I had forgotten the throb in my knee.

Holy shit!

A lightning strike. The bolt had been damn near on top of me. Everything lit up under this flash bulb with an intensity only the sun could understand. It was like seeing for the first time. Every leaf and pine needle on every branch, every cleft and crack in all the bark, every shard of gravel on the road in high definition, still visible through every raindrop freeze-framed in mid-descent. The world had been so bright that I flinched at its illumination. I have no memory of the sound.

My hands tightened on the handlebars. My head dropped. I began to shiver again, but not because of the cold. I wished I was under a shelter; I wished I was in a hotel; I wished I was home. But my legs kept at the cranks. What else could I do? Then the rain fell harder. Stopping wasn't possible. There weren't any houses or outbuildings in sight. It was a desperate situation.

Then something incredible happened.

My hands relaxed. My head lifted. I chuckled. An honest, happy-go-lucky, top-of-the-world chuckle. It was all out of my hands. Regardless of what I did, I had to take a chance and risk my well-being. I had no choice. My relief may have been counterintuitive, but it washed over me as sure as the rain. Yes, I chose to ride the route; yes, I chose to ride that day; yes, I chose to race the storm. But once I was in that storm and my choices limited, I was absolved.

The next fifteen minutes were the most incredible of my life. It was the first time I had ever lived in the present moment. It destroyed my illusion of life being a timeline. I took nothing for granted: not my sore knee, pruny skin, or low body temperature. My exhaustion was invigorating, and my numb hands could fend off giants. I felt Death running behind me, his skeletal hand on the bottom of my seat, pushing me along like a father teaching his son to ride a bike. I also felt life, in a new way, both foreign and familiar. It was like I saw the younger brother of a dear friend, the same features etched in both faces, but each with their own character. My legs kept pedaling, but now with Death pushing my seat as each brother took a handlebar. I experienced a calm, a comfort, a crowded solitude.

The hammer struck the anvil, again, right above me. And again, every detail was thrown into high relief. Every leaf and needle. Every cleft and crack. Every shard. It was seeing for the first time, and it was stunning.

● ● ●

"You must've come down the alternate, huh?" she said, seated below the level of the counter. My shaking hands dug for coins in my bag.

The lightning had passed. I took what it offered, and it had moved on. As it left the rain let up, and the throb in my knee returned. I stopped at a small gas station market in Grasmere. Drips of water ran up and down the aisles, marking my route through the store as I looked for something, anything that sounded appealing. I grabbed an orange juice and a Mars Bar, trying to match their price to my Canadian coins. I was 10 miles from the border.

"Yeah, I started in Elkford today and just wanted to get out of here, out of the rain as fast as possible." I cracked the seal on the orange juice and drank half the bottle in a single gulp. "Do you mind if I just hang out in here a bit while I eat this?"

"Of course not," she said. "You look like you need a break from the weather. Did you get hailed on at all?"

"Hail? No. You got hail here?"

"Yeah, no more than 20 minutes before you got here. It was good-size too." I couldn't believe my luck. The weather had been horrible over the last 30 miles, but it could have been worse. "And it was good you came down the alternate. The main route is just a few miles from here, up in the mountains and I know its snowing up there. You're lucky you didn't get caught up there."

My choice of route validated, I took the second and final gulp of the orange juice. We talked about the route and the race. Everyone loved to talk about the racers, especially since they had come through just a few days prior. My Mars Bar wrapper empty, I thanked her for letting me rest and apologized for the puddle I left in front of the counter.

"Oh it's ok. It will dry up before the next customer comes through anyway."

I stepped out into the rain again, threw my leg over my bike, and clipped my shoe into my pedal. I was almost to the border.

● ● ●

At the border crossing, I waited in line with the cars. My shivering wasn't constant; rather, it came in waves, big waves. Tremors started at my core and radiated outwards to the tips of my limbs. My hands were blind to my passport, unable to seize it on the first, second, even third try with my bluish fingers. It was such a trivial problem after the day I had just had.

Got it!

The border patrolman raised his hand and waved me forward. I circumnavigated the speed bumps, passport secured in my mouth as I rode up to him. What a sight I must have been. Despite my rain gear, I was completely soaked. Water still dripped from my helmet and ran down my neck. My cheeks were red, my hands blue, and my yellow panniers held together with that ridiculous glow-in-the-dark rope. I had a stripe of sand and dirt on my jacket, sprayed on by my front tire. I planted my feet, handed over my passport, and leaned on the padded armrests of my aerobars.

"Are you racing?"

Racing? Why was it the racers were the only ones that got respect? This route was a lot harder than you realized, bud. Anyone with the courage to attempt this route deserved a lot of respect. It must have been so easy where you were, sitting in your warm little hut, watching everyone go by.

"No. Just riding," I said. "For fun." I almost forgot to mention that part.

After a few standard questions, I was sent packing.

"There's a bathroom up and to the left if you want to …" he looked me up and down, "clean up." The patrolman's only contribution. I didn't even get a "good luck."

I did take advantage of the bathroom though and dug sand from my eyes and wrung out my gloves and jersey. The shelter was nice, but I had another 10 miles to cover, preferably before dark; it was already 7 p.m. As I emerged from the complex of buildings, I saw the sky for the first time since my first day riding. It was only a sliver through a small break in the clouds, low on the horizon, but it had a calming effect.

By 8 p.m., I made it to the town of Eureka. I had to talk my legs into moving, even at a few gears lower than usual. It had been a long day; 13 hours of riding that covered 110 miles. My conversation about the rain advisory with the nine-minutes-late-to-work hotel clerk was an eternity ago.

The hotel room that night was worth every penny. I unpacked everything in my panniers, washed my soaked clothes, and hung everything to dry. After I rinsed all the sand and silt from the tub, it was my turn for a soak.

I would later learn that the storm I had ridden through dumped almost two and a half inches of rain in as many hours. The area I grew up in, a region of non-irrigated farms, receives about 17 inches of rain annually. I experienced more than two months of rain in a single afternoon. Cold rain and a hot bath. It was amazing how different water temperatures led to completely different experiences.

Chapter 4

October 2011

"NATHAN, I've been meaning to talk to you."

"Yeah?"

"Well, you know Shane is leaving at the end of the quarter?"

"Yup."

Kevin led the way up the narrow trail to the slab of granite, me on his heels, both of us weighed down by large bags of climbing gear on our backs. There was a bite in the air. It was a late fall day, and despite the sun and cloudless sky, the briskness persisted.

We were hiking up the backside of Minnehaha, a large rock outcrop frequented by rock climbers. I worked for my university's outdoor program as a supervisor and teacher in the Rec Center's rock climbing gym. It was a sweet gig. That quarter, I taught one class and part of the curriculum was an outdoor climbing trip. For one afternoon, I got to leave everything behind and take a break from the stresses of school.

My boss, Kevin, and I were headed to the top of the outcrop to build anchors and set up ropes for our beginner climbers.

"Well, I was wondering if you would be interested in taking over some of his responsibilities?"

Shane was an upstanding guy and one heck of an employee and assistant manager. He was also one of my greatest friends. It would take two, maybe three employees to absorb all of the duties he had taken upon himself. Our rock climbing gym would not have run without him.

"Which responsibilities are we talking about?"

"Well, for starters, you would be made an assistant manager and would take over scheduling."

The heat rose in my face. Everyone knew Shane was graduating at the end of the quarter and would no longer be working at the gym. My other good buddy, Joe, had hoped, almost expected to absorb Shane's job and get the promotion to assistant manager. He was the staff member that had been working there longest. He was there when I was first learned to climb. Conversely, I took a year to rise from an unpaid assistant teacher to a teacher and prominent supervisor. But I had not expected my friend's promotion to go to me.

"Can I have a few days to think about it, Kevin?"

"Yeah, of course."

●   ●   ●

In college I developed what most teachers considered to be bad study habits. Everything was put off until the last minute. Not for a lack of time or effort, but because I thrived on the pressure. Whatever the task at hand was, finishing an assignment, studying for a test, writing a paper, I completed the task more efficiently if I did it last minute.

Now, even with the immense workload of my capstone class, I wanted more. The events of September still weighed on my mind, and I wanted to escape them. The pressure of a deadline could push anything from my mind, and it did. I equated more work to more clarity. Now Kevin gave me the chance to have it. The promotion and additional responsibilities would keep me busy, too busy to give thought to much else in life. That's what I was after.

"Joe, Kevin offered me the assistant manager position." He was quiet. For Joe, that was unusual. "What are you thinking?"

"Did you take it?"

"I wanted to talk to you first." He leaned back in his chair and sighed. "Are you mad?"

"Not at you," he said, "I'm just mad I didn't get the offer. I've been here too long to not be promoted or given a raise at least." After another moment of silence: "You should take it. It's a good job."

"Are you sure?"

"Yeah man. I'm happy for you."

That's a rare friend.

In addition to my usual responsibilities, I started to work with Shane and learn the nuances of his job. My schedule now overflowed. I left the house early in the morning and didn't return until late at night. My education and my job began to bear down on me, leaving me to act on instinct alone—just how I wanted it.

Chapter 5

HMM...IT'S RAINING.

My clock said 11:15, and I was just getting on the road. My late arrival to Eureka the previous day made for a late night, which had now become a late start. But I left the motel warm and with dry gear. The only thing to complain about was my fatigue. The 110 miles of the day before was the longest distance I had ever covered in a single day; my legs had no problem letting me know.

The first 10 miles out of Eureka were awful. The dreary gray of the rain had leaked down onto everything below. There was a complete lack of color to the landscape, as if it were a picture that had been spilled upon and the ink had run. I compensated with the bright fluorescence of my Jolly Ranchers. Soon, my tongue would be the most colorful feature in sight.

Twenty miles into my ride, I began to wonder if I should have taken a rest day. I wasn't sore apart from my knee, but I was so drained, so depleted, so defeated. That was not the best realization to have when at the bottom of a 15-mile climb through the rain. That was when the unthinkable happened: I ran out of Jolly Ranchers.

Savoring the last sugary morsel, I began a slow ascent using my lowest gears on the segments I didn't walk. I was on my bike, straining for every crank of the sprockets, when I saw more evidence of the day's dreariness. A large black mass approached the road from the downhill side, about 15 yards ahead of me.

Wait. Large? Black? Moving uphill?

Bear!

The pines grew thick here, right up to the road. He was nearly on the road when I noticed him; I jumped off my bike and yelled at him. He froze in his tracks, where he was obscured by a low pine bough. I remembered a book I had read, and when he didn't move, I barked like a dog. This technique was effective in the book, and it proved to be effective now. The black bear turned and bolted back the direction it had come, despite my horrible imitation and my florescent tongue.

Back on my bike, the pedals turned easier as the adrenaline coursed through my veins. Just like Billy said, he had seen a lot of bears. I was now more confident having not only survived my first bear encounter, but at having been the clear victor in our showdown.

Shit!

Another bear!

This black bear, much larger than the first, walked out onto the road 20 yards ahead of me. I repeated my sure-fire routine of bear scare tactics. My yells did stop him in his tracks, but only out of curiosity. He turned and stared me down. My heart rang in my ears and even the rain stopped to watch the two of us with our eyes locked in silence, each in the middle of the road. I half expected him to yell "draw" and pull his six shooter as tumbleweeds rolled between us. But all he did was stare. I yelled a bit more to no effect and was about to get back on my bike and coast down the hill when he lost interest. He turned his attention back to his own route and strolled off the road, showing no sign that anything had just happened. Well Billy, when you're right, you're right. I waited for him to get up the hill before I continued. When I pedaled past the point where he vanished, I looked up to find him staring down at me.

After my bear encounters, I met the day's next contender. The road was speckled with the wet, smooth faces of the rocks that halfway jutted out above the road surface. These were relief from the mud and loose stones scattered across it. All of this lay on a steep hill overlooking a valley, cut by the river that flowed below. Clear-cuts bordered the route and their wildflowers' petals frowned as the rain dripped from the ends, draining the landscape of its greens, purples, blues, yellows.

I alternated between walking and biking, but always kept an eye scanning the cleared swatches of forest. My two black bear encounters had put me on edge. Knowing I was in grizzly bear country took me past the edge to paranoia. Every blind corner of the windy road held secrets only revealed to me when I was lured in close enough to see. None of these secrets included the crest of the divide. The climb continued on and on, the top never in sight, the descent far off, like a cyclist purgatory.

Exhaustion set in, the rain persisted, and the road surface gave me and my glow-in-the-dark rope hell. I cursed the road and the climb, yelled at the clear cuts and the rain, and invited the grizzlies to try and mess with me. My will was bent, and my breaking point approached. After a shouting match with the mountains, I finally exhausted myself. So I ducked my head and kept pushing. I still felt defeated when I reached the top.

I looked forward to an easy descent; it was anything but. The rough surface did work on my panniers, which wobbled back and forth, their movement reinforced with every rock I crossed. Every few seconds, I gave a bear call to scare off anything ahead me, concealed by the blind turns. The ride down was as exhausting as the ride up.

When the odometer reached 40 miles, I stopped to have a snack and evaluate my situation. Cold. Tired. Hungry. My map showed a town 5 miles off route, only 15 miles from my location; a full service town.

Hot food?

A hostel with a warm bed?

Sounds good to me.

I didn't want to waste any energy to ride to the town for nothing, so I tried to call a few of the phone numbers provided on the map; I couldn't get cell service. I didn't complain, that was part of the route's appeal. I also noticed the map didn't provide a population for this town. Weird. Maybe it was a map error? Regardless, I wanted to rest, so I headed to town and hoped for the best.

● ● ●

Where in the hell?

I straddled my bike and looked between my map and the turn onto Forest Road 376. I had left the route over 5 miles back. The terrain was rolling, but manageable, and the rain had stopped. I had passed a few cars about a mile back, which I took as a good sign, especially when the driver of a pickup gave me at least three good wags of the "hang loose" gesture. I cracked a grin, laughed, and forgot my exhaustion for a moment while I appreciated the sign of support. But another mile down the road I had to face reality and admit I was lost.

Forest Road 376 … yup, right here.

I stared, puzzled. This road was south of Polebridge on the map, but I hadn't passed through Polebridge. How could I be south of it? The sound of an engine brought me back. A pickup approached me, heading north. Maybe he would know where it was. Or at least where I was.. In typical male fashion, directions were something I was too stubborn for. But this time, I began to realize how foolish pride could be. I still straddled my bike as I walked it to the middle of the road. The pickup stopped next to me.

"Hi there!" The driver was a middle-aged man and his demeanor suggested he would be helpful.

"Hey, I'm trying to find Polebridge and am hoping you can help me out."

"Polebridge? Well, I'm not sure where that's at. My wife and I are just up here for the weekend. I have a map though if you want to take a look."

Together, we examined both of our maps. I had missed it. My head dropped low, and I let out a long sigh. How had I missed a full service town?

"You look pretty beat. Can we give you a ride?"

I had swallowed enough of my pride to ask for help. I could do away with some more.

"Would you mind?"

"Of course not! Throw your bike in the back there and hop in."

The couple could not have been less concerned about how wet I was or how much mud I tracked into their pickup. The driver's wife had opened a bottle of Corona and put it into my hands before I had the door closed. They pummeled me with questions. Where did I start? Where was I going? Mexico!? How long will it take to get there? The kindness of this couple was the warmest experience I had in several days, the hot bath included.

Sure enough, I had missed the turn into Polebridge. When they dropped me off, it was obvious why. Also obvious was why the population wasn't listed on the map. There wasn't one to be listed. A mercantile, a tavern, a few small cabins, and the hostel were all the town consisted of. Full service, huh?

I entered the mercantile and hoped to find directions to a warm bed. Shawn was behind the counter, keeping the mercantile open after scheduled hours for no particular reason. He looked to be about the same age as me, and he could tell I was tired. We talked while he got me a hot dog and a cookie. He had come out to Polebridge for the summer from California. It was incredible to learn where the people in backcountry Montana had originated from; it made the world smaller. After I called the hostel, I set out from the merc in the wrong direction. Shawn's whistles and pointing got my attention and set my course straight. A half-mile from resting, and I almost blew it. Good thing Shawn was there.

I walked my bike up the pathway to the log lodge and was greeted on the porch.

"You must be the cyclist?"

"Yeah. Are you Oliver?"

"I am. Please come in." I had spoken on the phone with Oliver, proprietor of the North Fork Hostel and Inn. I couldn't quite place his accent then, but now speaking to him in person, I was confident it was German. "You look wet."

"Yeah, it's a been a few long days."

"Are you riding the Great Divide?"

I managed to chuckle. "I'm trying."

"You know, a girl stayed here two nights ago, also riding the route. She was looking for someone to ride with. I bet you could catch her. Her name is Allison. She left the web address for her blog, if you want to try to catch her."

"Yeah, I might do that."

Allison. A potential riding partner? A bit of outsourced motivation? My ride had been so difficult; the idea of a companion was irresistible. At least we would be miserable together. I copied her blog's web address into my journal and decided I would try to catch her.

Chapter 6

December 2011

DEAD WEEK.

As I understood it, that's what it was called at schools on a semester system. The week before finals, there would be no class, giving the campus a "dead" feeling. Students could use this time for the usual college stuff: to finish up papers, study for finals, drink themselves into a frenzy.

EWU was on a quarter system though. Our version was also the week before finals, but it earned its name by being the week when most students were on the verge. We still had lectures, we still had labs, and we still had all the parties. When a quarter was only ten weeks long, faculty and administration would not give up a week to give students time to "study." In fact, the only thing that changed on campus during dead week, apart from the increase of panic attacks, was the library's hours of operation.

The library was where I could always be found during dead week. Fall quarter of my final year was no exception. That was the week my group and I finished up the experimental portion of our crayfish study. During the study, only two crayfish had died and one vanished. Even after we replaced those three, we still had as many extra crayfish housed in the greenhouse. Our unpopularity had persisted among some of the faculty because of our water valve mishap, but I wasn't bothered by this. It actually appeased the guilt I felt when I interrupted a faculty meeting to talk to Dr. Hancock, whose good graces we had managed to climb back into.

I stuck my head into the room and scanned the faces that had become familiar to me over the last four years. It was a moment before I found Dr. Hancock. He didn't seem to be participating in the meeting, given how his chin rested on his chest with his eyes closed, his legs kicked out in front of him. Asleep? From across the room, I mimed to the professor sitting next to Dr. Hancock that he was needed. He wasn't asleep, just uninterested, and I, framed by the door with lab goggles on top of my head and a stack of spreadsheets in my hand, was a good reason for him to step out.

"Hey Dr. Hancock, sorry for pulling you out of the meeting."

"Oh, it's ok. What's up?" He eyed the data printout.

Dead week. This was a fitting term for our crayfish as well, but not because they spent any time in the library. The spreadsheets in my hand showed protein concentrations in the claw muscle from all of our test crayfish. They weren't going to give up the samples willingly; measures had to be taken. Regardless, lab protocol stated test subjects exposed to chemical treatments had to be terminated. It was an appropriate start to dead week.

"We ran the spec data, and apparently our concentrations are greater than one hundred percent. There's a problem somewhere in our procedure."

Dr. Hancock looked over the data on the spreadsheet, his hand cupped over his mouth and brow furrowed. He and I had talked for hours about the procedure for this analysis, and we were both under the impression that it was dialed in. Discovering after the test that we had made a mistake was a brutal realization. We had to do it again, which would be another four or five hours in the lab. It was dead week. We didn't have time for that.

"Well, Nathan, I'm not sure. Let's head back to the lab and take another look at the procedure." As most professors do, he set off at a pace faster than brisk, the spring in his step foreign to my eyes. He must have really wanted to get out of that meeting.

* * *

"Here it is."

We were back in Dr. Hancock's lab. The blank white walls closed in on us, pushing all the glassware and instrumentation into us. The one wall of windows looked out onto the courtyard at the building's center, now thrown into shadow. To find our mistake we had to search through our procedure, line by line.

"It looks like we did an extra dilution to our standards. The stock standards have already been diluted for us, which we didn't account for. Sorry, Nathan."

"That's ok. At least we know how to fix it." I glanced at the clock above the door. It was coming up on 4 p.m. Dr. Hancock followed my gaze.

"Listen, I'm going to head out of here around 5, but you guys are more than welcome to stay as long as you clean up and lock up on your way out."

I looked at my group members to see if we would stay. We had no choice. We needed the data to begin our statistical analysis. We still had to write a paper on top of that. Being given permission to stay in the building after close was an opportunity we couldn't pass up. We unpacked our sandwich bags filled with the pink-powdered muscles from the freezer and began again from scratch. Five came and went, as did Dr. Hancock, a few graduate students, and the cleaning staff. Our pizza was delivered at 7. The procedure was almost completed by 9. We got our data after 10.

Dead week.

• • •

There is something to be said about scientific research. Courses focused on research were my favorite, despite the high stress, lack of sleep, and hours spent pouring over journals and papers. I enjoyed the pressure, I enjoyed expanding my knowledge. But more than that, I enjoyed that moment of insight, of discovery, when after several weeks of effort and countless hours of searching through data I would see if the question we asked would be answered and what that answer would be. It was the intensity of the search that made finding the answer so fulfilling.

I sat in JFK Library as the clock approached midnight. My desk sat on the top floor at the very rear of the building and looked out over JFK Field, a patch of grass in the middle of campus stomped down during marching band practice, mashed down during flag football games, and blanketed in snow during winter. I was building a spreadsheet to analyze our data, but the students building snow men and having snowball fights on the field, bathed in the light of JFK Library, were a distraction. My chair gradually angled away from my desk and toward the window.

I gave a heavy sigh and shook my head. It was time for a break. I was too tired, too unmotivated to work. I checked my email instead and found a new message from an old friend.

The summer after I graduated from high school, I was part of an ambassadorial group that spent three weeks traveling through Eastern Europe. Megan was one of four delegation leaders. We first met at JFK Airport in New York, where our delegation convened, but we didn't have our first meaningful conversation until Prague. We were on Charles Bridge, walking through the various stalls filled with keychains, postcards, and t-shirts and occasionally pausing to examine a caricature artist's work or even one of the statues flanking the bridge. It was on the bridge that we realized there was a connection between us, a unique connection.

Megan and I were similar, and we had had similar experiences growing up. But because Megan was older, she was able to guide me through some of my internal conflict and help me develop as a person.

Megan was also an English teacher. Still unsure of what I wanted to do with life, I was considering writing as a career. As part of our trip's curriculum, we were required to keep a journal. By chance, Megan was the leader assigned to assess my journal. But I also kept a second journal, a more in depth, emotional examination of the trip. These were intimate thoughts of mine transcribed to paper— thoughts I considered private. But I had no problem trusting them to Megan; I wanted her to read my journal as much as she wanted to read it. Really, it became our journal. Megan would read it and write responses, pose questions, and instill deeper thought. Her insights were invaluable to me.

We stayed in touch after our trip and had seen each other a handful of times in the five years since. But it had been almost a year since we had last communicated. And out of the blue, here was a message from Megan.

I was not surprised. My thoughts had drifted to Megan more than once in the previous three months. She was someone I could be open with, and the understanding between us was impossible to quantify. Seeing her message, I knew she had tapped back into her eerily perceptive resonance with the universe. Somehow she knew I was in need of her help. Her message was short. Three sentences. Ten words. To the point.

I fired back a novella. I spilled my guts. My fingers raced as a professional pianist's, up and down the keyboard. Words appeared on the screen that I had been unable to say aloud, but had wanted to for weeks. My eyes teared. How I envied those students playing in the snow. How often had I sat in the library and watched them? They were so careless. Me, I was focused. I studied. I did my homework. I showed up on time. I did what was expected of me. How often had I missed the chance to be one of them?

I sent the message to Megan and felt some relief as a bit of the weight was lifted from my shoulders. Her reply would far exceed mine in length and would contain the responses, the questions, and the deeper thought I knew her for. It was the much needed encouragement I was after. And it was interesting how the universe conspired to give me exactly what I needed at the time I most needed it.

"Attention. The library will be closing in fifteen minutes."

I hated that ridiculous robotic voice, kicking me out as politely as its programmer could code. Hearing it once was always enough for me. I gathered my things and left the desk. What would happen to the snowball fight when the library lights went off? As I walked down the stairs, I imagined the blackout would only send its competitors into a frenzy, their snowballs now masked by the night, their own positions given away by their hysterics. I exited through the other end of the library. My breath was visible as I drew my coat around me and set off into the night, the air filled with laughter.

Chapter 7

DAY FIVE. After Oliver set me up with a bed in the North Fork Hostel and Inn the night before, I showered, ate, then passed out. I slept for nine hours, the most of any single night thus far, but I awoke several times through the night to search for my water bladder with a dehydrated desperation. It wasn't the most restful night. In the morning, my eyelids were heavy, waterlogged by the endless rain of the previous three days.

"Well, good morning," Oliver said. His accent added to his charm.

"Good morning, Oliver."

"Sleep well?"

"Yeah, I slept great." I put extra effort into lifting my eyelids. "You haven't heard a weather report for the day have you?"

"I have." He sighed, his smile falling to a scowl. "There is a 70% chance of thunderstorms today."

Great. More rain.

"I was afraid that would be the case." I surveyed the sky through the windows. Bleak. "Oliver, is it possible for me to stay here another night? I'm dreading more rain and I could really use the rest."

"Yeah, of course. After the last few days you've had, some rest is needed. You need to break into touring slowly, let your body adjust."

Oliver knew his stuff. He was no stranger to bicycle touring. Oliver left Germany for the US, drawn by her national parks. After he toured the continental US, Mexico, Canada, Alaska, New Zealand,

and Australia, he returned to the hostel he had begun to call home. He bought it and now plays host to cyclists of the route and various other guests to the area, many of whom are visiting Glacier National Park.

Polebridge is a few miles outside the park, and its rusticity would add to any traveler's experience. All of Polebridge is off the grid, meaning no power lines. The hostel's source of electricity was a small solar kit. The communal kitchen had one cast iron wood stove/oven and a second fueled by propane. The lamps were also propane, leaving a majestic network of copper tubing crawling up walls, through joists, and descending from the rafters of the ceiling. The subtle hiss of the lamps and their combusted aroma more than made up for the low light they produced and added to the quaintness of the place. All the walls of the converted cabin were covered in maps, postcards, paintings, newspaper clippings, and various odds and ends. Throughout the collage were various pictures of Oliver from his touring days. A small lean-to greenhouse stood along the south side of the hostel and gave my room the view of rich earth, green vines, sprouted herbs, and a planked walkway that lay beneath the coiled garden hose hanging outside my window. The nearby river had overtopped its bank with the rainfall of the previous three days, and its flowing roar accompanied the songbirds. The waning and waxing of sunlight added to the drama as the clouds above passed, unable to decide if they should release their payload. That was the first time I had seen the sun in three days; I almost didn't recognize it.

I used the day to catch up on my journal. Oliver also let me use his bike stand and tools to make some adjustments to my bike. I got her back in shape, except for the front shifter, which wouldn't engage the cable to move the derailleur from the second to the third chain ring. The shifter was too complicated for me to even want to mess with. I would get it taken care of in Whitefish where I would also replace my panniers.

● ● ●

I spent my last night at the hostel with Oliver, the two of us at the kitchen table, a single propane lamp lit above us. As the night grew late, Oliver began to floss his teeth. It was not in a meticulous way, like you would imagine a dentist would recommend, but in a very slow and relaxed fashion. If there was a pause in the conversation, the floss might go in, it might not. Oliver spent about 45 minutes unwinding the floss from one finger and winding it up the other, passing the wax coat carefully and unhurriedly between his teeth and only after his gums had time to prepare. It was such a trivial task handled with such patience. With the floss suspended between his two weathered hands, the low light cast Oliver, in his relaxed demeanor, as an embodiment of wisdom.

We talked as old friends, unafraid to say what we wanted. We talked about traveling, cycling, life and death, my motivation for riding the route. Oliver told me several stories from his own travels from which I found a renewed vigor and determination for my own trip. It was just like Megan's email. The universe had conspired to bring me the encouragement I needed at the moment I most needed it. In the next few days, I would be close to the home of my brother's in-laws. Our two families had grown close, which meant help was only a few phone calls away. It would be the easiest stretch to quit during. If the few previous days had planted a regretful idea in my head, then my talk with Oliver had extricated any trace of it. The next morning, I set out for Whitefish.

• • •

"Hey, you need some help?" Two pickups had come up the road behind me. The first stopped and the passenger leaned out his window to talk to me. I looked down at the blood flowing from my lower right shin, then to my shoeless left foot.

"Uh, no … I'm good."

I had woken to a dense fog back at the hostel and a forecast that was as bleak as the day before: 70% chance of thunderstorms. I thanked Oliver for the great conversation and set off into the ground clouds and freezing temperatures. It was 5 miles back to the route where my only climb of the day began. I stopped at the junction and removed my rain gear. The sun had broken through, and the fog had burned off. I was surrounded by mountains. The jagged, ice-capped peaks had been hidden behind a veil of clouds the entire time I had been in the area. I was astonished at what I hadn't been able to see. It was beautiful.

I continued on to the Red Meadow Pass. I'm not sure if it was an easier climb, having a rest day under my belt, or the fact that it wasn't raining, but the climb was fun. The only problem was the cleat on my left shoe; it felt loose. I wanted to keep my momentum and planned to take care of it at the top. But it became annoying, so I stopped less than a mile from Red Meadow Lake. I had not seen a single car that day, so I didn't bother to move very far out of the road before laying my bike over and removing my shoe.

I unscrewed the two bolts that clamped the cleat to the bottom of my shoe. The dirt and rock fragments that caked the cleat made it impossible to tighten. The components needed to be cleaned first. I held the cleat, the clamp plate, and the bolts in one hand and my multi-tool in the other with my shoe tucked under my arm as the two pickups came around the corner.

I jostled it all into one hand and picked up my bike with my free hand to move it further off the road. I lost control of the bike. It fell, away from me. I leaned trying to catch it and caught the large chain ring with my shin. The teeth dug in, leaving two deep channels just above my ankle.

"Having some problems with your shoe?"

"Oh not really. Just tightening up a cleat is all."

"Oh all right. Are you one of those racers?"

Maybe I should have answered yes. That would have avoided all the questions that come after saying no.

"No, but I'm riding the same route they are. For fun."

"Cool. Well, you want a beer?" The bed of the pickup had a few coolers and a stash of fishing and camping gear. I was flattered. This was the second beer I had been offered by complete strangers since entering Montana.

"Nah, but I appreciate the offer. I need to get to Whitefish before all the bike shops close."

"Well, all right. Have fun on your ride."

They rolled on toward the lake for what was sure to be a good weekend. Once they passed, I went back to my shoe.

Where was the clamp plate?

In my hurry to get out of the way, I had dropped it. I scanned the gravel for any glint or gleam for 10 minutes before I gave up. It wasn't absolutely necessary. I bolted the cleat back on without it. It seemed ok. I pulled my shoe back on and noticed a stream of blood had trickled down to the sock on my other foot. Was it too late for that beer?

"Give it a week, Nathan. In a week, you'll be well on your way, almost done really. Done with these stupid mistakes anyway."

Just give it a week.

I passed the lake and exchanged waves with the beer-toting fisherman. Past the lake I found snow on the road, but enough traffic had been through to carve ruts; it wasn't a problem. I finished the climb and began my long descent toward Whitefish.

Just give it a week.

Chapter 8

THE RIDE TO WHITEFISH was uneventful, a welcomed change. I did catch my first glimpse of a grizzly bear concealed behind some roadside shrubbery, but I passed him so quickly, I didn't have time to react. That was fine with me. The patchwork of clouds occasionally allowed me the company of the sun, keeping me content as well as my glow-in-the-dark rope, which hadn't been properly charged by the sun since I had purchased it. I passed Upper Whitefish Lake, then Whitefish Lake, and hit pavement, a sign I was approaching civilization once again.

A few miles from Whitefish, I saw another cyclist. He was pulling out onto the road. My downhill momentum allowed me to catch him and pull up on his left side.

"Hey, are you racing?!" Damn. I was annoyed by how often I had been asked. Now I was asking it too? Hypocrite.

"No. I'm riding recreationally."

"Very cool. Well, I'm trying to get to the bike shop and get some work done." I pedaled harder. "Maybe I'll see you later," I said back over my shoulder as I eased out in front. I was in such a hurry to get to a bike shop, I had probably passed up on some really good conversation.

Whatever. I was behind schedule. It was time to cover some distance.

Less than a mile after passing the cyclist, it began to rain. It wasn't heavy, but it had been enough for me to pull on my jacket.

Would any rain be heavy after Canada?

I made it to Whitefish and detoured from the route, heading straight into town. I got a bit turned around, but some locals set me on the right track to find Glacier Cyclery; it couldn't be missed. They had a whole lot of rental bikes sitting outside, as well as some bikes waiting to be worked on. I pulled my bike into a bike rack. I chuckled and shook my head at my panniers. The decision to stick with them was so long ago. Having now made it to Whitefish, I was happy with that decision. Yes, they had been horribly inconvenient, difficult to pack and load, and always had me worried that they would fall off. But what an adventure it had been with them. I walked through the double doors into the shop.

"Hi there, what can we do for you today?"

"Well, I'm riding the Great Divide Route, and my bike could use some work."

"Oh you are!? How's the ride going so far?"

I laughed and shook my head, thinking over the highlights. "It's been pretty adventurous."

After talking with one of the mechanics for a few minutes, a salesperson and I went outside to offload my gear so my bike could be put in a stand.

"Wow. You need to take a few pictures of those panniers before you take them off."

"Yeah, they've really added to my bike's character. I'm almost sad to see them go."

I pulled out my camera and snapped one last picture of my glow-in-the-dark rigging. As I unpacked them and took a knife to the rope, I realized I never actually saw them glow in the dark. With my bike in the stand and my gear stashed in a corner, I wandered out to find a bite to eat. The rain had stopped, the clouds had broken, and the sun shone. Figured. The nicest weather I had seen so far and I wasn't on the bike.

Fed, I returned to the shop. My bike wasn't ready, so I sat at a table outside and pulled out my maps. I traced the red line, examined the elevation profiles, poured over every feature, every bit of information. What would each of these upcoming stretches be like? How far would I make it in the next few days? Where would I stop to rest?

"Mind if I join you?" he asked, catching me off guard.

"Not at all. Have a seat," I said, squinting up at him, the sun over his shoulder.

His name was Martin. He was one of the mechanics at the bike shop. I was fortunate enough to be on my downtime during his lunch break. Talking with him, I learned he was fairly new to the area. He and has wife had visited Whitefish and had liked the area so much, they decided to move there, almost on a whim. When Martin had secured a job at the bike shop, their plans were finalized. I commended Martin on their spontaneity. There is a lack of spontaneity and courage to act on a whim these days. Might that be related to this country's high rates of depression and heart disease? That is to say, disease of the heart ... or heart dis-ease.

The conversation came back to the route, why I was riding, what I was looking forward to. I confided in Martin that I was intimidated. I had hardly covered any ground, but had had a lot of misfortune. Now looking at the map, especially the elevation profile, I felt worse about my lack of progress.

"Well, Nathan, if it makes you feel any better, I've heard Montana is the hardest section of the route."

Had Martin actually heard that, or was he just trying to be encouraging? I assumed the former, and it did make me feel better. If I could get through Montana, then things might get easier. That was similar to my logic of the first few days when I thought if I rode hard enough to make things difficult, then the rest of the route would be easier by comparison. I had not forgotten the difficulties of those days and cringed as I realized I had had no control over their difficulty. Maybe Martin's words weren't that reassuring.

Martin soon returned to work, and my bike returned to me. I loaded up my new panniers and left the old ones in a box to be shipped home. A photo of the new set on the bike completed the before-and-after transformation photos.

The few hours I had lost in Whitefish made me anxious to get going. My knee did not appreciate the extended break either as it had grown stiff with inactivity. I set off beneath the sun, my skin warmed by its touch for the first time in days.

I camped at an RV park that night. What a contradiction that was. I rode my bike down the gravel lane past 40-, 50-, 500-foot mobile mansions, complete with satellite dishes, air conditioning, and indoor plumbing. I erected my seven-foot bivy in the shade of a sapling, my bike in the grass beside it. If the bike loaded with panniers, a frame bag, and handlebar bag weren't odd enough, my bright orange bivy shouted exotic. I earned some strange looks that evening, but did get invited to dinner at a nearby RV and was later visited by some younger occupants of the park.

• • •

I slept late the next morning, an accomplishment given my bivy's orange illumination when the sun struck it. I ate, packed, and for the first time on the trip, I put on sunscreen. How optimistic. I pulled out of the park and waved to my dinner hosts Tom and Lynne as I went. The morning was dominated by the black top that crisscrossed the flats between Whitefish and Bigfork. It was a nice change of pace, the flat riding on a hard surface in nice weather. The sun hung from its blue curtain, drawn behind the peaks that flanked the valley. The only downside was the abundance of privately owned land that left houses scattered everywhere. Nature had called and it was difficult to find a discreet location to relieve myself. I eventually came up with a covert method that would be useful several times on the trip. I'll skip the details.

I ate lunch in Bigfork; a restaurant there sounded too good to pass up. Once inside I wish I had passed. It was a Sunday in the quasi-tourist town, and the place was packed. I was sat quickly, being alone, but it was chaotic inside and a bit of a wait for my food. It probably wouldn't have been so busy if it had been raining. Go figure.

I rode the 2 miles back to the route, crossed the Swan River, and left the pavement to climb back into the mountains. The day's heat had reached its maximum as I climbed. It was a welcome change to be drenched in sweat rather than soaked by the rain. At the top, I was exhausted. Pacing was something I needed to work on. As I began my descent, I began my bear calling as well.

Half way through the descent, I rounded a blind corner and every muscle in my body clenched. Two grizzly bears stood in the middle of the road. Shouting every few seconds at the top of my lungs for the past twelve minutes wasn't enough to alert them to my presence, but the squeak of my brakes was? They both looked at me and, to my surprise and relief, they both fled. The first bailed off the road into the thick growth. The second, bigger grizzly didn't like the steep topography. He ran down the road searching for an opportunity to escape. I was tired and did not have the best judgment. I wasn't going to let this guy slow me down. Hell, we were both going the same direction anyway. I let off the brakes and continued to chase the large grizzly bear, the one that could stop, turn, stand his ground, and leave me up a creek without a paddle. But he was a solid twenty yards ahead of me, and I only kept up the chase for about fifty yards before he scrambled off the road.

What a badass. I just chased a grizzly bear on my mountain bike.

I had a good laugh about it. Then I realized what I had done. How stupid. A grizzly running away? He was probably too young to realize he could have torn me to pieces. There had been no going back for me. Had he stopped, I would have either had to lock the brakes up and climb back up the road or blow right past him on the narrow forest road barely twelve feet wide. I had lucked out.

Paranoia set in as I reached the bottom of the descent. Somewhere, just beyond my field of vision, there was a hoard of grizzly bears seeking revenge. They were there, but every time I glanced over my shoulder they ducked out of sight. Cunning, those bears. Not enough to catch me though. I kept pedaling, with the hope they would tire before me.

I started to pass bulldozers and road graders parked alongside the road. It was Sunday. No work. The stalking bears' stares continued to crawl up my spine; they were out for my blood. Maybe I could increase my chances of nighttime survival if I slept in one of the graders. I stopped to see if one was unlocked. It was; the key was in the ignition even. Locks went unused at home too, and keys were hardly ever taken out of their ignitions either. Apart from that, the grader did not have any of the comforts of home. I did use it as a camp kitchen, its frame was the perfect height for a counter, but that was where its usefulness stopped.

The fatigue faded from my legs after my early dinner, so I kept riding. I rode and rode, the shadow of the mountain I had climbed earlier chasing and overtaking me. It was almost 9 when I started to look for a good camping site. As I rounded a corner, a grassy clearing adjacent to a creek looked perfect. Crossing the bridge that spanned the creek, I saw a tent already pitched in the clearing, a bike and a trailer next to the tent.

I knew that setup. That was the cyclist I passed outside of Whitefish!

Thrilled I had caught him, I pushed a bit further telling myself I didn't want to impose on his campsite; really, it was my ego that pushed me further. My exhaustion beat back my ego though, and I camped just a mile down the road. I set up as the day faded to black, and I began to regret not imposing. My bear paranoia had not worn off. I pulled out my camera, my friend, my confessional and explained why I might be killed in the night by a mob of grizzly bears. My body was more relaxed after I turned off the camera.

That day's descent was the last time I gave a bear call.

● ● ●

After I survived the night, I ate breakfast and began to pack up camp. Before I was able to break down the bivy, the cyclist I passed the night before came up the road and stopped. His name was Cefas, from the Netherlands. He invited me to ride with him, and I accepted. We agreed to meet further down the road, so he wouldn't have to wait for me to finish packing. I looked forward to riding with him. Apart from the mile or so with Freddie, I had been solo the whole journey.

As I loaded up my gear, another cyclist rode past my camp. He was an older guy with an incredibly light load. He must have been a racer. He was also the first northbound rider I saw (excluding Billy Rice of course, even though he was riding southbound when we met).

"Good morning," he said, a smile on his face.

"Good morning, how are you?" I replied as he drew even with me and began to pass by.

He called back a single word: "Free!"

Chapter 9

"NATHAN!"

It took longer to catch Cefas than I had anticipated. Luckily, he stopped for a coffee break at a dispersed campsite about twenty yards off the road. I rode into the site and, with a granola bar, joined Cefas at the trunk of a fallen tree that made a decent table.

"Can I offer you some coffee, Nathan?"

"No thanks, Cefas, I actually don't drink the stuff."

Cefas had always been a cyclist at heart, but life had forced him to work at it. The first time he was hit by a car, his bike's steel frame was bent to a right angle at the seat post, right where his leg was—you can estimate the degree of damage that was done. After years of crutches, wheel chairs, surgeries, physical therapy, and a second time being hit by a car, his leg wasn't exactly recovered.

"Yeah, at one time I seriously wanted the leg amputated."

"Amputated?"

"Yeah, I was so sick of being in pain all the time. I was in a wheelchair then too, my leg completely useless, so it wasn't like I would be giving up walking. But my parents kept arguing with me, telling me not to give up and to keep my leg. I listened to them and I'm glad I did too."

After our breakfast prelude, we set off together, me with two good legs and Cefas with one and quarter. It was another beautiful morning and the riding conditions were mellow enough that we could talk.

"Oh man, that makes a lot more sense. I was wondering why you were moving so fast when you passed me outside of Whitefish."

"Whatever, Cefas. It's not like that. I just thought it would be cool to ride with her," I said.

Cefas laughed. "What's her name again?"

"Allison."

"Uh huh. Fun to ride with her. And how do you know where she's at?"

"Well, I don't know exactly. But she has a blog for the trip. I can get a sense of where she is and how fast she is moving from that."

"You are just out here chasing girls aren't you?"

"No, Cefas! I'm riding with you aren't I? Oh, wait," I paused for effect, "I guess you're right."

"Shut it, Nathan!"

"I'm just kidding. Besides, I chase other things out here." I told him about my descent the day before, when I came up on two grizzlies.

"Wait," Cefas managed to say through his laughter, "you actually chased him down the road?"

"Yeah, not the best idea, but at the time it was awesome. Afterwards I got paranoid though. I thought about sleeping in one of those graders we passed. I even thought about camping next to you, but that seemed like a dick move. I didn't want the grizzlies to kill you too."

Cefas was still laughing. "Whatever, you could have camped with me. I wouldn't have minded."

Cefas had heard about the route the first year of the race and had wanted to ride it ever since. And why not? He had already won a Dutch reality show in which handicapped athletes and able-bodied models were paired up to compete in team challenges. And don't let me forget that he competed in Athens as a paralympian. Cefas was just the type of guy I expected to meet in the backwoods of Montana.

"So you've been traveling for how long?"

Cefas: "Since January."

"With your girlfriend?"

"Yes."

"Where have you been?"

"We started in Southeast Asia and then went to Nepal. There we did a trek, climbing a trail across the valley from Mt. Everest." All with a bum leg. Nobody told Cefas his leg should slow him down. Maybe he just wasn't listening. "Then we went to India. After that, we split up so I could do this route while she does a mountaineering trip in Pakistan. We are going to meet in Denver and head to South America."

"That is awesome. Where are you headed in South America?"

Our mellow ride came to an end. We began to climb, and it became apparent that we had different abilities. I hiked my bike more than I needed or wanted to, but it was worth getting to know Cefas.

We stopped at Clearwater Lake for lunch and dipped in the calm, cool waters. But as mountain weather does, it changed in a heartbeat. As we left, we opted out of a steep 5-mile climb to avoid possible snow and certain misery and, instead, descended through the rain to cruise along the highway to Seeley Lake.

We rented a tent cabin there. The rain was disheartening after a day and a half of riding in the sun; the forecast wasn't any better. If the weather wasn't agreeable in the morning, we would take a rest day. I still felt rested and didn't want to take another rest day so soon, but the prospect of rain and Cefas's company was justification enough.

• • •

Thump.

Thump, thump.

The spatter on the canvas roof and the dim morning light woke me. I had been excited to sleep on a cot, an improvement over the ground and sleeping pad, but it allowed air to circulate beneath me. Cefas and I both woke in the night, our backsides chilled. Given the rough night and wet morning, I didn't leave my sleeping bag; we weren't going anywhere. The spatter slowed to a steady drip, paced by the pine tree that grew next to our shelter, its branches extended above us.

Cefas and I rode to the opposite end of town to find the grocery store. We filled my backpack and rode back to camp with bags of groceries hanging from our handlebars, the flimsy white plastic flapping in the breeze. The sun started to make the occasional appearance and let us use our picnic table for good food and good conversation.

"How about *V for Vendetta?*" I asked through a mouthful of

tortilla filled with cheese and lunch meat and topped with a dollop of chili.

"Yes! Love that movie," Cefas replied, already making his next tortilla. "It's so blunt in how it addresses political scare tactics."

"I love the ending, how the people overcome their fears and stand up to the government."

"All in the mask!"

Cefas and I spent a long time talking about fear, and for the first time, I looked at fear from evolution's perspective.

In all my hours of number crunching as a biology student, I learned there are only two possible statistical errors: a false positive—when you wrongly answer your question in the affirmative—and a false negative—when you wrongly answer in the negative. If you pair this with the basic idea of evolution (that organisms who survive are the ones that pass on their genes), you can see a possible origin of fear. Animals that lived in fear, that is made a "false positive" type mistake, were the ones that survived. "Did you see that shadow? Was that a bear? Run!" Of course the friend who saw it only as a shadow didn't run and maybe he typically survived. But the one time he made a "false negative" mistake, the one time it actually was a bear, well, you know what probably happened.

Now give that false positive a few million years and rename it. Fear has a place, but our society and lifestyle have skewed the context in which it is most useful. Fear did not get that memo.

"So how does someone recognize their fears?"

Cefas and I pondered that for a long time. We shared our experiences, those events that made us reevaluate what we were doing with our lives; those that made us seek what we actually wanted; those that had us out there, trying to ride our bicycles thousands of miles through lush mountains and barren deserts, through bad weather and bad emotions, through sunrise and sunset.

"So a lot of introspection after an experience of great emotional significance can help you realize your own fears, like you being hit by a car."

Cefas looked skyward for a moment, then he nodded his head. "Yeah, or like you and your mom."

I watched my toes flex in my sandals. "Yeah, exactly."

"Does that make us the lucky ones or unlucky ones?"

I laughed. "Have you seen *The Matrix*?"

"I was just about to bring up the scene with the steak!"

Together we recited a line from that scene: "Ignorance is bliss."

It was an enlightening discussion about fear, and I coupled that concept with our skewed notion of time and found a new understanding of people. We are taught to plan for the future, to be forward thinking. We forget today, lost in an imaginary world known as tomorrow. The torrential rain in Canada had been a great experience; never mind the horrible conditions. The fact that I was in the moment, seeing from such a different and fulfilling perspective, more than made up for it. All of the philosophy that I had read in the past year had started to click. I realized what it meant to "do," how living and thinking about living are different. Thinking is given meaning through action, ideas given power through illustration and demonstration.

That was what I wanted from this journey: empowerment.

• • •

Our second night in the tent, we both slept on our insulated sleeping pads on top of our cots. We woke rested and pedaled into an overcast morning. The forecast wasn't good, but there was no end to the rain in sight. Luckily, conversation is a good distraction from the weather.

Cefas and I stopped in Ovando to have lunch and were updated on Billy Rice's progress by the locals. He was in Wyoming fighting a lot of head winds.

After lunch, the sun broke and warmed us for a few hours while we crossed the flat expanse of a valley floor that hoped to be confused with big sky country. The crunch of gravel beneath our tires stirred the butterflies from their bent blades of grass, called them to surf the waves of our wake, to glide alongside us with only the occasional beat of their wings. They laughed, splashed in the air, and then returned to their beach of leaves to bathe in the sun until the next big set.

That afternoon, we fended off rain as we climbed Huckleberry Pass. The clouds threatened us, the drapery of rain ebbing up and down the valley, dropping a light rain on us occasionally. The threat was increased by our slower pace, but I maintained my patience. How could I pass up the opportunity to ride with a guy ballsy enough to do the route without two fully functioning legs?

On the last stretch before the top, two cyclists caught us. They were two middle-aged guys that said they had been following our tracks all day. We chatted a bit, enough to find out they were from Seattle. Fellow Washingtonians. They had started at the border and were trying to cover as much of the route as they could before they had to return to work. We were soon in eyeshot of the top, and I witnessed Cefas's competitive edge. These were the first cyclists we had seen since we had been together, and Cefas wasn't about to be passed. Cefas kicked into high gear and reached the divide before them.

"Nathan, they said they had been following our tracks all day, right?"

"Yeah, they did."

"Well, they can keep following them. Let's fly down this descent," he said, a fierce smile across his face.

"Hell yeah, Cefas!"

We descended to Lincoln and left the Seattle boys behind. We ate a mediocre meal at a diner where we passed on dessert. Instead, we went for pastries at the grocery store.

"You're buying my dessert, right?" Cefas asked through raised eyebrows as we stepped up to the cashier.

"Maybe, but why would I do that?"

"Because I'm crippled."

I doubled over with laughter. "Cefas, if you are voluntarily riding the longest mountain bike route in the world, something most able-bodied people wouldn't do, then you have already forfeited your right to play the 'crippled card.'" We both laughed as I handed the cashier my credit card.

As we stood in the parking lot munching on turnovers, Cefas burst into laughter. In response to my raised eyebrows, he pointed. By coincidence, we had parked our bikes on the sidewalk right in front of a handicap parking sign. Cefas pointed to the sign and then to his leg.

"I guess not everyone agrees that I can't use the crippled card."

We almost choked on mouthfuls of cherry turnover we laughed so hard.

Refreshed and recovered from our fit of laughter, we rode a few miles outside of town and camped among the pines, alongside a stream. We settled in early knowing tomorrow would be a long day.

We had to cross the Continental Divide three times to get to Helena where we would meet my brother and sister-in-law. I lay awake in my "grizzly-bear-snack-sack" (Cefas's new name for my bivy) hoping we would make it.

* * *

"It's been good, man. I'm glad we got to ride together."

The sun was high, and there wasn't a cloud in sight. The day had grown hot while we took our lunch break after the first Divide crossing. Cefas and I had set out in the early morning, riding in the cool shade of the mountains so that we could get to Helena. Our first crossing had been too slow and involved a lot of hiking. We had covered about 20 miles in the first four hours of the day; we still had another 35 to go. At the bottom, we stopped for lunch.

I was the first to cook my food. I was the first to finish eating. I was the first to be repacked. I was the first to be back on the bike. I was worried we weren't going to make it. This wasn't lost on Cefas.

"Nathan, why don't you go on without me? I know you want to see your family, but I don't want to be the reason you don't get to."

"Are you sure?"

"Yeah. We can both ride at our own pace this way. If I don't make it to dinner, at least you will."

So we went on our own. We agreed on a campground to meet at, but I wasn't sure Cefas would make it. Neither was he.

"It's been good man."

"Shut up, Cefas. I'll see you at camp in a few hours."

"All right." He scowled through his lie.

We parted ways. Cefas and I had become good friends in the four days we had been together. It was difficult to imagine riding without him, even though most of my ride *had* been without him.

It did feel good to ride at my own pace though. I climbed steeper terrain than I had been with Cefas and hiked far less. I covered ground much faster. I hit the highway about 7 miles outside of Helena in the late afternoon. At the junction was a cell phone tower, which I took advantage of to call my brother and confirm plans. Then I rode the last few miles to the campground, worried Cefas wouldn't make it. The second crossing had been more difficult than the first. Add a third, and that made for a long day.

I had a few hours to kill before my brother would arrive, so I set up camp, ate, cleaned some clothes, and sat in the cold river water for the benefit of my legs. I had just become comfortably numb when I heard a loud whistle. I turned to look back up the bank in the direction of my camp.

"Cefas!"

"I made it!"

All smiles, Cefas strolled down the bank and plopped down next to me, showing no hesitation toward the cold water. We sat for a few minutes and talked about how grueling the day's ride had been before getting out and preparing for dinner with my family.

• • •

Jared and Whitne picked us up at the campground. It was a warming relief to get a big hug from each of them. I had lived with them the whole of the previous December in the town of Bozeman, and I had only seen them once since. Because they were only a few hours from the route, they wanted to see me and make sure I was doing all right. I introduced Cefas, and we headed for Helena.

We went to a nice restaurant for dinner. After we were seated, I reached for my glass. I cringed. Chlorinated water. For almost two weeks I had been drinking mountain stream water. When I raised the glass to my mouth a second time, I could almost see the chlorine boiling off the top. Where was my water bladder? I needed to rinse.

The conversation was also fumigated with the standards of politeness. Most of the conversation regarded the trip, but not from the perspective I found most interesting: the sapio-spiritual. It rated as small talk in my book, and though I would loved to have brought the conversation around, it was difficult to know if they could understand. The conversation was awkward at times as well. Jared, Whit, and I might have started on a tangent that regarded nothing and no one Cefas knew about, so it would be put to rest. The rest of dinner was filled with the dull questions regarding the small details of someone's life that may not have any significance. I tried to guide that conversation by throwing in details about Cefas, or asking him to tell the story about the one person in the one place and how they did that thing.

I had grown accustomed to being alone. Every conversation was the only chance I had to connect with someone else. After four days, I knew Cefas better than some of my closest friends. Solitude has a way of wringing out the dirty water from the sponge that picks up everything in our lives where the mundane things number so great that the fantastic gets diluted, forgotten.

We finished our meal (I had barbecued pulled pork—delicious) and set out. On our way back to the campground, we stopped at a grocery store to get supplies. Cefas and I shopped in a droll fashion, Jared and Whitne in tow. We wanted specific items, items that could be in one of several places in the store. Up and down, up and down the aisles. This way, then that. This way, then back. All necessary items procured, Cefas and I got a cheesecake to split for dessert. Jared and Whitne refused their own portions. We didn't argue.

It was late, dark when we returned to the campground. We all said goodbye and with one last hug, Jared and Whit got back into their car. Cefas and I stood at the picnic table, bathed by their headlights as they backed up. It had been a good night. The first week and half of the ride had been hard, and seeing them helped strengthen my resolve. I felt a lot of strong emotions as they left, the color rising in my face and moisture collecting at the corner of my eyes, when a stranger strolled into camp.

Staggered actually.

Obnoxious and loud.

Drunk.

This southern girl was with two other friends a few campsites down. They weren't there to camp, just to have a good time. Now that they were about to leave, she was worried about the embers in their fire ring; she wanted us to make sure they didn't start a fire. They had drowned enough of their misery to forget to drown their fire.

"You know, I don't want to burn down Montana the weekend before the Fourth of July." I had to give Miss South Carolina some credit to have that kind of concern while inebriated. Hopefully she would be heading south again soon to spare Montana any more trouble.

Jared and Whitne still sat in the car, backed out of the parking spot, but not leaving until they knew it was all right that some strange person had wandered into our camp. Jared flashed his headlights. I extended my hand behind the girls back and gave a thumbs up to my brother, one that she was unable to see. She mistook my subtle communication as an invitation. She stepped closer to me and threw her arm around my shoulders to give me that awful drunk side-hug. That was how I watched my family leave, embraced by a stranger, shrouded in an ethanol fog, and listening to Cefas failing to hold back his laughter. At least we had cheesecake.

Chapter 10

February 2012

I GRADUATED from high school not knowing which direction I wanted my life to go. College was a popular decision, and I loved learning. Writing was something I had in mind, but the hard sciences were something I did well with in high school, and these could lead to a promising career, so my advisor threw me right in. My first quarter, I took calculus, chemistry, and English. My workload was a shock for a guy that had breezed through high school, but I figured things out, and adopted that model for the next five years. Science classes dominated my schedule; general education classes were fit in whenever I could get to them, which was not often.

This is why I didn't like my class schedule winter quarter. I had left behind the stresses and time requirements of my senior capstone for the lower level classes I considered leftovers. I wasn't thrilled about my enrollment, but it was necessary to graduate. History and geography moved slow for the freshman that didn't know how to study, too slow for my liking. I sat in the back of those classes. Now, it was also a habit to take science classes whenever possible, especially biology. I wasn't excited to leave behind the four hundred-level classes, but no other biology class fit into my schedule. So it was back to a low three hundred-level class, back to school with the students fresh out of General Bio, wet behind the ears.

I wouldn't have had such an issue with this class were it not for the group work. My real problem was with the lack of maturity of some classmates, but it was the group work that forced me to interact with them. One aspect of this group work came in the form of group quizzes.

One day, half way through the quarter, I walked into class to find everyone sitting in their assigned groups. Great. Quiz day. I sat down with my group and the four of us crammed for the quiz. Once we were handed the quiz, it took ten minutes for the whole class to finish. Then it was time to move forward with the lecture. But this quiz day was different from the rest. One student decided it was important for him to abandon the desk he had taken his quiz at and move back to his usual desk. As luck would have it, that was the desk I was in.

I didn't know this person well and didn't care to. Our school was small. I knew several people who had socialized or worked with him, and it was general opinion that he was an unsavory character with some despicable habits. I had no desire to interact with him. But he walked up to the front of the desk I occupied.

He reeked of that high school immaturity and preteen manipulation that every parent must fear. What the hell was he doing? He stood there for a long moment, staring at me.

"That's where I sit," he said.

My chest expanded as the beat of my heart accelerated to a hum. "I'm sorry?"

"That's my desk."

My mind spent a lot of time wandering in those months. I didn't have any difficult classes that demanded every spare moment and every ounce of my energy like I did in the fall. Work at the climbing gym hadn't been enough to keep my mind occupied either. I even took on the task of creating a newsletter, a project three other assistant managers had failed to complete. Not me though. I searched for something to take up the time. I was on the verge of depression, drowning in self-pity. I wanted help, but was too proud to ask for it. I wanted someone to rescue me. Why didn't my friends say or ask any of things I wanted them to?

I was angry. This dick trying to reclaim his desk wasn't helping.

"That's my desk."

Your desk? I hadn't realized we had assigned seating. I hadn't known you couldn't handle not sitting here today when it hadn't been a problem on any other quiz day. Sorry, I had forgotten the trivial crap most high schoolers base their life around, like which desk is his.

My heart hummed still. I stared back at him, at his sense of entitlement. What were my possible courses of action? I could've stood up and hit him. That would probably have felt good for a moment, but be regrettable later. What if I stood my ground? What if I refused to move? What could he have done? He couldn't even pretend to be intimidating. But what if I conceded?

I continued to stare back at him. The whole class was silent, stricken with an unusual tension, all eyes on us. I made a decision. I didn't hit him, even though I wanted to.

"If it's that important to you," I said.

I stood and grabbed my bag and notebook. I moved forward two desks, the closest one available, one he had walked past. He had demanded his desk, which I thought ridiculous. Wouldn't I have been on the same level of ridiculousness if I had defended the desk as my own? No, I wouldn't be brought down like that. Neither he nor the desk was worth it. My heart slowed after I sat down and the lecture began, my opinion of that person not improved any.

• • •

The rest of the quarter was much the same: me in a terrible frame of mind, concealing my emotions under a hard exterior and wearing a good face for the world. And again, the contradiction. I wanted people to address my pain, but only if I could hide it. This emotional pride began to overflow into other facets of my life. I sacrificed my grade just because I thought my essay would have been better if I didn't follow the criteria. I was right, and I ignored my professor's suggested edits. I wasn't remorseful over my actions, just my motivation. Too much pride.

There was one good thing that quarter though. Her name was Ariana. Ari, for short, was also in my Biology class. She was the only one that made it bearable. In our class's weekly lab we examined various vertebrate specimens. Each week we experienced a new variety of sights and smells. Skeletons, pickled fish, stuffed birds with dusty feathers older than everyone in the class, and even a shark with a half-digested octopus in the stomach. Each lab was preceded by a quiz that covered the previous lab's material. And every week, the class would congregate outside the lab to do some last minute cramming.

"Are you ready for the quiz?" she said as she sat down next to me on a couch in the hallway.

"Not really, but I'm not too worried. You?"

"I think I have most of it down."

And thus began the weekly ritual. I showed up to study and would find a couch. She would show up a few minutes after and sit beside me. It was such a small act, but it was helpful. There weren't any flirtatious undertones; there wasn't a need for help with the material; there wasn't that much conversation even. Ari was just pleasant, a sweetheart. I looked forward to those five, maybe ten minutes every week when we sat together. And when I felt low, I told myself one thing: "Give it a week. That's all you have to do. Take one week at a time and you can get through this. After another week, you'll be back on the couch with Ari."

Just give it a week, Nathan.

Chapter 11

"YOU SHOULD easily be able to see that I'm struggling!"
Two words: Lava Mountain.
Lava? More like hellfire.

• • •

After our brief encounter with the southern discomfort of the night before, Cefas and I split that cheesecake. Then I drowned the neighbors' embers to make sure Montana didn't burn down. We left the next morning in good spirits and in good weather. I had missed Jared and Whitne before I had even embarked on the bike; add the stresses of the trip and my desire to see them had grown. My brief interlude with them wasn't satisfactory, but it had been enough. I pulled out of the campground, my memory surreal as though the night before had just been a dream. My current lifestyle stood in stark contrast with the life I remembered when I was last with them. It had been ages ago.

I let Cefas lead so that he could set our pace. The day was going to be beautiful. We rode a couple of miles down the hard packed dirt road before we turned off onto another nameless road, its only identity a number. The forest road immediately began to climb and there was a switchback fifty yards ahead of us. The road crossed into the morning shade of the ridge that we would be climbing. Perfect. It was always a relief to climb in the shade (assuming it wasn't raining). But as we rounded the first switchback, Cefas dismounted. It was too steep for him to ride.

I gave the hill an incredulous stare. Hadn't Cefas climbed terrain just as steep in the past few days? Why not now? It was the morning. Our legs were fresh. Our bellies filled the night before. My odometer showed that we hadn't even covered 3 miles yet. My daily frustration with Cefas was beginning earlier and earlier every day. It wasn't that I had a problem with a slower pace. My problem was not traveling at my own pace. I was not listening to my body; I took orders from Cefas's body instead. This wouldn't have been a problem if I hadn't set out with the expectation of listening to my own body and the goal of pushing my own physical and mental limits. At the end of every day with Cefas, I could have kept going. I wasn't challenging myself like I wanted. The solo aspect of my ride was dissolving. Cefas and I needed to split up. I decided Butte would be a good place to split.

In the meantime, I held my tongue and pushed my bike alongside Cefas, but the road deteriorated and loose stones and gravel covered most of the surface. Finding a good single line to push a bike up was difficult enough, so we pushed single file. The sun arced high enough to find us, and we lost our shade.

There was little conversation on the push up the next 5 miles as we jumped back and forth, on the bike then off the bike, cycling then hiking. Near the top was a small reservoir.

"Do you feel like a swim, Nathan?" Cefas asked. The water did look inviting, but it was still early and what we had just done was nothing compared to what was to come.

"If you want to Cefas, go ahead. But I'm going to push on. I'd rather get to Lava Mountain before the heat and get it over with."

Was Cefas getting frustrated earlier and earlier with me too?

Cefas passed on the swim, and we rode further into the mountains on a nicer road with a slight incline. I stopped every several hundred yards to wait for Cefas. On those breaks I started to have negative thoughts. What if? What if I wasn't waiting for Cefas all the time? What if I had been riding at my own pace? I'm sure I could've left Montana behind by now. The sun was high now, and while it burned me from the outside, my own frustration and self-loathing burned me from the inside. I didn't like those thoughts, but I couldn't help thinking them.

Three miles later, we found our next turn. The map described this segment as a "rough four-wheel drive track." Really? I would have loved to watch someone try to drive that road. The track was really more like a one-time set of ruts that water had found and transformed. It more closely resembled a gully now than any road. The steep uneven surface was a patchwork of dirt, clay, gravel, cobbles, and boulders. The runoff that coursed through it during precipitation events had cut below the base of the adjacent trees and shrubs. Gnarled roots had a dissatisfied appearance like gnomes removed from their subterranean network of tunnels, baking in the sun that was far too bright for their beady eyes, wishing to return to their dark and sheltered world. The clouds passed overhead and cast strange shadows over the roots, and their canopy counterparts reached out for us; it was straight out of a Tim Burton film. To make it better, the endless rain of the previous weeks had left water trapped every few feet. It was one thing to push through puddles and mud, but quite another to deal with the mosquitos that they harbored.

We started up. Slowly. One step at a time. Hiking alone was exhausting. The map's "virtual wall" in Canada had been steep too, but it was short. We had more than 2 miles of this torture to cover before we would get to the top and start back down. If the other side was similar, we wouldn't spend much time riding on the down side either.

Yeah, hellfire.

It wasn't long before the gully worsened and both Cefas and I began to slip in the loose substrate. Some segments were so steep, not even our disc brakes would arrest our bike's backward progress. It became frustrating, but especially so for Cefas. His bum leg was another burden on this climb that I couldn't relate to. He took half steps, only able to push forward with his good leg. Soon he was struggling, cursing under his breath.

It was a few minutes before Cefas's mumbles were loud enough to hear over my own strained breathing. To say I was surprised at what I heard would be an understatement. My foot slipped as I pushed off my toes; my forward leg caught my weight, but began to slip too; I locked up the brakes and pulled myself up by my handlebars.

"What did you say?!"

"You heard me! Fucking American!"

Apart from being insulted, I was lost. What had sparked this explosion? How should I have reacted? The climb was getting to both of us, so I ignored it, let it go. At least for the time being.

We pushed and slipped and slid and struggled. The climb did not get any easier, and I could have sworn we weren't even covering ground. Finally, we reached a flat stretch. I leaned on my handlebars as I watched Cefas mount his bike, intending to let him go first. He couldn't get his right foot clipped to his pedal. There was a problem with the cleat on his bad leg and he couldn't reach his shoe to check.

"Will you check my shoe to see if anything is stuck in the cleat?"

I laid my bike down and walked up to Cefas. He held his foot as high as he could and, sure enough, a small pinecone was lodged into the cleat recess. I dug it out, satisfied. He had criticized the particular cleat design I was using (different from his) because mine was known to become lodged with trail debris and clog up.

"Got it. A pinecone."

Before I could criticize his cleats he mumbled to himself, "Finally, he fucking helps."

"Cefas, if you want help, speak up!" I was pissed. My body tensed, and the heat in my face rose further. "I'm not just going to fucking help you because I think you need it!" I took a few breaths. I was still breathing hard from the push up the hill. "What if you don't think you need it? I'm not going to risk insulting you or hurting your pride by stepping in just because! If you want help, ask!"

He clipped his right foot to his pedal and rode off without a word, without any kind of response. I waited a moment to create a comfortable riding distance between us, but also to cool off, contain. I mounted my bike and stared at the puddle in front of my bike. Winter quarter of my last year in school I had acted just like Cefas was. I needed help and had just expected it. I had been too proud to ask. When it wasn't just offered up by any of the people I thought should, I was let down, even angry. How unfair of me to put my friends in that kind of position, especially when I pretended everything was fine. Did they even know something was wrong beyond the obvious? I doubted it. But if they had, would it have really been up to them to address it? Would they have felt they were overstepping their bounds, that they were intruding on my private life?

I pedaled around a bend in the trail and found Cefas pushing up another steep incline. We hadn't pedaled fifteen yards from where I had found the pinecone in Cefas's shoe. Awesome. I dismounted and began to push as well, catching back up. Progress was slow and apart from our strained breathing, progress was quiet. That was until we reached the steepest stretch. It was short, about ten yards. At the top was a network of roots of the nearby pine tree. My geology training showed me how rain would fill the gully and cut the hill back, but leave the soil at the top, anchored by the roots to make the hill steeper and steeper. It was a process similar to the formation of a waterfall. We were almost to the top and the root system proved to be problematic for Cefas.

"Nathan, can you please help me?"

I didn't miss a beat. I bent down and grabbed the back of his trailer with one hand and balanced my own bike by the neck with my other hand. "Push." Together we overcame the roots that held him back.

"Thanks."

"You're welcome."

The exchange was so natural. It wasn't bitter, and it wasn't overly polite. It was as though we had been acting like that all along, that we were well practiced. When I reached the top behind Cefas, I sighed relief. Being upfront keeps things so much more simple. Human interaction has enough complexity without having to read someone else's mind.

We stopped for lunch, still on the ascent. Again, I was listening to Cefas's body instead of my own. My body felt fine, and I wanted to continue until we reached the top. Instead, we found a shady spot on the bank of the gullied trail, surrounded by a few large puddles and their mosquito guard. I unpacked my stove, started some water towards a boil, then bumped the lid to my stove. It fell and rolled on its rim, in slow motion, all the way down the bank and straight into a mud puddle. Cefas laughed; I clenched my jaw. I retrieved the lid and rinsed it with boiling water. I was silent.

"Sorry for laughing, Nathan, but that was funny."

"Yeah, I suppose it would have been if it wasn't mine," I said too politely.

The steam started to roll off of my noodle concoction. A few spoonfuls of peanut butter and a handful of trail mix kept me occupied while it finished cooking.

"Are you ok, Nathan?" Cefas said. "You seem angry." Really? I seemed angry? I was blown away that he had to ask if I was angry.

With calm condescension, "I probably seem that way because I am."

"Because of the trail?"

Match to fuse.

"No Cefas, not because of the trail. Not because of the route. Not because of the weather. Not because of my bike or my gear. You are making me angry, Cefas. Your negativity is bringing me down."

"Well, I'm sorry, but this is hard for me. I don't have two full legs like you do. I can barely push my bike up this crap, and that's frustrating. This is one of the hardest parts of the route!"

Explosion.

"Exactly!" Our voices had progressively risen. I paused to organize my thoughts before giving them voice. "Cefas, you're right, this is one of the hardest parts of the route, but you are out here doing it, man. You're covering ground despite the difficulty and despite your leg. Why are you so frustrated by that? That should feel good, man. Most people couldn't do this. Most wouldn't want to. But you do. And you are. That should be awesome regardless of who you are. But you, with a bum leg, you should feel empowered."

That shut everyone up. We finished eating and cleaned up, tired of fending off the mosquitos. My body was much less tense after telling Cefas what I thought of his crappy attitude; my own attitude improved because of it. That pseudo-speech was not something typical of my behavior. I usually kept thoughts like that to myself, but Cefas had forced it out of me. I was glad he did too. I felt better for it, and his silence told me I might have struck a chord with him as well.

"Ready to go?"

"Ready."

We left our shady spot that had gradually been intruded upon by the sun as we sat there. The day had grown hotter during lunch, and we still had to finish our push to the top. Soon, the ridge seemed to be somewhere out in front of us instead of above us. We were able to look through the trunks of the trees uphill from us instead of staring at the underside of their branches. The trail improved. With a lower grade, the erosive power of water was also decreased. Roots weren't completely unveiled here. Fewer shrubs grew along the trail. The gully filled back out into a trail, one resembling a four-wheel track. There was less gravel and fewer cobbles, though still the occasional basketball-sized boulder, and the puddles were much larger here. We were close. More importantly, there were tire tracks left in the mud the puddles had shrunk back from. Bike tracks were always a welcomed sight. They let us know we were headed in the right direction. We hadn't seen any on the way up, and I wouldn't have been able to imagine the despair if we had taken the wrong trail and realized it just then.

We topped out and began the descent. Luckily, the trail wasn't as steep on the descending side, so we were able to ride most of it. There were still sections that were nothing but sand and very difficult to ride through, while other sections were incredibly steep and full of rocks. It was a test of our braking capability.

Cefas broke the silence while we walked one of those difficult segments halfway through the descent. "Nathan, I'm sorry I've been in such a bad mood. I've been thinking about what you said, and you're right."

"I'm sorry I got so angry with you, Cefas. I guess neither of us has been in the right frame of mind."

"Yeah, well you helped me realize that, and I'm getting back to the right frame. This has been a tough hill, huh?" a smile emerging.

"Hell yeah, it has been," a full smile manifesting on my own face. We began to laugh. Emotions on the ride were like the weather. It wasn't as though they just changed at the drop of a hat; really, it was the same changes I experienced in everyday life. Out there though, emotions were so much more intense, so much closer to the surface that the changes were drastic when I experienced them. And like the weather, there was no way to hide, or hide from your emotions. They were overwhelming at times.

"So do you think this will be the hardest day?" Cefas said, both of our good moods in full swing now, as though the anguish of the morning was a clouded memory.

I thought for a moment before I answered, reflecting on all my false assumptions and inaccurate imaginings of the route thus far.

I gave a somber, "No, I don't think so."

"Then which day do you think will be the hardest?"

"Well," I pursed my lips, "everyday." I didn't want to admit it, but this was a suspicion I had formed back during the Canadian rain.

Our trail terminated on an actual road, a very welcomed change of terrain. However, it too was short-lived, and we were back on a quad-track once again. As we cut across a meadow, we were given one of the best views of the day, looking out over the rugged terrain that was hard to imagine crossing—but that was exactly what we were doing.

I had read repeatedly that cycling was such a simple life. Even after starting the trip, people said they were envious of such a simple lifestyle. Well, let me set the record straight. These people are confusing the concepts of simple and easy.

The confusion of these words is justifiable though. I can't hold that against anyone. Easy and simple are very similar—but not in this context. Simple is a lifestyle. On the bike, it's time that makes this lifestyle simple.

Our skewed perception of time, our mental construct of life as a timeline, our habit of always looking to a future that never arrives, that's what makes this life simple. It eliminates all the planning and wondering and brings you back to the present. As in everyday life, where every decision had consequences. But out there, the consequences were instant by comparison. It was the immediacy of actions that made it appear simple. If you were thirsty, you drank. Don't have water? Better look for some. It was the fact that not taking action, not implementing a plan right then, in that moment, could be dire. Don't have a job? Well, maybe I'll look next week. Need to study for a test? I can put that off until the night before.

Yes, this life was simple, but only because decisions were simple, the possible outcomes so clear-cut, my judgment unclouded by the fog of foresight. The routine of ordinary life, however, can mask those outcomes, hide the best decision, or cloud your judgment, because the consequences are going to occur so much further down the road. Don't pay your mechanic, don't get you bike back, don't get back on the trail. Don't pay your taxes, well, we'll check back in few years. It's that immediacy that is lacking from common perception. The only day anyone will ever have the opportunity to change things is today and that is a fact that has been forgotten.

To be clear though, this does not mean this lifestyle was easy. In fact, it was damn hard. Several of the hardest days of my life occurred on this trip. So what's the difference? Just because the process of making a decision has been simplified, that doesn't mean the decision itself—the course of action you've opted for—is going to be easy.

Apart from the physical exertion, which was much more demanding than the average day of everyone I knew, you had to constantly worry about water; plan your meals days in advance; worry about weather; worry about injury, which could occur miles from the nearest town (which likely didn't have a hospital or clinic anyway); worry about mechanical break downs, mental breakdowns, and emotional breakdowns; and don't forget to mention the wildlife, such as mountain lions, grizzly bears, and wolves. Easy? Yeah, 2,700 miles of easy.

This is what I meant when I told Cefas everyday would be the hardest. It was in the moment he asked that I realized the difference between simple and easy and the common mix up between the two. Just because decisions were simple, that didn't make my course of action easy.

Cefas and I made it down from the mountains to the town of Basin. On the way, the road evolved from the overgrown quad-track that cut through the meadow, to dirt, to gravel, to pavement. The descent was an amazing ride with little climbing and there were even a few instances where we went so fast we risked going over the edge of the road, down an embankment. Some calls were too close to be comfortable.

In town, we had a few celebratory cokes and onion rings to commemorate not only our crossing of hellfire, but also the personal growth we sustained coming over the top. Cefas and I had both crossed two divides, only one of them material.

With some advice on the route, which we could always plan on receiving in these small towns, we decided to continued on, Butte in our sights. When we returned to our bikes, Butte became even more important: Cefas discovered a problem with his rear wheel bearing.

Chapter 12

"DO YOU THINK you could have made it to Butte?"

"Yeah."

"Do you think you could have gone past Butte?"

"Probably."

"Sorry."

Cefas and I had left Basin with the goal of finishing the day in Butte. The route paralleled the interstate the whole way, following a "non-maintained cattle access trail" before it transitioned to an old railroad bed. One climb, short but steep, finished Cefas off for the day. We made camp just a few miles further on. I had hoped to make it to Butte, but I had to admit, camping was much more convenient than trying to find a place in town. Cefas apologized for holding me back and also for his earlier behavior. I dismissed him on both counts and told him not to worry, but that it was time to part ways. We agreed to ride to Butte together and then say goodbye. We set up camp and then sat and talked over our dinner about philosophy, travel, and life in general. It was another insightful conversation, the continuation of which I would miss. But it was time to return to my solo journey.

We were slow to start the next morning and allowed our gear to dry from the night's dewy deposit. I took the opportunity to rework my packing scheme and moved my sleeping bag from a pannier to the top of my cargo rack. A piece of glow-in-the-dark rope I salvaged back in Whitefish held it down. As I packed, tires disturbed the gravel on the rail bed. Our campsite was well concealed, but we could still see the tracks. It was the Seattle boys, the two cyclists we had lost three days before as we crossed Huckleberry Pass.

Cefas's competitive edge kicked in again. I told him to go ahead while I messed with my packing scheme and that I would catch up. My recycled rope wasn't functioning very well. I had to stop a few times to mess with it and I had travelled almost 4 miles before I caught Cefas.

"Hey, I was beginning to wonder where you were."

"Yeah, my sleeping bag was giving me problems. My rope doesn't hold it down very well."

"Well, I saw the Seattle boys. They crested that hill in front of us just before you came up."

With a devious smile, I said, "Think we can catch 'em?"

We didn't, but our banter persisted along the frontage road we travelled down. It was the most traffic I had seen in a while. Obviously some of the interstate travelers knew what we were doing, giving us a honk and even a few waves. I smiled. I closed my eyes and felt the sun on my face. The ride was all downhill to Butte.

• • •

We pulled into the Outdoorsman bike shop at about 10:30. The Seattle boys were inside making some adjustments to their set up. Cefas spoke to the owner about the problems he was having with his rear wheel. He dropped his trailer in the corner and pushed his bike back into the shop for a mechanic to work on. I spoke with the Seattle boys who had taken an alternate route that missed Lava Mountain. They had heard it was a hellish stretch and wanted to avoid it. Cefas and I looked at each other, both of us smirking. It had been a hellish stretch. That's why we were better for having taken it. The grueling gully of a trail made for a better story than the straight, flat pavement the boys had taken.

The Seattle boys called it a day. They had woken up early in Boulder and had already logged 40 miles. A heat advisory had been released for the day, so they wanted to reach Butte before the heat. Cefas and I left our stuff at the bike shop and headed to a sub shop for lunch.

"Did you check Allison's blog?" Cefas said, sipping on his straw.

I swallowed a huge mouthful of sandwich before I could answer. "Yeah. She still hasn't updated it since Helena. She must be three days or so ahead of us."

"Well, I bet you can catch her."

When we stepped outside after eating, it was apparent the temperature had risen dramatically. The heat pressured me to get going. I became irritated. I hadn't anticipated being in Butte so long. Time was wasting.

We returned to the Outdoorsman, and I prepared to leave. I was speechless when I learned Cefas's bike was fixed and ready to go again. As Cefas spoke to the owner, he kept using the pronoun "we" in regard to future riding. My irritability worsened. Whether Cefas managed to get his bike fixed or not, I had planned to continue on solo. Had I not made that clear? Did he think we were still riding together? I continued to pack and focused on reworking my sleeping bag into a better position.

"Nathan? I have a gift for you before you leave."

"A gift, Cefas?"

"Yeah, I have these two straps. They would be perfect to hold down your sleeping bag."

"Yeah? You aren't using them?"

"Nope."

"I'll give them a shot."

He went about his own business while I reworked the sleeping bag configuration. The two straps seemed solid. They would be helpful, because it would be disastrous to lose my sleeping bag. The gift was a relief, as was the realization that Cefas knew I would still continue solo. I finished packing up and checked the weather report. The heat advisory would be in effect for four days, which coincided with my crossing of the more arid parts of Montana.

"You could just say thank you," he teased.

"Damn it Cefas, I was saving it for the goodbye. It's not going to mean as much now that you called me out," I said, both of us smiling.

"Are you about ready to leave?"

"Yeah, I am. Thank you for the straps. They're great."

I put on my helmet, pulled on my gloves, and slipped into my backpack. I walked my bike to the door, Cefas in tow. Outside it was hot, and now it was 1 p.m. Butte had been a longer delay than I had wanted, and now I would be pedaling out just in time to experience the heat of day.

"Listen to your body, Nathan. Don't push yourself too hard."

"Come on Cefas, you know I'm going to push. I have to go 'see about a girl,'" I said, bringing some comedy to our glum goodbye. In our hours of conversation, we had talked about several movies. One of them was *Good Will Hunting*. So naturally, Cefas stole a line from the movie to characterize my effort to catch Allison.

"Yes, Nathan, go and see about that girl," he repeated back through his laughter.

We finished our goodbye with a hug. It was strange to leave Cefas. We had bonded, seen each other at our highest and lowest, we had laughed and argued, we had talked very openly. We had become good friends. Even more strange was that I didn't even know him the week before. It was bittersweet to press on without him, and though I was excited and relieved to be back on my own again, as soon as I left Cefas, I started to think about our next bike tour together.

Chapter 13

THE SUN BORE DOWN on me with a vehement grin. I was 7 miles outside of Butte when I began to feel like Atlas, except I held the more immense and searing sun. My bike groaned under the weight and I almost saw my tires' tread melt away. The first day of the four-day heat advisory, it was obvious my body had been adjusting to the cold and wet weather.

At the bottom of my first climb since Butte, I was passed by a teenager in a car who shouted profanities at me. Hormonal imbalance? Trying to impress his girlfriend? Searching for satisfaction within a mundane routine? I wasn't sure. Maybe he was just rude? Most of the profanity I heard tossed my way and most of the inconsiderate drivers I saw were within a ten-mile radius of Butte. That was not a good representation of my Montana experience, but it did encourage me to move on from the state.

I laughed about the teenager as I climbed a section the map described as having heavy timber cover, but there must have been a fire since its publication. The timber was thin, short, new growth. That meant very little shade. I was beginning to distrust my maps, even with their updated addenda. The solar radiation—in addition to the heat I generated—forced me to stop. I laid my bike over in the shade and walked into the stream that flowed down the glen. The water was cool relief, a layer of armor that Atlas never had to protect his shoulders. I removed my gloves and helmet, my backpack and jersey. I soaked my jersey, dunked my helmet, rinsed and wrung my gloves, and redressed in my much heavier, cooler clothing. I continued the climb at a lower temperature and with a refreshing drip, drip, drip of water from my helmet, the padding of which had retained a substantial amount of stream water.

By the top of the climb, I was dry. A mile further, I was soaked in sweat again. As I started to search for another roadside stream, clouds started to collect, offering occasional shade that turned off and on like an incredibly slow strobe light. I was grateful for the change of weather conditions as I began climbing towards another Continental Divide crossing, the second of the day, the first without Cefas.

I listened to music as I climbed. Music was always a great help; it distracted me from the less enjoyable aspects of the ride. The burn in my lungs, the soreness of my legs, the boredom of the long flat stretches of pavement. All were diluted through music. This climb, I listened to Florence and the Machine. It was empowering music, not just through the melodies, lyrics, and incredible vocals, but because it had such great memories tied to it. Cefas and I had bonded over a lot of music and found we had very similar tastes, both of us having loved this particular album. My ride with Cefas was just one more memory added to those associated with Florence.

I reached the summit and my sixth Continental Divide crossing since Banff. The intermittent bouts of sunshine had ceased, and from the vantage point, I could see two storms approaching: one to the southwest, the other to the southeast. My route lay between them. I had flashbacks to Canada that made me cringe, but I clenched my jaw and rode on. The thick growth of trees faded into open meadows filled with sage and barbed wire, and as I descended further, these meadows were dotted with pines that flanked large stone outcrops, fractured fortresses that were crumbling. Above them, the bannered sky was striped with the fall streaks of rain. I looked to these fortresses for potential shelter as the storms sandwiched me, but the steep walls barely broke the wind.

The storms blended above me. My small strip of sky vanished. I saw lightning to the west and heard thunderous responses to the east. It was bizarre, but intimidating. It was like being in the middle of a football stadium filled with the fans of the home team as they chanted back and forth to each other, across the field; the jeers of one side reflected and reinforced by the other. The wind finally brought the rain down to me, sideways. It wasn't heavy, but moved fast enough to sting my skin. What had happened to my heat advisory?

The rain was nothing compared to Canada. I rode through it, seeing that my two storms were moving north as I approached the southern edge of both. The rain picked up as I began to climb a steep hill to a watershed divide.

It was over. I saw blue skies and a large green valley. The storm ceased precisely at the watershed divide. The transition was paradoxical, abrupt but congruent with the geography of the valley. The sky was again a patchwork of cumuliform clouds cut at the horizon by the peaks of the Pioneer Mountains. Here was my heat advisory. The descent from the divide to the valley floor crossed through familiar, fenced meadows that lacked the sage found on the other side of the divide. I stopped at the bottom for a snack and to pack my rain gear. The straps Cefas had given me had loosened on the descent; not a lot, just enough to let the sleeping bag rock a bit. I wrenched them tight and continued on.

The good weather held for the rest of the day as I climbed up Fleecer Mountain. This was the final approach to the notorious Fleecer Ridge, a short and extremely steep descent, so steep it is recommended that riders leave the trail—which is bad trail etiquette—to make switchbacks across the hill. Supposedly that is the safest way down. I thought I might make the descent that day, but 3 miles from the top, my body refused to go further.

I set up camp, alone, a much different experience from camping with another person. I did try to communicate with a squirrel that had invaded my space, me in my tent and him on the stone fire ring that contained my failure of a fire, the wood too wet to burn. My storm had passed through here before it had gone to greet me, like this squirrel did now. Our conversation was short, though, and he disappeared as the light faded. As I journaled, I saw another animal from my tent. This one I had no desire to talk with. It was a canine, somewhere between white and silver. He walked right down the middle of the road, apparently the owner. Despite a slight limp, he carried himself very well, with a pride I found disconcerting. My breathing ceased while he was within the twenty-five yard stretch of road visible from my campsite. I told myself it was a coyote. We had a lot of coyotes back home on the farm. I had never seen one walk down a road like that, though, or with that coloration. Yeah, I had to sleep. It was just a big coyote.

Chapter 14

"BATTERIES?"

I dug to the bottom of my pannier looking for replacements.

"You are wasting time, Nathan ... on batteries. Unbelievable."

My campsite was wet when I woke up in the morning, but the clear blue sky visible through the tree tops promised another warm day. I wanted to get going early to avoid the heat as best as I could. My first obstacle was a wrong turn. I only did 2 miles extra before getting back on track, but that was 2 miles that took me nowhere. I still wasn't confident I had taken the correct road until I reached a cattle guard at the bottom of Fleecer Ridge where it became obvious that I was in the right place.

The ridge had no trees, but was guarded by vast forests on either side that sloped down and away from the backbone of the mountain. Instead, it was a thick growth of grass freckled with the yellow petals of a vast population of dandelions. The road devolved into a two-rut track that snaked its way up the ridge, eroded by the rainfall, and dug deeper into the hillside. Beads of water still clung to the blades of grass and the road was still wet with the night's rain. It wasn't long before I had to push my bike to avoid sinking in the mud. It wasn't much longer before it was too steep to ride anyway. A few times I turned and aimed my camera back down the hill, the immenseness of which grew the higher I climbed. The cattle guard at the bottom was hardly discernible any more, even though I knew it was there.

When I made the turn off the main track to cut across the

meadow, the batteries on my GPS tracker called for a change. My map indicated I should aim for a "solitary 'fence.'" I saw a single wooden fence post. That must have been it. I leaned my bike against the post while I worked to replace the exhausted batteries.

It was warm for the early hour. The heat was coming. I needed to get going. Of course, my extra batteries were buried under everything in my pannier. Once I replaced them, I jumped back on my bike and followed the flattened grass looking for a "steep downhill track." I found it and turned onto it. The track was narrow and the sage was thick. It grew right up to the track and the branches were high enough to catch my feet as I passed by. I made it about halfway down before I dismounted and began to make the suggested switchbacks through the grass and sage. Then I noticed another track coming down the hill to my right. Weird. It was farther down from where I had turned, but both tracks originated close to the same point. It also looked like they terminated close to the same point at the bottom of the hill. No worries then.

I fought the sagebrush all the way down the hill. It snagged my shoes, tripped me up, clogged my drivetrain, and grabbed at my tires' spokes. It was frustrating. No wonder it had a notorious reputation. I made it to the bottom, where the tree growth began again, and started searching for a stream that cut through the trees. My map indicated it was to the left, but I couldn't find it. There was a second trail though, the one I saw coming down the hill. It would have been possible for the turn to be to the left of that trail, but to my right. I turned my bike around and began to push it back. No luck. I found a stream, but no clear trail. The undergrowth was thick and the ground soft; it was difficult to walk through. How could a bike trail have cut through that? I pushed my bike outside the tree line, following the downhill contour to see if the flora thinned at all. Sage snagged me the whole way.

I was lost. Pushing the bike was a waste of energy until I had a destination to push it to. I laid it out in the clearing, visible from a large portion of the hill, and hiked farther down the drainage hoping to figure out where I should go. As I hiked, I took an oblique line slightly uphill to gain a vantage point. The sage started to thin, but only because loose rocks the size of baseballs and volleyballs inhibited its growth. Now instead of being tripped every other step, I rolled an ankle every third. My vantage point gained me no advantage and the hill went on and on. I doubled back, all the way past the point I initially explored. Then it clicked: the map addendum.

The sun climbed higher, and the moisture began to burn off the grass and sage covered slopes. The addendum to this map had better directions for the mileage at which I made the turn down the hill. When I read them, I knew I was in the wrong place. I cursed myself for being in such a hurry. The five minutes I had "wasted" to change the batteries had led to more than an hour of pushing my bike all over that hillside. At least my GPS tracker had fresh batteries to track all of my doubling back and directionless wandering that looked like a child's scribbles when superimposed on a map.

I pushed my bike back to the bottom of that single track. My spirit was crushed when I looked up the hill. I had a strong desire to cry, but I couldn't. I know. I tried. I decided it was frustration that made most people cry. I was certainly frustrated at this point, but I was frustrated at knowing what I had to do. This was different from the frustration resulting from not knowing what to do. Because I had a course of action, I couldn't cry. There was still something to be done, still some hope that the situation could be redeemed. My body wouldn't allow me to cry while there was still a chance like that. It was another example of this life's simplicity. Ride down the wrong hill, push your bike back to the top.

I examined the hill and decided on a course. The sage that had tried to prevent me from coming down the hill would now try to prevent me from going up. This time though, gravity was on the side of the sage. Covered in sweat and drained from my route finding, I took a break to hydrate and eat a few granola bars before the big push. I ran out of water. I had camped next to a stream, but planned to fill the bladder on the descent from Fleecer Ridge. I had plenty for that, but I hadn't anticipated getting lost for more than hour. Now beads of sweat formed on my skin just from sitting. The break was over. From that point, I could only lose water. I needed to minimize the time until my next drink.

I pushed my bike up a portion of the hill that wasn't as steep. I still lost my footing repeatedly and cursed the thick sage all the way to the top. I pushed for thirty minutes before I crested the top and found the correct path. My legs were scratched beyond belief from the knees down. I dripped sweat, and it was only 10 a.m. I breathed easier though, being back on top of that hill. But my relief was laced with self-resentment for not checking the addendum that morning.

As the track emerged from the grass, I cursed my stupidity. Somewhere around a hundred racers had been through here in the previous week. The track I found was a strong indication of that. It was clear the single track I had mistakenly followed was not crossed by hundreds of tires. I should have realized, should have noticed there were no tracks. It had become a habit to search for tire tread in the mud, and I had let that habit lapse just long enough to cost me.

When I found the actual notorious hill, it was easy by comparison. I did walk down it, but I hiked my bike straight down it without leaving the trail. No sagebrush nipped at my ankles, no rocks slipped underfoot. It wasn't even as steep as the hill I wrongly trekked. It was a disappointment then.

The left turn at the bottom was obvious, as was the stream I was supposed to find. More bike tire tracks. Still headed the right direction. I rode another half-mile before I stopped to filter water. I shook my head and slowly unpacked my filter. What a dunce. The last day of my second week and I made a huge mistake like this? Hadn't I been polishing myself into an experienced rider? Hadn't I been slowly losing that newbie status for the last two weeks? Nope. Newbie status reinstated.

Refreshed by the water and the shade, I descended all the way to pavement, reaching back occasionally to tap my sleeping bag to confirm that the straps were still tight. I reached the junction with State Highway 43, the junction where an alternate route rejoined the main route, an alternate that avoided Fleecer Ridge. If I had taken the alternate, I would have passed the junction the day before. I shook my head at the notion. Fleecer Ridge was some of the most challenging terrain on the route. Better to fail at something hard knowing you tried than to the succeed at something easy knowing you didn't need to. I smiled at not having even considered the alternate.

● ● ●

The sun was glaring. There was no shade along the road. It made me envious of the fly fisherman hip deep in the Wise River. I coasted into the town of the same name and ate lunch outside the mercantile. I sat on the ground next to the ice machine and was fending off mosquitos as two bikes pulled up to the merc. Not bikes of the pedaling nature. Street bikes: big engines; bigger egos; complete with scantily clad females. The two couples walked into the store and came out with ice cream and bug spray. They sprayed each other with the bug spray, arms outstretched like the messiah. I slapped my leg, killing three mosquitos simultaneously. Maybe the reinstatement of newbie status was a bit harsh. Their conversation turned to the unsightliness of tan lines. I glanced down at my hands. Each arm was dark to the wrist, where my glove sat all day, shielding my white skin from the sun's rays. The difference in color produced the illusion of gloves even when I wasn't wearing any. Newbie was definitely too harsh.

The bikers left, and I followed a few minutes after. I rode a 40-mile segment of pavement through the heat of the day, but stopped several times to cool off in the river. The water was cold and allowed me to essentially ice my legs to cool down.

After another climb and great descent, I made Polaris where I stopped at a hotel bar for dinner. There was need to celebrate. Polaris was the last town on the first US map of the route. I had finished my second map. Only five more to go.

Polaris also marked a dramatic change in the scenery. Instead of the pine forests and mountain streams, I had entered an arid area with more sage and barren soil than I had seen so far. I rode 20 miles to Bannack State Park where I planned to camp for the night. It had been a long day, piling my Fleecer Ridge mishap on top of my highest mileage day since riding with Cefas. A $23 camping fee extended my day. No way would I pay that fee for ten hours of camping.

Eight miles down the gravel road, I was tired. I needed to stop. The problem was private ground ran right up to the road. There was no decent place to camp. It was time to ask someone for help, something I had become more comfortable with. I pulled into the driveway of the first house I came to. A beautiful golden retriever met me halfway up the driveway. If he could speak English, he probably would have told me to get the hell off his property. That's what his bark implied as well as his growling and stalking of me as I approached the front door, refusing to turn my back to him.

I explained my situation to the older couple that lived there. They suggested motels and campgrounds, all which sounded like a substantial distance away.

"Really, all I need is a patch of ground to set my tent up on. I noticed all the land around is here private, so any public land of any kind would help."

The husband spoke: "Oh. Just try the end of the road then, about another mile down. The road splits there and the right of way would be a good spot."

"Awesome. A mile? Thank you for the suggestion, I really appreciate it."

The retriever really appreciated me leaving. He escorted me all the way to the road. It was about 2 miles to the end of the road, but I had already learned not to trust people's distance estimations. Car miles and bike miles are not equivalent. But the man was right; the right of way was perfect. No water, but I still had plenty, and the sage there was big enough to conceal my bright orange grizzly-bear-snack-sack.

I set up camp and prepared dinner. The valley I had come down was flanked by mountain ranges on the east and west. The barren landscape was like a familiar desert, a desert that lacked red wounds. Sunset was a spectacular substitution though. I crawled into my tent, watched the last bit of sun fade through the branches of the large sagebrush, and listened to the hum of the hundreds of pairs of beating mosquito wings just outside my bivy.

Chapter 15

Spring Break 2012

I HAD NEVER been in a desert before. But here I was, looking out at the reddest rock I had ever seen, bands of it cutting diagonally through its tan counterpart. It was 8 a.m., and I had been awake for more than twenty-four hours. I was invigorated.

Trip catchphrase: "Damn. That's some red rock."

Winter quarter had dragged on, but I had made it to Spring Break. Rather, Spring Break had pulled me in.

A few weeks before, Megan had been in town for business and we were able to see each other for the first time in more than four years. I spent the night out with her and some of her colleagues, but as the night progressed the number of our companions dwindled. By 3 a.m., it was just the two of us. We had dropped off a colleague at his house, which was not far from my mom's house.

We pulled into the driveway, and I turned off the headlights. We didn't leave the car. Everyone inside was asleep. I told Megan how my year had started, about the day Axel had died. Megan held my right hand as she listened to me spill my guts, listened to me say a lot of things I had wanted to say, but just hadn't been able to. I cried. It was the first time I cried in front of someone since that day. We sat there for a long time; 4 a.m. came and went. We finally left so Megan could catch her flight and when we did, I felt I had been unburdened.

By 5 a.m., we had recovered Megan's things from her hotel and had made our way to the airport. On the way we discussed what I called the "eerily perceptive resonance" she seemed to have with all the universe. She told me it was all about recognizing the signs and the feelings that accompanied them.

The signs.

A week after Megan had flown out, that's all I could think about. I had been supervising the climbing gym when an older gentleman approached our front desk and poked his head in to watch the climbers. Motivated by the requirements of my job, I approached him and struck up a conversation. Soon though, I was engaged by the guy. He was an experienced rock climber who had given up the sport a few years earlier because of injury. He told great stories and suggested a lot of places to climb. One of the places he raved about was Red Rocks, outside of Las Vegas.

"Yeah, if you ever get the chance to climb at Red Rocks, go for it. That's such a great place to climb, and even if you don't climb, it's still beautiful."

"Really? Red Rocks? It's strange you should say that, because a few friends of mine are planning on going there during Spring Break, and they just invited me."

"Do it, man. It's incredible."

A complete stranger. A man I had never seen before and haven't seen since, recommended I visit a place I was just invited to.

Sign?

I had been looking forward to not having plans for Spring Break. Being on the more introverted end of the social spectrum, the week was a good opportunity to relax and recharge. I slept on it. I decided to go for it.

A few days later, the four of us were committed to a climbing trip. Another older climber, John, was headed there too. John worked in the Biology Department, so I knew him on two fronts. He was in charge of the stockroom, so all of Fall Quarter, I was in and out of his office trying to keep the crayfish experiment on track. Conversely, he was in and out of mine too—the rock climbing gym. I also featured John in the climber's newsletter I got off the ground, publishing his climbing trip report of the Nose route on El Capitan in Yosemite National Park. I respected John's opinion, to say the least, as well as his suggestion to head to Vegas.

The last few weeks of the quarter I was in and out of his office again, this time in regards to climbing instead of crayfish. For the first time that year, I was excited. Things started to look up, and I began to feel good. After my talks with John, I would stop to talk to Ari as well, who just happened to work in the stockroom with John. Sign? Personal relief just seemed to be flowing out of that room.

• • •

"I say we get breakfast."

"Yup!"

"I'm in!"

"Let's do it!"

Winter Quarter had ended the day before. My friends and I had our bags packed and ready to load after the last final was finished. We left town at 3 p.m. and drove through the night. We were in Las Vegas by 7 the next morning, and we were hungry.

After a stack of buttermilk pancakes slathered in syrup, we headed for the campground outside of Vegas. On the way, we stopped at the Red Rocks overlook to use the bathroom, stretch our legs, and throw around a ball in the empty parking lot, riding a sugary syrup high the whole time. We took pictures of the rock formations, the ones with the large bloody wounds that turned the desert red. That was some red rock.

We sat on a short stone wall and looked out over the desert as a hoard of cyclists rolled into the parking lot. They enveloped the bathroom and drinking fountain, claiming their territory with the click-clack of their cleats on the asphalt. Their bright, skin tight clothing, aerodynamic helmets, and expensive looking bikes told me these guys were hardcore. They began to take off, one by one. As the herd thinned, I picked one off and started a conversation. Nice guy. They were some sort of cycling club.

"So where do you ride mostly?"

"This loop we are on. It circles out of Las Vegas, past the park, and then back in to a different area of town."

"Really? We just came out of Vegas the direction you guys are headed. How big of a loop is it?" I had expected a large number.

"It's about 17 miles."

"Seventeen?" My respect had begun to dwindle when I asked, "Well how many times do you do it?" trying to imply how many laps.

"Usually twice a week."

Twice a week? Seventeen miles? Maybe I was a tad judgmental, especially considering I wasn't a road biker, or a mountain biker for that matter, but only 34 miles per week? Usually? I wasn't impressed.

My eyebrows dropped even further when I looked out over the road; it was essentially flat. A flat 17 miles?

After all the cyclists left, we continued on, in the direction opposite theirs. We found our campground, found a campsite, and tried to catch a few hours of sleep before embarking into the park to climb.

This was when I opened to the first page of a new notebook. Ever since traveling with Megan, I had made a habit of writing during any trip. This was no exception, but it was my first time writing in several months.

I'm finally doing something. Something fun and liberating. Something good for the soul... That's why this trip is so important.

Me just being here represents my new will for a change.

This much needed change of scenery helped clear my head. Even though we were so close to the indulgences of Vegas, we lived simply at our campground. Days spent hiking and climbing in the desert heat were a form of meditation for me. Being away from it all allowed me to start examining myself and my life—writing about it helped too.

Overall, it was an epic Spring Break. After several days at Red Rocks, which had become incrementally more crowded, we left early, spent a night in Vegas, and then camped in Zion National Park, where we did some hiking and canyoneering. We drove a lot, but most of it was at night and was filled with either good conversation or good music. It was on this trip that I first listened to Florence and the Machine.

Chapter 16

"SHANE! How the heck are you?"

I had slept deeply and was not woken by any cars on the nearby road, but I did hear the subtle crunch of gravel as I drifted to sleep and a voice trying to determine which way to turn. Another cyclist. Riding in the dark? Must have been a racer. I couldn't understand the language in which he cussed his map.

I woke early. The sun had not yet crested the peaks on the east side of the valley and the tops of the west peaks only showed a sliver of light. The sky was deep blue, accented with the subtle wisps of cirrus clouds. It was going to be a hot day. I ate, packed, and snapped a few photos of the sun as it broke into the valley to mark the start of my day.

I had an easy 3 miles of pavement before I turned onto the "very remote" gravel road that would be my only company for the next 57 miles. The extra resistance provided by the gravel alerted my legs to their fatigue; the day before had been more draining than I had realized. I stopped to fill my water bladder and unpacked my mp3 player again for some additional motivation.

No juice. Kaput. Dead.

Great.

I tried to push through the fatigue and boredom that developed. The first few miles of road had the occasional ranch to look at, but the arid scenery started to repeat itself. Not only was it uninteresting, but like a broken record, it began to annoy me. The same tree, the same fencepost, the same rocky outcrop, over and over and over. The terrain rolled, which didn't help my legs or my attitude, and began to deteriorate the condition of both. The heat didn't help either.

Saddle sores had started to develop during the heat advisory. I had to stop and drop my shorts to apply more chamois cream to my backside; the icy burn hurt so good. I pulled my shorts up and stared at my bike, lost from the moment. I was in the shade of a high ridge and a part of me wanted to sit in the shade all day, but the shade wouldn't last. So I dug the trail mix from my bag and fixed it to my aero bars. I pedaled again and snacked on the trail mix as I went.

My mind was plagued with crappy feelings, and it conceded to the struggle; I was having a hard time staying motivated. I daydreamed about the end of the trip: what I would do when I was home, who I would talk to, what I would say. I reached toward my bag of trail mix to grab a handful and bumped another hand. Wait, another hand? My eyes followed the hand from the bowl of nuts, past the elbow, past the shoulder, and to the face.

"Shane! How the heck are you?"

"I'm doing good," he said as he threw the nuts into his mouth and washed them down with an IPA. He set the glass down on a dark wooden table top. The red brick walls were dimly lit and reflected back the chatter of the other occupants. I knew this place. It was the Post Street Ale House. "How's your trip going, man?"

I took a drink from my own glass, cold and slick with condensation. "I'm struggling right now, but it's been a hell of a trip."

"Nice, but why are you struggling?"

"Well, I'm on a pretty desolate stretch of road. I'm tired from all the miles I covered yesterday, and it's hot. I'm actually riding through a heat advisory right now."

"No way?"

"Yeah. It's nothing compared to the rain advisory I saw in Canada, though. Let me tell you about that day."

I analyzed my trip, thought about the most important parts to tell him. I went through the whole trip, day by day, but instead of examining it, I told Shane about it. I spoke out loud to him, shared my trail mix with him, and I sipped an ice cold IPA from my camelback. Our conversation was pretty one sided, but there were times I tried to imagine what he would say or how he would react, so

I could keep the dialogue going. And that was how I passed the next 25 miles: with my friend Shane. I spoke and laughed and even shed a tear or two, as though he were there.

Shane's presence, in a way, was an escape—even if just in my imagination. Shane and I were always able to be very open with each other, to share ideas and thoughts we weren't sure the world was ready for. Having that spirit of support kept me going.

As I talked with Shane, I noticed tire tracks on the road. The tracks were sunk below the surface of the road, accompanied by footprints in the places that had been too muddy to ride through. Bikes had come through here when the road had been waterlogged. How old were those tracks?

When I crested the divide I had climbed toward all day, I looked back down the treeless valley. It was a straight, narrow valley, nestled between the Tendoy and Beaverhead Mountain Ranges. The last 10 miles of the road were a straight line that arced up and over the rolling terrain all the way to the horizon. Incredible, to see an hour's worth of pedaling from a single vantage point. Even more incredible, I had covered the ground with my achy legs and fatigued body through the intense heat, but without noticing any of those things. How could I have noticed? I was at Post Street with Shane.

On my ride down from the high point, I encountered a headwind. The further I went, the narrower the gorge I was in and the stronger the headwind, but I was still moving fast enough to reach back and tap my sleeping bag after the bumpy sections to make sure the straps hadn't loosened. I stopped at a stream to cool down and refill my water bladder and debated whether to eat there or to wait another 10 miles until I was in town. Ten miles was another hour of riding, but I put off eating with the intention to visit the Yesterday Calf-A, a restaurant that had been recommended to me back at the North Fork Hostel and Inn.

The wind made things difficult, but I combatted it with Jolly Ranchers while I crouched on my aero bars. As I emerged from the desolate landscape, the wind carried the smell of garbage to me; the putrid rot and bitter sting in my nose didn't seem an appropriate welcome. I rode past the dumpster and into fresher air as I made my way to Dell.

The Yesterday Calf-A was an old school house turned restaurant. It was delicious. Homemade everything. I ordered a hot beef sandwich with mashed potatoes and gravy and tried to savor it as best as I could, but failed miserably as I scarfed it all down. I journaled and allowed my stomach to process before I ordered pie: warm sour cream cherry á la mode. It was the best slice of pie I'd ever had.

Stomach bursting, I left the cafe and rode 9 miles to Lima. I was still tired, especially now with a full stomach, but it was only 2 p.m.—too early to end the day. Instead, I took refuge at a local rest stop to avoid the heat and planned to continue on later in the afternoon if I felt up to it.

* * *

"Hey bicycle man."

"Hi there."

A lot of interesting people come through rest stops. Lima was right on Interstate 15, so I saw a lot of travelers. Small families, big families, families with adopted children. People with small dogs, big dogs, dogs that misbehaved. People in cars, SUVs, RVs, vans spray-painted black with passengers whose faces had black accents to match their dark clothing. Yes, a lot of people came through that rest stop during the few hours I was there.

I set up on a covered picnic table, offloaded my gear, and inverted my bike to clean the drive train and replace the chain. I also found an outlet to charge my mp3 player with, but it still didn't work. That was disappointing. After I charged my phone, I used it to check Allison's blog. She had posted up to Lima the day before. A day behind? I was gaining on her.

From her blog, I gathered she was now riding in a group and that during the desolate crossing I had just completed, they had been rained on. Were the tracks I had seen theirs? I was excited when I found out how close I was. I had thought she was several more days ahead of me. So after my rest, and with this new energy, I headed to the local gas station to get some supplies before leaving town.

I was smiling at the ice cream in my hand when a man pumping gas started a conversation with me. His daughter was riding across the country on a bike and stopping every few days to help build houses.

"Are you doing something like that?"

"Not exactly. I'm riding from Canada to Mexico, but just for myself. Not for any kind of fundraising or humanitarian reason."

"All the way to Mexico? You've still got a ways to go."

"Yeah. Hopefully I'll be there in a few weeks though."

"Is this all your gear?" he said as he eyed my bag-laden bike.

"Yup. No support crew, so I just have myself to rely on."

"Oh. Yeah, my daughter doesn't have to carry anything. They have a van. And she's on a road bike too."

"Well, I'm riding a lot of dirt and gravel, so I need the mountain bike."

"Wow! All the way to Mexico, huh?"

"That's the plan."

Riding a high from the ice cream and conversation, I left Lima.

• • •

"Hey, you look like you're racing," I said, pulling off the road toward another cyclist.

My good feelings had lasted as far as Lima's city limits. I was fatigued as I climbed the first small hill out of town. I was desperate for some music, but my mp3 player didn't work. It wasn't the battery, it just wasn't functioning. My phone had some music, so I turned it back on and opened its mp3 player. The music got me going, but only just. Luckily, about 6 miles out of town, I ran into another cyclist who had stopped on the side of the road to eat.

"We can ride together if you'd like."

"Yeah, that would be great. I'm dragging, so anything to keep me going. I'm Nathan by the way."

"I'm Ralph, but my friends call me Yukon."

"All right, Yukon it is."

Ralph was a hell of a guy. He was indeed a racer and had started with the Grand Depart in Banff just three days before me. I was thrilled to have caught him, especially when I learned that he had not taken any rest days yet. He was surprised I had caught him, so I refrained from telling him just how many rest days I had taken. But don't let me sell the guy short; Ralph was in his sixties.

"Well, before I came out, I went to the doctor just for a check up, you know, to make sure everything was ok. I didn't mention anything to him about the race, or anyone really, just in case I want to drop out. But the doctor, he looks at my tests and comes back into the examination room and guess what he says to me."

"I have no idea. What?"

"He says, 'Ralph, you're looking good for the most part. My only recommendation would be to get more exercise and lose a little bit of weight.' Can you believe that?" He started laughing, "I said, 'Doc, that won't be a problem.'"

And it wasn't, not for anyone riding the route. Obviously the exercise part is straight forward, but everyone lost weight. That was to be expected when you burned several thousand calories every day.

Ralph and I talked the entire 30 miles we rode together. He was a professor, and even though he was in the race, he occasionally stopped at a library to do some work for an online class he was the instructor for. That's right, he was racing and teaching. And even though he was at the back of the pack, he was still racing. A third of the racers had dropped out by that point, but not Ralph. What a guy.

I told Ralph about my experience on the route thus far, about chasing the grizzlies and becoming paranoid.

"I actually thought about sleeping in one of those graders," I confessed.

"You too, huh? I actually did sleep in one of those. It was a long night. The chair wasn't very comfortable," he said laughing.

"Then I'm glad I passed on that option."

I also told Ralph about my ride with Cefas and about my big mishap on Fleecer Ridge. It turned out Ralph had made the same wrong turn as me. I was glad I wasn't the only one.

"And now I'm trying to catch a girl named Allison."

"Oh yeah? I rode with a group for a day that had an Allison."

"Really?"

"Yeah, a group of five. They went pretty fast down the hills, a bit too fast for me. Even the girls." I felt even closer to catching Allison now.

Ralph and I camped together that night, just off the side of the gravel road we had been following. I was thrilled to stop. Even though I had felt tired and unmotivated for most of the day, I had ridden another century. That was my second day breaking 100 miles and having Yukon for the last 30 miles was how I was able to.

Chapter 17

"DID YOU HEAR that noise this morning, Nathan?"

"No, what was it?"

"I'm not sure. Animals of some kind. I think it may have been cows."

I had slept through it. I was glad for it, because I had just had two big days in a row and had another Continental Divide crossing coming up. I needed all the rest I could get. What I didn't need was Ibuprofen; my knee had stopped throbbing as expected, after two weeks. Ralph took off ahead of me while I cooked something for breakfast and packed up. It looked to be another day of riding through an exposed, arid landscape. Hopefully it would be the last day of the heat advisory.

I caught back up to Ralph within 15 miles. I could see his bright, neon yellow, long sleeve shirt just at the crest of the hill ahead of me. Beyond the hill, a cloud of dust rose into the clear sky. When I crested that same hill, I found out why. Yukon had been right about the noise—it had been cows. And now the two of us were stuck behind a cattle drive. We happened to catch that herd right at the Lakeview Cemetery, where a local lifelong resident and his granddaughter were performing the cemetery's upkeep. Ralph and I chatted with him and learned about the history of the area before I looked at the board that listed the occupants of the cemetery.

No one had been buried there in more than fifty years. Of the twenty-five or so names, several were infants or children. Even more surprising was the lack of names for plots; instead, the names of the people the person in question had worked for were listed. It was a good reality check, a reminder of just how privileged I was to be taking a trip like that.

The cattle drive terminated just past the cemetery. The half-dozen cowboys herded the last few cows through the fence alongside the road, and the herd dispersed into the pasture, their momentum rapidly decaying as they found new shoots of grass to nibble at. The cowboys headed back the way we all had come and tipped their hats to us as they passed. Ralph and I climbed back onto our bikes and hadn't even covered half a mile before he told me to go on without him. My pace was just too fast for him. Ralph had been good company, but I had been enjoying my own pace and did as he suggested.

The route brought me through the Red Rocks National Wildlife Refuge, which encompassed two lakes and the surrounding marshland, a refuge for waterfowl. I passed several cars parked along the road while their camera-toting drivers chased butterflies through the plush meadows of wildflowers. These flat, open meadows were bordered by a perfect line of evergreens that covered the intermediate slope leading up to the large peaks of bare rock, eroded in such a way to produce shelves, some with trees, others unoccupied. The gullies and deep shadows still held their snow, the slow melt sustaining the greenery below. It was easy to see why so many photographers were there.

After I left the refuge and did some pushing, I crested Red Rock Pass. I took the customary Divide crossing picture, me in the foreground, the pass marker in the back. While I took the first photo, I noticed a fencepost opposite me, and I laughed. Several blogs seemed to have the same picture at this pass. The weather and the subject varied, but the vantage point never did. Now I saw the reason why. I placed my camera on the same fence post that had held dozens of cameras before mine and set the self-timer. I ran back across the road and stood next to my bike in front of the sign. Now I was one more person that had the same picture. It was a club of sorts. Membership granted.

The ride down to the next town took me off-road and onto trails that circumnavigated gates that would deny the typical driver. Not me and my steed though. The only thing I was worried about was taking the wrong trail. Gates were not where the map indicated they should be. The trails and roads I followed were marked on the map, but had no signs in reality. I started to scour the ground with my eyes, searching for tire tracks. It had become a habit.

There! I spotted some and regained my confidence. I rode another mile through a pine forest spotted with the occasional meadow before I passed two cyclists headed in the opposite direction. Day bikers. No panniers, no backpacks. I didn't even see water bottles. Was it their tracks I had seen? Was I going the right way? Hopefully.

That was a weird aspect of the ride. Most of the route is so far removed, so remote, that bike tourists riding the route were the only people out there. That mentality became so engrained in my mind that I was surprised when I saw cyclists that weren't riding the route. Then, to see people not carrying supplies—not even water—that was mind blowing. I couldn't comprehend the thought.

I made it to the highway by 1 p.m. The day was getting unbearably warm now, and I sheltered in a small resort lodge for lunch. All the establishments along this stretch of highway were sustained by tourism. Even the map admits it, showing how the outline of the town traced the highway, hardly branching away from the pavement.

After I finished lunch, I crossed the road and wandered into the gas station that doubled as a small market. It was incredibly hot and I had a few hours to kill. Not being on the bike, I felt I should have been doing one of two things. Eating or sleeping. I wasn't tired, so I bought a pound of strawberries and a chocolate pastry. It was the perfect dessert to follow my lunch.

I sat against the outside wall of the gas station in the shade with my strawberries as four-wheelers went up and down the gravel roads. A line of ATVs sat outside the lodge where I had eaten, their uniform color indicating their rentability. It seemed like the more popular form of transportation in the area, which was strange to see. We had an ATV growing up too, but it usually pulled a chemical sprayer or a trailer that we would fill with rocks. In other words, it was for work, not for errands. So were these drivers locals and this just a different social standard? Or were these people tourists, trying to blend into the "rural" setting?

At 4 p.m., I was too antsy to sit any longer. It was still

uncomfortably warm, so I bought a few sport drinks to combat the loss of electrolytes the heat would cause. I poured one into my camelback and filled the remainder of the space with water. I examined my map one last time before setting out. The main route followed an old rail bed, while the much longer alternate followed gravel and pavement. The main route was flat for the most part with a slight downhill grade, while the alternate had much more climbing and descending. It seemed like an easy decision, but the catch was this: the rail bed was "extremely soft volcanic soil" on par with a fine sand. I had read about this stretch, and it sounded like a challenge. That must have been the reason an alternate was created, an alternate almost 20 miles longer with a lot of climbing. I weighed my options with Fleecer Ridge in mind. I had felt satisfied at the junction where the paved alternate rejoined the route, satisfied with my choice to take the more challenging route.

I left town through the conglomerate of small cabins and houses, each with their own ATV, some of those with coolers secured on the front. I crossed the Henrys Fork River and turned south onto the rail bed. Wow.

And again. Wow.

It wasn't just a sandy rail bed. Because it was a converted rail bed that granted access to lots of different trail users, it had been torn up. The all-terrain tourist cooler carts had thrown sand all over and created ruts, berms, and washboarding. Crisscrossing trails intersected with the main bed to create wave patterns. Knobby tires had thrown sand off the bed, extending it into the bordering vegetation. There was no hard surface to be found anywhere. After a hundred yards, I stopped and deflated my tires to their lowest recommended pressure. Then I deflated them further.

The sand was soft. "Extremely soft." Incredibly soft. Pedaling from a stop was difficult; the rear tire just wanted to dig into the sand. Once you had momentum though, pedaling became easier; it was the steering that became difficult. Turning the wheel pushed the sand instead of pushing the tire in the desired direction. Steering became a balancing act where direction was determined by hips. Good thing the rail bed was nearly straight.

"Well, Nathan," I said to myself, "at least it's only 30 miles."

Only.

The sand was hard work. The heat made it harder. Once I found my groove though, it was a lot of fun. I put the hose of my camelback into my mouth for a drink early on and the hose never came out. The heat was enough that I nursed the diluted sport drink the whole way. I focused on my front tire and tried to keep it from pushing sand instead of rolling over it, and the further I got from the town, the more uniform the sand surface became. I did go down once, falling onto my shoulder, but hey, it was such a soft landing I couldn't even get angry about it. All I could do was laugh.

I was happy with my decision to ride the sand. From this route, I was able to see a historic cattle-holding pen, a rustic cabin, a rock with old and new engravings of names, and my first glimpse of the Tetons. Even more exciting than those was an elk. Apparently, he hadn't seen me until the last second. Spooked, he ran out from the vegetation on my left, crossed the sand bed, and disappeared into the vegetation on my right. He crossed immediately in front of me. If I hadn't been in mid-flinch, I could have reached out and touched him. And if I had been on a harder riding surface, I probably would have gone over my handle bars with how fast I locked up both wheels. Overall, the sand was difficult, but that's why I took it. The writer in me decided that would be the better story.

• • •

"I figured I'd let you pass. You are working a lot harder than me," he said from the seat of his ATV.

"Yeah, it's not easy. I appreciate it."

An ATV, without a cooler, had been approaching me from the front on the sand. We could see each other a long way off, so I postponed moving for him to conserve my momentum. As we drew closer to each other, he pulled off the rail for me. He had a jolly demeanor and, more importantly, an understanding of my experience. It made me smile, the only person I had seen in almost 20 miles acknowledging the effort I was exerting. Maybe others had an idea of the effort it took too. Maybe that's why I was the only non-motorized vehicle I saw on the entire stretch of sand.

The last few miles before the Warm River Campground, the rail bed lost its soft texture and became a solid rock base as it dropped down into the ravine that wrangled the Warm River. It was early evening. The heat had subsided and shadows had grown. I looked forward to reaching the campground where the trail terminated and getting some shut eye. It was a USFS campground, so I didn't expect much. Rather, I expected a basic, low-key campground.

The trail dropped off the rail bed and followed a single track that paralleled the river and dropped lower and lower down its bank. I was almost at the river's level when I left the trail and emerged from the tall grass into the campground's parking lot.

It was the Ritz. A blacktop road circled through the tall evergreen and deciduous trees, its cilia filled with the ostentatious displays of the working-man's wealth. Massive camper trailers and RVs with their extended slide-outs filled every spot. Bicycles laid unused against the sides or against the picnic tables, their new sheen still visible in the failing light. And the chopped wood. Piles, stacks, towers dominated several camping spots, the occupants clearly not planning to leave their fire for the duration of the week. Children ran rampant down the road and along the river, scaring the stocked trout from the fisherman's fly. Adults were just as rampant, though they didn't run. Why risk spilling their drinks? Then there was me, soaked in sweat, covered in dirt and sand, everything I needed on my bike, which was just as presentable as me. I drew some attention.

I was not excited by the scene. Maybe I should have expected it. The Fourth of July was only two days away. I was less excited when I found the information board at the camp entrance which told me it was a $15 nightly rate. To camp there? This didn't compare favorably to the $5 fees I had been paying at USFS campgrounds. I was unsure about camping there to begin with. Factor in the money and it was almost time to go. But I was exhausted. I had almost hit 90 miles that day. And it was late. I was just about to ride back up the trail to look for a suitable spot away from the RV park when I saw the campground host pull his golf cart into his camping spot. Must've been making the rounds. I succumbed to my exhaustion and decided I may as well ask. It seemed every time I asked for something, I got it. I rode my bike around the backside of the host's trailer and pulled up next to his golf cart. He still sat in it, staring off into space.

"Hi there. Are you the camp host?"

He blinked and turned his face to me, not leaving the golf cart. "Yeah, can I help you?"

"I hope so. I was just looking at the camp fees and was wondering if there was any way I could proposition a bargain with you?"

"A bargain huh? Well, I can't do that. Those are the prices set by the Forest Service. I don't have any say in the matter."

"Yeah, I figured that was the case. It doesn't hurt to ask though."

"You must be doing that race that comes through here, huh?"

"Nope. I'm not racing, but I'm following the same route as the racers."

I planted both feet on the ground and leaned toward him, arms resting on my aero bars. He turned further toward me with each exchange of words. It wasn't long before we were having a full conversation that covered the race, retirement, golf, and being a campground host. The guy looked tired of the Fourth of July crowd already, on the second of July. We talked for twenty minutes or more, and though it was nice to talk with someone, the light had now left the canyon. Twilight told me to find a place to camp soon. But I didn't want to leave. I felt the situation was about to produce something worthwhile.

"You're just wanting to stay the one night?"

"Yup, I'd be gone early tomorrow morning. Be here twelve hours at the most."

"I'll tell you what," he said, turning and completely facing me now, "in the other loop, across the river, there's a tent spot. I call it the honeymoon suite, but only because it's a little ways up a hill and hidden behind some trees. Its hidden well enough that no one would know you were camping there." He emphasized that last part: "Not even I would know."

"Really? Are you sure? I don't want to cause you any problems."

"Yeah, of course. It's fine."

"Across the river you said?"

"Yeah, cross the bridge and go straight. The parking spot is marked with a T for 'tent' and you'll see the trail."

"Well, I can't thank you enough. I'm Nathan, by the way."

"Nathan? I'm Paul."

We exchanged pleasantries for a few more minutes, and right as I was ready to leave, Paul told me if I wasn't happy with the tent spot, I could set up in his site. He told me I could use his picnic table and fire ring too.

"I appreciate it Paul, but I'm sure it will be fine. You should see some of the places I've camped."

"Yeah? Well, this place is pretty nice by campground standards."

I laughed, saying, "Yeah, it is. That's why it will be nice to be in the tent spot and away from all the noise, so I can sleep."

We shook hands, and Paul wished me the best on my ride. I rode back through the campground, having to avoid fewer stares this time now that the barbecues had been fired up and the satellite dishes turned on. I had to smile at the prospect of camping to be closer to nature, all the while undermining nature in the process. How many of those satellite receivers were tuned to a nature program when a better nature program lay just beyond the confines of the campground?

Chapter 18

WHEAT.

    Potatoes.

    Tetons.

    "Give it a week, Nathan."

    Wheat.

    "Just give it another week."

    I woke early. The campsite was quiet; all sound was muffled by the collective haze from the several fire rings that still produced smoke from the almost dead, gray embers. Above the haze, the brilliant blue told me that even though I had survived the four-day heat advisory, the heat wasn't gone yet. I packed quickly and without sound. I pulled on my jersey and socks, still cold with the river water I used to rinse them the night before. I ignored my skin's complaints; the cooling effect would be beneficial in a few minutes on my climb out of the river's canyon.

    No one stirred at the click of my rear hub or the clang of the bear-proof dumpster I deposited my garbage in. The enormity and number of the brown receptacles was another indication of how lavish the campsite was. I wouldn't produce enough garbage on my entire trip to cover the bottom of one. They would all be full by the end of the next day. I pedaled my farewell to the campsite, riding around the speed bumps on my way out, and gave a final wave to Paul, the only person to be up and about in the campground.

    I began my steep climb out of the canyon and left behind the smooth river and the trees that drank at its banks. At the top, I was greeted by a grid of roads that overlay the large, irrigated expanse of agricultural land. I climbed steadily, at a low grade, but the land was so uniform it was hard to tell I was climbing at all. As I crossed through the landscape, I passed large sprinklers that guided themselves through the fields, their tracks memorized by the dirt below while their arced conduits framed the distant Tetons; the water they distributed caught and scattered the light and drifted to bathe me in its cool glow. Fields of potatoes and wheat took their morning drink before a hard day of production. The wheat, still a dark green, had large heads atop the slender stalks, and the leaves had only just begun to show the darkest tans and yellows in their tips.

Was the wheat back home this green? It must have been close to turning itself. The grass—having produced its seeds—would die, dry, and turn a rich green landscape to gold. These Idaho fields may have had the Tetons as a backdrop, but our fields back home had hills, our fields had character, and in many respects our fields were unique. In our fields, the wind didn't blow; it danced. Stand atop a saddle that adjoined two hills and you could watch the wind wrap around you, bend the wheat stalks in unison up one side of the hill and back down the other, all the while the waves moved around you on the hills above. An appropriate canvas for the wind, the wheat anchored and textured, unlike the waves of a lake or an ocean. And the hills, the rolling hills allowed for a rhythmic dance of the wheat displayed in every dimension, all ordered and stochastic at the same time. It was nothing like these two dimensional fields that extended beyond the limits of my vision, that lacked character, that disappeared over the horizon of uniformity.

My ride through the wheat fields only resulted in more thoughts of home; thoughts of home led to thoughts of family; thoughts of family led to thoughts of friends. All these thoughts led to despair. I was alone. There was not even anyone to be seen anywhere I looked. There was nothing of comfort.

Just wheat.

Just potatoes.

And the Tetons.

Tears collected in my eyes as I guessed what my friends were doing at that moment. At that early hour, and in a different time zone, they were probably still asleep. At home, warm in their own beds. Not a down sleeping bag and inflatable sleeping pad, but an actual bed with blankets and pillows. I missed the physical and emotional comforts of home. Even with such beautiful scenery, my head hung.

"Just give it another week, Nathan. The feeling will pass."

My breathing more level and eyes drier, I left behind the farmland and crossed through a tree line onto a gravel road. The road was wide, so wide that traffic had failed to produce any ruts devoid of loose gravel that would make riding easier. Instead, the coarse gravel would slip and spin under tire and slow progress. The first mile, all I did was cuss under my breath and shake my head at the road. The second mile, all I did was cuss under my breath and shake my head at the heat. The sun's intensity increased, and both my sweat glands and water bladder noticed. Maybe that heat advisory should have been extended another day.

I removed my phone from my backpack and plugged in the headphones. I searched for music, not by name, but by emotion. I found the music I needed. M83. The *Oblivion* Soundtrack. I saw the movie before I began my trip, and the soundtrack was the best part. Just as I had done in the desolate stretch through Montana, I stepped out of this reality and into another. I didn't go to the Post St. Ale House, though, and Shane was nowhere in sight. Instead, I stepped up to a conductor's podium, baton in hand.

The theater was archetypical: auditorium chairs of red fabric and classic wood armrests; a second balcony set back above the lower tier; private boxes flanking each wall from the balcony to the stage. The house lights were down, the stage lights dimmed, and a single spotlight fell on my podium.

I brought in the strings section by section, softly. Next, the keys of the piano created overlying melodies that brought complexity to the music and filled the theater. Then all at once the brass and percussion brought drama to the show with an entrance that shook dust from the velvet-draped walls. As my baton cut through the air and as sweat started to collect on my brow and at the hem of my cuffs, it became apparent that this was an odd scene. Not because I had no experience or skill as a conductor, but because the theater was empty. It was the performance of a lifetime, and no one was there to see it. Even the instruments were without performers: the strings sang of their own accord; the brass blew through their own valves; the percussion pounded their own surfaces—all at my direction. It was the performance of a lifetime, and I had the only available seat. My arms moved with a passion, a fury as they tried to play all the instruments simultaneously.

The crescendo.

The climax.

The resolution. My arms hung limp at my side, my baton with a slight bend. As the last strings bowed out of the emotional conclusion, the audience erupted. I turned, dismayed to see every seat occupied. Then the audience rose from their seats. A standing ovation. Only after the last note ended had they appeared, only able to catch that last bit of resonant sound that echoed back from the walls. The sweat dripped from my brow, and the baton hit the floor.

The sweat dripped from my brow and my phone battery died. The heat was more intense than when I had left my bike for the podium, and while I was gone I had crossed into Wyoming. I was too distraught over my dead battery to think about the significance of my concert. This parallel world though, this imaginary construct of escape did manage to capture my interest. It reminded me of a movie … a specific movie.

But now it was the reality of the Tetons that I had to face while I crossed their northern flank. The road was not graveled or wide anymore. Instead, it was narrow and rocky, tan with clay and organic deprived soil, and spotted where bedrock protruded to reach for the sky. The sun was high now and shade sparse. The road was windy, steep, and rolling. I kept a hopeful eye open for a misplaced tuxedo and baton on the side of the road.

Instead, I found a cool stream with a series of four-foot waterfalls. I cooled in the pools and considered staying there for the afternoon while the temperature dropped back down. But it was before 1 and the real heat hadn't even set in yet. I had another 15 miles before I reached Flagg Ranch and finished the first half of the map. The last 12 miles were downhill.

"Let's do it."

• • •

I finished the rocky climb and descended. I had been so distracted by the road that I had forgotten I was skirting along the edge of Yellowstone as I climbed. I rode the last mile on pavement and the bike coasted so easily that I didn't need to pedal. At Flagg Ranch, I ate lunch in a dining room much too fancy for my appearance. Fortunately, it was empty apart from one table.

Eight obnoxious individuals about my age occupied a table in the center of the room. They were on some kind of summer road trip, and according to one, he had a dish with a barbecue sauce that was beyond tangy. In fact, it was "twangy" and made him feel as though there was a "banjo in his mouth." I would have been impressed with his use of imagery and word-blending if it hadn't sounded so rehearsed. How long had he been waiting to use that line? Their good natured waitress, also about my age, laughed and continued to humor them beyond their meal and well beyond their welcome.

I had to chuckle as the waitress assured them they would be able to make the drive to Idaho that day. If I had covered the distance on a bike, I was sure their van could handle it. They still didn't seem so sure as they stood up, but they headed to their van regardless, but not before they all hugged their waitress goodbye. After the group left, another waitress approached her.

"I felt so sorry for you. They were being so ridiculous." The waitresses spoke freely. They either didn't care I was there or had forgotten me. I guessed the latter.

"Yeah they were, but it was worth it. I got what I wanted from them."

Laughter: "Yeah? How much?"

"Tip was 60 bucks," she said, her smile now more genuine than any she had given to the group.

"Nice, girl!"

That was my cue. Once I was reminded of the day of the week, paid for my meal, and retrieved my phone from the bar where it was left to charge, I left the restaurant. I wandered the resort's small grocery store to kill time by calculating calories. I purchased some cinnamon rolls, ate two, and returned to the bike. I had spent too much time in the immediate vicinity of too many tourists. I already missed the solitude.

Flagg Ranch would be the first of many ranches I passed that were economically dependent on tourism. Though I wasn't a fan of so many people, this ranch was a supply oasis. But once I got what I needed, I was happy to leave and cruise along a flat, 35-mile segment of pavement. After just 12 miles though, I had to stop.

As I crouched over, elbows on my knees and eyes fixed on the ground, I thought back to home again. One harvest when I was maybe thirteen, I drove truck. It was in August, and August was always hot and dry. I was prone to nosebleeds when I was a teenager and that harvest may have been the first incident. I sat in the truck when the blood started to flow. I jumped out before I dripped blood all over myself and the interior of the truck.

I stood in the shade of the truck, desperately clutching at the bridge of my nose to staunch the flow. After twenty minutes of bleeding I started to cry. After twenty-five, the rest of the crew began to wonder where I was and why I didn't answer their calls. After thirty, the other truck driver found me standing over a pool of blood. We weren't far from my mom's house when he had found me, so I took my shirt off and used it to staunch the flow while he drove me to the edge of the field.

Mom did what mothers are good at and calmed me down. That made it easier to stop the bleeding. She also saw to it that I took the last few hours of the day off, and wouldn't hear any arguments against it. She was the type to go to war for her children.

I laughed with the memory as blood dripped from my nose along the banks of Jackson Lake, the Tetons reflected in the water. I aimed the steady drip of blood to miss myself and my gear as I dug through my frame bag searching for my toilet paper. That wasn't a scent I wanted on any of my stuff in bear country.

It took about fifteen minutes to clot and clean up. Like I had learned back during my first harvest in the truck, a bit of lotion up the nose can go a long way. Because I didn't have lotion, I used chamois creme.

The remainder of the day was uneventful as I pedaled along pavement, 14 miles of which were brand new black top. It was so smooth, so new, still unpainted, and still flanked by cones and construction equipment.

I paid a $10 campground fee that night, guilt free after the free night Paul had given me. Plus, this campsite had bear boxes—good storage for my two remaining cinnamon rolls.

Chapter 19

THE TETONS DOMINATED the horizon again the next morning. But this morning was different. I was on the opposite side of the Tetons, and they were bright, illuminated by the rising sun, free of the shadows I had experienced the day before. I was on the opposite side of the emotional spectrum too. I was ready to go, ready to cover some ground. I wolfed down my two cinnamon rolls and set off into the sunshine to start up the first pass of the day: Togwotee Pass.

The first 8 miles of the day were on gravel and a remote dirt road that dumped me out at another tourist lodge alongside the highway. The lodge was a complex of buildings, all made of logs, guarded by rows of ATVs, snow cats, and passenger vans, all parked to create perfect row after perfect row.

The route transitioned to the highway, which made for an easy climb. The hard surface at a manageable grade had me in good spirits and feeling sorry for the motorcycle owners that passed me, some of them decked out in leather, while others pulled trailers. Nine miles of steady pedaling brought me to the Continental Divide. Here, the route followed a dirt road into the mountains. It was not a good road. It was washed out, bumpy, and after a mile of being jarred, my legs began to burn. Why was I still climbing if I had already crested the Divide? My question was answered by the road's first view.

I saw an immensity. Mountains extended past the horizon, each successive ridge achieving a lighter shade of blue until the snow of the furthest peaks couldn't be distinguished from the distant pale-blue clouds; it was as if the clouds had chosen not to precipitate, but rather, just laid themselves directly upon the mountain tops. The pines were a patchwork: green with growth, brown with burning heat, gray with decay, all shades present between the sun and the shade. My road laid at the top of the meadow that extended down slope and fanned out below me. The crisp blades bowed to the wildflower's blue hue and the patches of dandelions, still yellow in their late bloom. A line of trees wandered through the meadow to mark the path of its stream that was fed by an alpine lake trapped somewhere above me. I couldn't move. My breathing had stalled until my first, long, deep breath brought the wind and colors and emotions of the mountains into my lungs.

I breathed vitality.

Somewhere below me, hidden, was a line of cars. If their passengers were lucky, they might look away from the road, their phones, their headrest monitors long enough to see a minute detail of this landscape. I stood at the top and looked upon the landscape as a whole. That was how it left me: feeling whole, feeling like I could go anywhere.

I started down and found gravel. Fortifications rose from the landscape, large rock walls that guarded the perimeter of Brooks Lake, the steep faces polished by the weather. The earth's age, a geologic time scale, was visible in the rock, the striped horizontal layers that were ledges for the snow to rest on. Another lodge sat nestled in the valley, corralled like its horses. Past the lodge, I began to see more people: hikers, fisherman, campers; it was the Fourth of July, so I had expected nothing less.

The road became steeper when I left the lake. Steep roads caused me to overuse my brakes. If the road surface was covered in a loose substrate, sharp turns would make my body pucker in unspeakable places while my face was pelted by the small particles flung from my front tire. Even worse than descending a steep hill was being stuck behind a timid driver on that hill. I wanted to pass the dark blue sedan, but the road was too windy and the gravel too loose. The driver braked in the wrong places and forgot the accelerator. My disc brakes grew hot while I tried to not rear end the car. My temper grew hot, too, when the car's tires began to throw the road's sunbaked dust into the air.

"Well, at least it's not raining."

The car turned onto a different road after a few miles, and I was free to coast to my bike's ability. I moved fast enough now to think to reach back and tap my sleeping bag, another new habit. I came back to the highway I had left only 10 miles earlier and tightened the straps on the sleeping bag. The pavement was dreary compared to the mountains. My vantage point was so low that I couldn't see outside of the valley. The darkness on the horizon didn't help either.

• • •

Fifteen miles later, the horizon was gone, and the darkness extended past my position to engulf that which lit my way. I had started up a 4-mile climb the map referred to as "hard." After I began to push my bike up a steep section, a pickup rounded the corner in front of me, a trailer with three ATVs in tow, and slowed enough for the driver to lean out his window and instruct me on the proper use of a bike.

"You're supposed to be riding that thing!"

Had the guy ever used a form of transportation where he was the source of propulsion? I doubted it. I also doubted he was still in range of my bear spray. Too bad. Once he was out of sight and I was pushing again, the clouds above me burst. "Hard" the map had said. These directions were tailored to me.

The rain fell heavily. I rode past the corner that hid the hillside and found a long section of road before me, only visible to the next switchback. The road, dried by the heat and pulverized by the traffic, was in a fog. Fog? No. Dust. The heavy rain drops stirred up several days worth of dust to create a light brown haze in the two feet above the surface. Within the minute, the rain had cleared the dust and had brought it back to the surface as mud. The collective splash back of the rain-drops-turned-mud-drops created a dark brown mist in the six inches above the road. Water collected quickly, but the runoff didn't drain from the road. Instead, the road directed the water. Ruts helped cut channels. Banked turns funneled water through switchbacks to worsen the washboarding. The road had become the hillside's gutter.

The climb was hard, just as the map had said it would be. I hadn't imagined it like this though. I had fallen victim to my misconception about these maps. To that point, they had been my guide, my key to success, my whole journey planned out. To that point, I had forgotten what a map really was: a representation. Geology taught me about maps, about their usefulness, about the subtle nuances that made them worthwhile to those who knew how to use them. But I also learned about their shortcomings, their inaccuracies, and the fact that they are only a representation and nothing more. I had depended on these maps to tell me what to expect, what to prepare for, what I would experience. But they were just maps. Just a representation. Just a piece of waxy, weather-proof paper incapable of capturing reality. They were just a plan.

Rain wasn't always enjoyable on the trip. It often drove me inwards to escape. On this climb, the inward trip included the ideas of these maps, these plans. I had always done that, tried to live my plans. I always tried to stick to the red line. But those plans, those maps, those lines, they were just to orient, to give direction. The real experience was beyond the plans, beyond control, and I had been missing out. I had tried too hard to live my plans, to strive for a life I had imagined instead of trying to live the one I already had: the one beyond control, raw and unplanned. The one that actually existed. That was the life that those maps could never capture, the one course you cannot know until you travel it.

I emerged from my mind back into the rain. The storm front now extended miles across the valley as it chased the sunlight. Water splashed underfoot as the road drained the hillside. It was miserable, but I was off the map now and back on the hill. Sometimes I hoped the occasional car or pickup would stop to offer me a ride, but none of them even hesitated. I finished the climb strong, on my own. The rain had passed over me and swept across the valley in a narrow band, much more narrow than it had led me to believe. The road, with several days of intense heat stored within it, began to evaporate the rain as soon as it stopped falling. Wisps of steam rose from the whole surface, a natural fog machine of sorts. Meanwhile, the sun broke on the higher elevation clouds and reflected down to illuminate the storm from every side. It was spectacular.

• • •

The sun had been short lived at the top of the climb, and the life left in my legs was lacking. Thrown back into the shadows and still wet from the rain, I looked for any relief. My map (just a plan) hadn't shown a lodge nearby, so I followed the signs and the directions of an ATV operator. The Crooked Creek Lodge was another tourist destination, a central log building, complete with food and drink, surrounded by small log cabins to rent. I sat at the bar and ate my late lunch when I was recognized by the woman in the trio next to me.

"Oh! That was you we passed?"

"I'm sure. I haven't seen any other cyclists in a few days."

"Well, I'm sorry. I told my husband we should stop and see you if you needed a ride."

"Oh don't worry about it. I would have turned it down anyway."

They were in the area camping and had been on a hike when the rain began. They had retreated to the confines of their trailer, but I supposed boredom had driven them to the bar for a drink. What a luxury to be dry and disappointed.

I finished my sandwich and left the lodge with a simple goal: go as far as I could. My plan was to ride to Pinedale the following day and take the remainder of the day off. I hoped it would be substantial enough to qualify as a rest day, but that meant I had to ride as far as possible after another Continental Divide crossing today.

I followed the road above a narrow gulch cut by a stream. Inside one of the meanders was a fly fisherman, upstream from the gravel bar. What a simple life. What a simple hobby. On the surface, most everything is simple. The fisherman stood back far enough to prevent his shadow from falling on the water, even though the sky was clouded. Even his dog stood back and stared at the surface to evaluate each rock and ripple, every pool and riffle to imitate his master. Where were the trout? Behind that rock? Under that bank? What were the trout eating? What insects were hatching? Dry fly or wet fly? Reach cast, roll cast, or backhand cast? Simple, indeed.

The rain traveled against me and crested the Divide before me. Visibility was zero compared to my earlier view. Instead of the endless ranges that blended into the horizon, the rain now masked the closest range behind its veil to leave a vague outline. My lunch had not settled well and now my bike made a horrendous noise. My rear bearing sounded gritty, shot, and begged to stop. I examined it, but like anything, bikes are only simple on the surface. It sounded bad in either direction, but worse when spun backwards. I did not have the knowledge to diagnose the problem or the tools to fix it if I could. The nearest bike shop was in Pinedale. It was another simple decision: keep going.

I crested the top of Union Pass while I ushered cows off the road and out of my way, the rain keeping us all miserable. The second climb had done me in. The cold rain had made sure of it. I consulted my map for a landmark, a goal, a reason to keep going and reward myself with food. The only landmark was an outhouse a couple of miles down the road. It would do.

I checked on my rear wheel before I began the descent. It seemed fine for the moment. The road cut through a long meadow, cold and exposed, at the mercy of the rain. I was at the mercy of the road, one of the worst roads on the entire route. Sand and cobbles. No gravel. No hardpan. Just sand and cobbles. Without a front fender, my face was covered, the sliminess of the mud and the abrasiveness of the sand perpetual. The rain fell harder. There was no longer a view of any kind. Just dismal gray. To add to it, my descent was through rolling terrain, and once again, it was difficult to tell I was losing elevation given all the climbing.

The rain worsened, as did the riding. Up and down, up and down. Dim light was filtered further through squinted eyelids that defended against the abrasive sand and dirty water. Pull a mouthful of water from the water bladder. Rinse sand and mud from mouth. Spit. Drop jaw again with the strained breathing of a tired, unacclimated body riding at too high an elevation for comfort. Hope for more oxygen. Close mouth again. Collect sand from front teeth with tongue. Water. Rinse. Spit. More sand, raise eyes from grainy bombardment of roadway to battering of rain. Squint at water, flinch when the perfectly placed drop strikes eyeball and shifts contact lens. Blink to secure contact and clarify vision. Lower head. Squint. Sand. Breath. Rinse. Spit. Repeat. Breathe. Pedal. Repeat. Breathe. Pedal. Repeat.

Gray streaks blocked out all warmth and color. Only dark, earthy tones were visible. The dark green of the meadows, the forest green of the evergreens, the black and gray bark, steel gray streams with the dull pearl froth of runoff. The torrent left me cold and wet. I had read a blog, a few years old, of a cyclist that rode south to north. The only precipitation he experienced on the whole trip was a hail storm that lasted an hour. How unfortunate for him.

I rounded a bend in the road and found my landmark: the outhouse. Or three? An older one stood alone, locked, closed for business. The two newer, typical USFS stood further back from the road, the shared building's eve negligible. But I propped my bike under it as best as I could with the rain only occasionally advancing below the eve, at the whim of the wind. Peanut butter had begun to taste bland. With each mouthful, the butter thickened, and became harder to swallow. Maybe it had mixed with the sand and formed some sort of edible concrete, caloric concrete. The jar made me think of warmer days, how the heat had melted the peanut butter and created a smooth surface when it resettled. The peanut fragments had settled to the bottom because of this. I had to work extra hard to get to them.

While I ate, I unfolded my map and took in its full extent. I was still 60 miles from anything. There were a few primitive campsites farther down the road, but in a national forest, anywhere is fair game. I felt the peanut butter in my stomach, its weight, its thick consistency; I shuddered and put the lid back on the jar. My map wasn't motivating. No good landmarks were in reach. I sighed a defeated sigh. I knew I wasn't going anywhere. It was still early, only 4 or 5, but another mile would have been twice as long as the same mile after resting. I was too tired. I needed sleep.

I did a quick survey of the area for a suitable place to pitch my grizzly-bear-snack-sack. I shivered as I wandered and began to cringe at the idea of being in my bivy for several hours before I fell asleep. I wasn't claustrophobic, but I was accustomed to wide open spaces. My shelter was too small to fully stretch out in, to sit up in, to roll over in. It was fine while unconscious, but for several hours of wakefulness? That goes without mentioning the rain. I still had not experienced a night of rain that did not leave a heavy deposit of water on the inside of the waterproof material that drenched everything, including my sleeping bag. I was already wet and wanted to escape the moisture, not subject myself to further exposure.

Hey. A roof.

I noticed it, not for the first time, but in a different light.

I walked around the outhouse just to confirm the eve wasn't accommodating. It was not. The ground adjacent to the building was drenched all the way around; there was no rain shadow even. I walked back to the front where my bike leaned against the wall between the two doors that separated males and females, straight-legged stick figures from triangle-skirted. I leaned against the male door and weighed my options consciously, searching for any justification for the decision I had already made subconsciously.

I opened the door to the male side and poked my head in. Not clean, but not terribly dirty. I closed the door and leaned against it again. In front of me, the small clearing extended to the road, beyond which laid a meadow. There was no horizon, no end to the rain in sight. I turned back and opened the door once more, then walked in this time. Yes, definitely big enough to lay down in. The bike would fit too. I looked back out at the rain. Well, no reason to dawdle.

I grabbed my bike by the handlebars, the pressure on my gloves making the wet fabric more apparent to my palms. I watched the back wheel and listened for the noise as I rolled the bike a few inches. I did not hear it. But from the tire, my gaze moved to the triangle-skirted figure. I leaned my bike back up against the wall. I reached for the door handle, but felt compelled to knock first even though I knew it was empty. Societal norms? The knock resounded in the emptiness. I stuck my head in. Just as I had suspected. Not clean, but not as dirty as the men's side. Gender norms? I backed my bike in against the wall. I stepped back and considered it one last time, looking back out through the open door framing the landscape. I closed the door and locked it.

I unpacked my bag and bivy, inflated my sleeping pad, and situated the trio as far from the toilet as possible. I changed and hung my wet clothes on the hand railing and from my handlebars. I was still hesitant for the first half hour or so about sleeping inside of an outhouse, but rain had the tendency to drive me inwards.

Sand collected in the corner of my eyes as I sat on my sleeping pad writing in my journal. The grains tried to dislodge my contacts. I had to dig the sand out; losing a contact would be disastrous. The process blurred my vision, the image of the name on my journal's page. Amber. She had worked for the US Forest Service during summers, back in Washington. She had usually been trail crew, but had switched the summer before to campground maintenance. She had told me a few horror stories about campground outhouses and how she had to clean up the mess. I cringed. Then I told myself a girl like Amber was in charge of this outhouse. Knowing her compulsion for cleanliness, that was a comfort. Besides, I would reach Pinedale the next day where I would be able to clean my stuff. What a relief it would be to wash my hands of this place.

I wrote a substantial amount in my journal by headlamp; the entry stressed my complete lack of shame in the decision. It was hard to argue against a night of dry rest. Necessity had trumped pride, which is why my sleeping pad and bag lay inside my bivy, limp without its poles, on the hard concrete floor. A small amount of light, whatever the rain allowed, came through the window in the upper outside wall above me. The crack beneath the door let in the cool air, and I could hear the rain.

My friends, they were probably all celebrating the holiday. I could see the barbecues, all the steaming food, served by the spoonful onto their paper plates, the clear sky above them alight with the bursts of strontium, magnesium, and copper, the colorful oxidation reflected in their dreamy eyes. They would never suspect that I lay on the floor of an outhouse, my only fireworks the thunderclaps of the storm overhead.

Happy Fourth of July, Nathan.

Chapter 20

March 2012

PIZZA AND BEER.

Netflix.

Relaxing.

Spring quarter had begun. I had finished off my general education classes and was now back into the sciences. The days grew longer, the sun shined, and rain fell less frequently. Things had improved, like I had brought back a small piece of the desert from our climbing trip to Vegas. In addition, one of my classes, Field Ecology, had us doing research on Turnbull National Wildlife Refuge, 18,000 acres of channeled scablands, a unique environment covered by ponderosa pine forest and dotted with ponds and lakes that served migrant water fowl in addition to the resident fauna. Permission was needed to do anything on the refuge, so it gave me an air of privilege; but, more importantly, it was just plain beautiful.

The second week of class had just begun. I had not been overwhelmed by any projects or essays yet, and I still had a few weeks to work out any graduation kinks. I took the time to relax while it was available. I picked up a pizza and some beer and headed home. The warm pizza box sat on the coffee table as I pulled up Netflix and grabbed a bottle opener from the kitchen. I plopped down onto the blue couch my mom had given me when I moved out of the dorms and scrolled through the movies Netflix had to offer. I had been on a documentary kick, so I went to that section, scrolling, scrolling, searching, eating pizza.

Ride the Divide? I had seen the title several times in the past months but had not watched it. I read the description anyway, ready to pass over this documentary again. But, Canada to Mexico?

I had been thinking of what I would do when I graduated college. One idea was to hike the Pacific Crest Trail, which a friend of a friend was doing. I wasn't dead set on the idea. I hadn't given it the full thought it deserved, but I had wanted to do something like that. Another friend thought he might road bike from the west coast to the east coast that summer and invited me along. That seemed pretty cool too. And it definitely captured my idea of what cycling should be—unlike the Vegas cyclists I met during Spring Break. A guy I once worked with on the family farm had done something similar after high school. He and a friend started in Canada, rode down the west coast, and finished at Mexico. He said it had been one of the best experiences of his life. That was what I wanted, something on a grand scale, something that would impact my life, something that would challenge my physical, mental, and emotional capabilities. Biking from Canada to Mexico? The Continental Divide?

My first piece of pizza was gone, so I selected the movie before I ate the whole pizza trying to decide. The more of the movie I watched, the more appealing the route sounded. Maybe it was the full belly. Probably it was the beer. But, it wasn't the race that had caught my attention, but what all the racers had said about the route. It was empty, beautiful, full of solitude. They were alone and physically pushed, which was expected. But the emotional challenge had caught some of them off guard, and the producers caught more than one breakdown that resulted in tears and talk of quitting.

I was fascinated by the idea of riding down the rocky spine of the continent. I was enthralled with the idea of doing it alone. This route was a combination of my other ideas' best elements. This was a mountain bike route that avoided the large cities and concentrated populations that road biking would not. It was out in the mountains, removed like the PCT, but I would still have the greater mobility and high rate of travel of a bike.

When the movie ended, only a few slices remained in the box, the greasy stain outlining the missing pieces. As I put my leftovers in the fridge, I filed those thoughts away. I returned to my desk and began to search for scientific papers. I still needed to graduate before I did anything like that. I needed to focus for the next nine weeks, and get my degree. Then I could entertain those ideas.

I had no idea then that I would end up on the route. Despite the appeal of the route, or any of the other ideas I had, I was scared to act on those desires. It wasn't characteristic of me to take big chances like that. I had always been the good student, the one that never stepped out of line, the one molded and prepared for a quiet life of complacency within society. I was accustomed to doing what I thought was expected of me instead of doing what I wanted. Riding the route would break that mold, and I wasn't sure I could do that.

I never thought I would find the courage;

I never thought I would break that mold;

I never thought I would reclaim my life;

And I certainly never thought I would have no problem sleeping on an outhouse floor.

Chapter 21

IT DEFIED GRAVITY.

Did it know? Did it understand what gravity was? Probably not. I think of gravity as the force that holds me down. But did it even have a concept of "down"? Was it looking down at me or out at me? He was very still on the wall, except for that one leg that couldn't pick a position. It looked like a twitch, but I guess he was just ready to move.

I laid on my back and stared up from the floor of the outhouse. As soon as I moved to scratch my shoulder, his legs scuttled across the wall to carry him away from me. To be that small would be a bizarre experience. The forces of the universe would have a different influence. If I asked that spider what he thought of gravity, he might say, "What the hell is gravity?" It was hard to grasp his experience.

If I wanted to understand, I would need to change my perspective.

I had survived my night in the outhouse and found the company of spiders preferable to that of bears. I crawled from my sleeping bag, opened the door, and emerged into light. The meadow reflected the sun's rays with droplets of moisture still clinging to the bent blades of grass, while water dripped from the outhouse roof and surrounding trees. I sat outside and ate my breakfast of macaroni and cheese while I took in the sun and fresh air. I had slept, but was still exhausted. It was my second day all over again when my body performed as though the sleep never happened. Was this a consequence of sleeping at an elevation higher than I was acclimated to? Regardless, I only had 60 miles to go before reaching Pinedale, and they were mostly downhill.

When I set out, I realized the lack of rain was the only improvement from the day before. The road's moisture still glued sand to my tire, which was thrown into my face; the cobbles still turned and rolled to make my bike sway and tires slip; and the landscape was still rolling. There were several short climbs that forced me to hike. That left me vulnerable to the newly hatched mosquitos. They were thirsty, and my repellant wasn't effective against them.

On a downhill stretch, a USFS pickup passed me from behind, and an employee leaned out of the passenger window to give me a thumbs-up. The gesture took me back to Polebridge where I had been given the "hang loose" sign. I smiled, even though the pickup's rear tires threw sand as it passed. The memory faded, though, as I hiked up the next hill with my wake of mosquitos out for blood.

The further I rode, the more cows I encountered. I was cutting through ranch land and crossed a cattle guard every few miles and saw cows every few hundred yards. One downhill bend concealed a few grazing cows from my sight until I rode around. None were in my way, but off to the side of the road. My appearance frightened one though, which took to running and crossed up onto the road right in front of me. It was my encounter with the elk all over again, but this cow was not as fast or as graceful as that elk. I braked, but my tires slipped in the sand and cobbles. I cursed the cow and prepared for an impact. But it did not come. I managed to slow enough to avoid the cow while my yells herded her across the road and out from in front of me. I continued to yell after I passed it. That let out a lot of frustration.

Several miles further, to my disbelief, the road worsened. Great protrusions of bedrock erupted from the road to make it uneven and bumpy. My front shock absorbed a lot of the road's rough rhythm, but my bike's hard tail had to feel every ridge and pockmark in the bedrock, every rough transition back to the cobbles, every washboard ridge. And the road still threw sand.

The road also had signs of people—the tire tracks of pickups and ATVs. After a rough segment, I actually passed a pickup, the second vehicle I had seen that day. Its passengers both waved.

Another rough and steep section of road brought me down to the valley floor and onto a smoother road. I sighed and looked over my shoulder back at the hill, glad to leave behind that awful road. I pedaled half a mile on the new road before I reached back to tap my sleeping bag. Huh? I reached back again. Nothing. I locked up my brakes.

"Where the hell is my sleeping bag?!"

It was rhetoric, frustration, dramatization. I knew where it was: laying on the side of the road where it fell as I crossed a rough patch. I cursed myself for having been so stupid. Everyday the straps had loosened. Everyday I had reached back to check the straps. Everyday I had stopped to wrench the straps tight. Why would I do all of that if I didn't suspect I might lose my bag? Now it had happened. Now I had to climb back up an incredibly rough road to search for it. I didn't have the energy or the patience to do it. What choice did I have though? Answer: a simple one.

I turned my bike around and followed my own tracks backwards, through the mud. My head was heavy and wanted to hang, but I held it up as best as I could, keeping an eye out for the white and black stuff sack that held my sleeping bag. Maybe I would get lucky. Maybe it had fallen off recently, and I wouldn't have to back track far. Maybe? Yeah right.

Wait. What was that sound?

ATVs. Three. They came from the direction I should have been heading. I stopped the leader and explained my situation.

"Your sleeping bag?"

"Yeah, I lost it on a rough section of the road but didn't realize it until a few minutes ago. Can you just keep an eye out for it? If you see it, just set it on the road or if you're heading back just bring it?"

"Well, I suppose. Which road did you say you came down?"

"There's a turn just a couple hundred yards from here. I came down the road on the right."

"Oh, well we are going to the left. Sorry."

The older guy, mid fifties, pulled away without so much as a goodbye. The next two ATVs followed his lead and their occupants didn't say anything as they passed and then disappeared over the next hill.

"Selfish pricks!"

They went on, not wanting to help, not even caring. This was the first time I had asked for help and had not received it. It wasn't that I had expected them to go out of their way to help me, but a little compassion and empathy would have gone much further than they did. They had had no idea the effort it would take me to backtrack to find something they could retrieve in a few minutes. I hated those ridiculous side-by-side, bench seat ATVs. They didn't look all-terrain with their small wheels and low ground clearance. Probably modified for a ranch. A tourist ranch. That would explain the kids in the trio. I had probably ran into a family on vacation, out to see the countryside so the parents could instill good values and such in their children, like avoiding weird cyclists in the middle of nowhere.

Bad thoughts continued to pervade my head and body and a tingle manifested in my toes. Maybe that was the fatigue. Even so, I still knew what needed to be done, and I continued to follow my tracks backwards. As I crested the hill the ATVs had disappeared over, a familiar pickup crested the next one and stopped when I came into sight. I began to coast and tried to avoid rocks with my front tire while I kept an eye on the pickup. Why had it stopped? When I got to the bottom of the hill, it was obvious the driver had rolled his window down, because his arm reached out. In his grasp, my white stuff sack.

I pumped my fist into the air to acknowledge that what they had found was mine, but also because I was relieved at them having found it. It was a celebratory gesture. I pulled up to the driver's window.

"This must be yours?"

"Yes, thank you so much. You have no idea how much trouble you've just saved me."

"Yeah, well, we passed you and found this shortly after. I figured we travel faster, so it would just be easier to catch you."

"I can't tell you how much I appreciate this. I really don't think I'm capable of explaining the relief I'm feeling right now. Thank you so much."

Adam and Christine were too modest in their heroics. They were in the area for the holiday weekend and were out for a drive when they passed me and found my sleeping bag. I explained to them my trip and my goal to get to Pinedale that day.

"Well, the road gets a lot better just a mile down the road. It gets a lot flatter too."

"That sounds great. This rolling terrain has been killing me since yesterday."

I re-secured the bag, extra tight this time, and from that time on I tied the surplus webbing of the stuff sack to my seat post. I shook Adam's hand, and we both turned around and went our respective directions. I had no illusions about my luck. It may have been terrible losing my bag, but to have it retrieved and returned by a perfect stranger was immensely good luck. But more than luck, it was an answer. I asked for help and that's what I received, just like so many times before. This time though, the answer came from an unexpected source.

• • •

Adam was one of the few motorists I talked to that got it right. His observations about the riding conditions were accurate in regard to the state of the road and distances. The flat terrain made things easier on my fatigued legs, but the mud did not. The road cut down the middle of the valley where it became very broad, and a mile stretch of the road and surrounding flood plain was mud. I had to walk most of it, but it wasn't uphill, and it wasn't raining.

Campers and RVs littered the meadow the farther downstream I rode. Just 3 miles from the pavement, 3 miles from the end of the national forest, a huge dumpster stood at the intersection of two roads. Its faded and chipped green paint, its animal-proof cage top laced with rust, and its swarm of black flies were signs of civilization. The large amount of trash it held was a sign of the holiday weekend. It was out of place. Not even its camouflage paint job could hide its sharp, unnatural angles, its pungent smell, its hum of wings. It was a tragedy to see something so ugly somewhere so pristine and all for the convenience of the campers who couldn't "pack it out." What? They couldn't manage with all of those ATVs I saw?

I hit pavement and crossed the last cattle guard the national forest could lay in front of me. I was 5 miles from a cafe. My depleted fuel cells demanded that I stop. The glowing neon was reason for celebration as I pulled up to the rustic log structure. I leaned my bike against the porch, removed my helmet, grabbed my map, and turned off my GPS locator. My legs were heavy as I pulled them up the few steps onto the porch and then across it. Their weight was nothing compared to the door though. Everything had tried to keep me from food. How heavy would the menu be?

I stepped inside. Hardwood floors. Wood paneled walls and ceiling. The place had a golden glow from all of the lacquer. Heavy wooden chairs and tables and a stone fireplace. I walked to the bar and climbed onto the tall bar stool. I was handed a menu and immediately ordered a Pepsi. My body yelled for the liquid sugar. After looking at the same standard menu I had memorized back in Montana, I ordered the special, a pork sandwich that was unique to the cafe. I talked with the bartender and another customer about my trip and about the racers. A fair number had stopped at the cafe on their way through. The bartender made them out to be pure muscle, athletes to the extreme with a personality to match. They were just go, go, go… only there long enough to eat

The food and drink did an excellent job on me. I took the time to eat every last bit of the enormous portions I was served and washed it all down with a third Pepsi. Sitting and not pedaling was doing me good. I outlasted the other customer and was there long enough for another to show up, a local rancher. He told me about the bear problems he had been having. His hired men had found several cows, mauled and killed, in the grazing land I had been on the last day and a half. A bear killing a cow wasn't rare, but he had seen an incredibly high number that summer. He guessed the bear population was too big for the area to sustain. Comforting. I just rode through an area overpopulated by bear. Even better, the rancher was having the population surveyed. That week, a government official in charge of the survey returned to his pickup to find wolf tracks surrounding it. The smell of the stain on his driver door indicated the wolf had claimed it. Either that, or the wolf didn't like the make. Hearing about the area's wildlife, I was glad I had sheltered in the outhouse. Cefas had named my bivy the grizzly-bear-snack-sack for a reason. They assured me I was in the clear though. The scenery's greenery would soon end.

I left the cafe feeling good. I mounted up after I checked the straps on my sleeping bag and hit the road. I was within 30 miles of Pinedale, but there was no way I could call this day a rest day. Given my fatigue, I would need to stay in Pinedale longer than I had wanted.

Chapter 22

"I'M SORRY, we're all full."

"That's ok. I was just passing by and thought I'd swing in and ask."

"Well, it's a busy weekend in town, but what you can do is go to the Chamber of Commerce. They keep tabs on all the motels and hotels there, so they should know who has room."

"Awesome, thank you."

I had made it to Pinedale. Lunch had held me over until the last mile. I coasted into town on fumes, and as I had expected, the Fourth of July weekend had made finding accommodations difficult. There was always the Motel 6 or Holiday Inn, but I didn't want to pay those national chain prices. I had pulled into a few places to ask before being directed to the Pinedale Chamber of Commerce. Inside, both employees were on the phone. I browsed through some tourist brochures, the colorful pages showing beautiful weather, rich and lush vegetation, and most importantly, smiling faces. The pages painted enjoyment, a worthwhile experiences not to be missed. What would the brochure for the GDMBR look like? Would advertisers try the same tactics? Doubtful. I folded up the brochure and returned it to the rack of its brethren. Anyone that wanted to do the GDMBR would know they couldn't smile and have fun the whole way. That wasn't the purpose.

"Can I help you?"

"I hope so." I showed some teeth and turned on the charm. "I'm passing through town and am hoping to find a place to stay. If I can, I want to stay here and take a rest day." I was still wearing my backpack, helmet, and riding gloves. I assumed they could piece it together.

"Well, things are pretty busy, being that it's the Friday of the Fourth of July weekend and all."

"Yeah, I figured it would be, and I've actually already stopped at a few places. I was told you might know what motels had vacancy. I'm on a budget, so I'm trying to avoid the big chain hotels."

"Well, not all of the hotels work with us, but let me take a look."

After I ruled out the only campground another 10 miles down the road, they suggested three motels and gave me directions. The first one I had already been to. The front desk had been unattended, but a sign explained there was no vacancy. The second was closed. I mean shut down, doors locked. I called the phone number just to be sure only to have a robotic voice explain that the number was disconnected. Ok, number three it was. I pulled into the third motel. The parking lot was empty. Not a good sign. Neither was the notice taped to the office door which explained the motel's electricity would soon be turned off due to nonpayment. I didn't return to the Chamber of Commerce. There may have been a disconnect between the Chamber and the local businesses.

I did find a nice place, small, but more expensive than I had preferred. It was for one night though. I could ride the 10 miles to the campground tomorrow. A short ride would have been good for the legs anyway. I walked into the office, trying to look tired and pathetic; it didn't take much effort. I spoke to the owner and explained my situation. She gave me the AAA discount. How sweet of her.

I dumped my stuff into my room, which had a fridge and microwave, the definition of luxury. Two blocks away was a grocery store, and I was all smiles on my way there, excited to put some weight back on. I craved donuts and ice cream. It was going to be Eureka all over again, trying to pack back on all the calories I had burned during that first 100-mile day.

Inside, the floors were bright, polished to a shine. Hard to believe with the amount of foot traffic I encountered while I wandered up and down the aisles. People were making their last preparations for the weekend. Shopping carts went by full of hotdogs and hamburgers, chips and pretzels, beer and beer and beer. People at the checkouts had cases of water and cases of sports drinks with bags of ice balanced on top. Everyone knew what they wanted. Me on the other hand, I couldn't choose what to put into my modest hand basket. I had had a voracious appetite minutes before, but now I didn't want to eat at all. I went with my initial craving and found some ice cream bars and pastries in addition to some fresh fruit. Nothing appealed to me. Dehydration maybe? I added a bottle of juice and a few sport drinks to my basket. It was time to quit lingering and get back to the hotel room. I was light-headed and felt a pang in the pit of my stomach. Was I dizzy too? My condition was deteriorating, and I would have rather ridden the bike while I had the ability.

The two blocks of pedaling with weekend traffic did not return my appetite. I tried an ice cream bar, but it was difficult to swallow. My stomach refused everything my mouth offered. Even the fluids wouldn't go down without effort. I didn't feel horrible, so I busied myself with other tasks. A rest day is only restful for your legs. There is always something to be taken care of. So I filled the bath and laundered my clothes.

The water was filthy enough to inspire a second "cycle" for the clothes. The hard white surface of the tub was cold on my rear and the brown water warm on my feet. Dirty bubbles collected around my shins and at the edge of the water. Before my clothes were rinsed, I was incapacitated. My whole body ached while I sweated and shivered. No fluids would go down now, my stomach still in its temper tantrum.

I crawled into bed and hoped to fall asleep and pass whatever ailment this was. I couldn't sleep. I stared at the popcorn textured ceiling wide awake, but un-alert, unaware of my environment. Not even the TV could lull me to sleep. My shivers returned below my blankets and, finally, something did appeal to me: a hot bath. I laid in the hot water with legs bent, too long for the modestly sized bathroom. My knees developed goose bumps while the rest of me sweat. What was this? My stupidity coming back to haunt me? Was this the ghost of overnight-outhouse-past?

My symptoms: nausea, fever, cold sweats, body aches. What did they indicate? I didn't reach a conclusion. I did narrow down the cause though. It was either the outhouse or the cafe. I had felt crappy that morning, but had attributed that to the high elevation. I had made it down from the pass fine, apart from the exhaustion, and was fine at the cafe, where I ate pork. It wasn't until 3 or 4 hours later that symptoms had begun to show.

Why did it even matter? I was on the verge of panic. Not hysterics, but a quiet, contained panic in my mind. I stepped out of the bath. The air was cold and sapped the heat from my body I had gained from the water. Where was my phone? I found it and set it on the lid of the toilet to play music. What was done was done. No need for an unnecessary freak out. I turned off the lights and slipped back into the water. The music of Dax Johnson, one of my favorite musicians, filled the air. It had the desired effect and almost put me to sleep.

But the water became too hot. I was on fire. I crawled out and sat on the edge of the tub naked to air dry and cool myself. I grabbed an ice cream bar from the freezer and managed to get the whole thing down. A little water went with it, but only a little. Back in bed, the night sky had finally emerged and concealed the light that came through the blinds.

That was my bathing routine for the night. Cold? Into the hot bath. Hot? Back out. Nibble on an ice cream bar. Sip some water. I finally crawled into bed around 1 a.m. I fell asleep, but that didn't last. I woke after an hour, with an urgent need to urinate. I went to the toilet only to squeeze a few drops. I sipped a bit more water and went back to bed. This pattern continued. Sleep. Wake. Pee. Sip. Sleep. Every hour. My body aches persisted, but my stomach did distinguish itself from the dull sensation, its aches much worse. I tried to vomit, I tried to defecate. Nothing and nothing. Hardly anything went in and hardly anything came out. At about 3, I was worried. At 4, I was plain scared.

Aunt Lea. She was a nurse with years of experience. She might have been able to help. Call her? What about calling an ambulance? I hadn't been this sick, maybe in my whole life. I had always taken pride in my immune system and its effectiveness. Just a cold was rare for me. But this was no cold. I was debilitated. And with all of my sweating and lack of fluid intake, dehydration was a serious concern.

Any medical attention would have probably ended my ride. My family would have gotten scared and insisted I come home. Maybe I would have been too scared to continue on. It hadn't exactly been an easy ride thus far. But what would have happened if an ambulance did come? They would have probably been as lost and just stuck a straight saline IV in my arm. What would that have cost me? Money; pride; the experience of a lifetime? I walked back to the bathroom and refilled my paper cup from the tap. I drank as much as I could manage, a few gulps. I went back to bed, resolved not to make any decisions until the morning. If I was still in bad shape, I could call whoever. But for the rest of the night, I would fight.

* * *

I woke up again, this time to daylight. My body didn't ache as much, but my stomach was still unsettled. I had improved enough to be glad I hadn't made any regrettable phone calls. I pulled on the only dry clothes I had and went to the hotel's breakfast bar. I only picked at my blueberry muffin, but did get some juice down. I spoke to the owner about staying another night. I told her how I had become sick and just couldn't function. She understood and made it happen.

I forced down more fluids back in my room. For a few hours that was my only concern. I tried to nap, but couldn't, even with as broken as my sleep had been the night before. Sitting around didn't help me feel any better. I needed to do something. I took my bike down to the local hardware store and spoke to a bike mechanic about the grinding sound I had heard at the top of Union Pass. I left my bike with him and walked back to my hotel.

The town was calm for such a big weekend. Everyone must have been out in their RVs, riding their ATVs, and filling the large green dumpsters that littered the river valleys. I appreciated the lack of people. I walked down the empty sidewalk, the sun bright in my eyes and warm on my skin. It pushed the stomach pains to the back of my mind.

Back in my room, I finished the laundry I had started the night before and scattered it across the room to dry. Wet clothing hung from the closet, the luggage bench, the TV wall bracket, the towel rack, the curtain rod. I managed to eat a few more ice cream bars, but for the most part, I didn't eat or drink the rest of the day. I tried to sleep again to no avail, and I wasn't motivated to write in my journal. I looked up Yukon instead. He would finish the day in Pinedale. Maybe if I got lucky, I would ride out with him the next morning. I also checked Allison's blog. She hadn't updated her blog in almost a week, the last entry being all the way back at Lima,

Montana, where I first met Ralph. I was sure I had been close to catching her, but now she was extending her lead over me again.

I retrieved my bike from the hardware store and returned to the hotel just before it started to rain. It was a brief, heavy, heavy rain like the one I had to climb in after I had been told how to use a bike. It was strange to see the water strike the blacktop of the parking lot. It was violent without the soft dust to buffer the impact. Water splashed everywhere, and every drop made a statement disproportionately audible. I may have felt like garbage, but I smiled at the roof over my head.

* * *

"Can I help you?" The maid was on double duty: laundry and front desk.

"Yes. I'm wondering if there's any chance that I can stay a third night. I have just been so sick and don't want to find another place to stay."

"Well, the problem is we have your room booked for another person tonight. Let me talk to the boss though when she gets here, and I'll see if we can't work something out."

"Ok. I'll be in my room if she needs to talk to me. Thank you."

My second morning at the hotel I was able to eat a whole muffin. I also gulped down a couple of the cheap plastic juice cups with no problem.

I had listened to the suggestions of friends and family and decided to stay at the hotel for a third night so I could fully recover. The reservation problem was worked out early, and I was allowed to remain in the same room. The incoming guest stayed in a nicer room without the rate increase. That appeased my guilt for displacing her. So, with another whole rest day in front of me, I headed to the supermarket in search of food. My appetite was returning.

I wandered the same polished floor, up and down the same aisles. Now my indecision originated from the abundance of choices, not the indifference of a sick stomach. I wanted this. I wanted that. I wanted those. So many calories, so little time. I also had to plan meals for the next few days. Once I left Pinedale, my only chance to resupply was in Rawlins, a solid three days away.

My basket full, with a few fresh donuts on top, I stepped into line at the check out. I scanned over the magazine and tabloid covers and looked at celebrity faces I didn't recognize, at diet names I didn't care to know, at exercise programs that promised to lift and firm my butt. My eyes closed as I pinched the bridge of my nose. Being removed from that stuff had made it more grotesque. It was more trash to fill the green, rusted dumpsters carelessly thrown into the environment as an eyesore. I pulled my eyes away. Then I saw her, a face I recognized from a blog.

She had come up one of the aisles and emerged between the tall shelves. Her eyes searched the lists above the next aisle to see if it held what she was after. I had been trying to catch Allison for more than two weeks. Now, here she was. But how? My brow furrowed as I considered it. I hadn't gained any mileage in more than a day and a half. So I had passed them somewhere. Maybe they rode the Jackson Spur? Or maybe they ventured into Yellowstone? That would explain how I passed them without knowing it.

She vanished back into the shelves. Behind her, two more people appeared, obviously cyclists. Members of her group. I stepped up to the cashier who started to unload my basket. Should I talk to them? They looked like they were in a hurry, and I knew how it felt to have someone delay your progress. It was just after 11. Best case, they would have had only a half day advantage on me when I set out the next morning. Given how I had overtaken them in a week, I figured I could catch them in two or three days.

I walked out of the grocery store and glanced along its long windowless brick wall. Sure enough, three bikes leaned up against it, all laden with gear. It was by chance my own wasn't with them. I had left my bike at the hotel and walked to the store. I was spurred. I wanted to get my bike and take off. My competitiveness stirred and tomorrow couldn't come soon enough.

I spent the rest of the day eating and drinking as much as I could. I still wasn't able to nap, my body doing much less than it had grown accustomed to. I went to bed that night in decent health. Not great and not recovered, but dang near. I had told the owner I would leave early the next morning and had arranged to leave before the office opened. My gear was all packed and ready to go. I had managed to pass four people that I knew of and my sickness allowed them all to catch me. My planned partial day of rest in Pinedale had turned into three nights and two days. It was time to leave.

Chapter 23

Monday morning.

Week four.

Day twenty-two.

I left Pinedale early, as planned. The day was beautiful, the big blue sky whitened only with cirrus clouds. The first 30 miles of the day were along a flat and featureless stretch of pavement, a reflection of the landscape to the south more than that to the north, the River Mountains of the Bridger Wilderness. When I left the pavement, I left behind civilization. I was alone again. No more towns; no more people; no more TV; no more magazines. Solitude. Clarity.

The landscape was a blank canvas. Not much existed there, but it didn't carry that air of desolation. Perhaps it was the mountains to the north that loomed over and looked on that kept me company. The road slowly morphed from gravel to dirt.

Apart from fatigued, I was feeling good. Fifty miles into the day, I stopped at a creek to replenish my water where the topographic divot stuck out, lush and green, from the dry brown landscape. After I filled my water bladder, I took cover under a shrub and slept. This was the nap I had tried to take the last two days. When I woke, I was recharged and ready to go. It was well worth the lost hour of daylight.

Just 2 miles beyond the creek, I crossed the Continental Divide for the tenth time. The road extended like a scar across the landscape, the dirt white and raised above the landscape to trace the Continental Divide, to flirt with it. I had good weather and a slight tail wind to push me along the hard-packed dirt. It was one of my favorite stretches so far.

It was also on this segment that I experienced something bizarre. I could see for miles, in every direction. I was on the highpoint of a flat expanse that lacked vegetation or anything else that might be used for concealment. I was the only one out there. But the feeling persisted: I was being watched. I wasn't threatened. It was not the feeling that makes the hair on the back of your neck stand right before you catch a stranger staring at you. It was a calm as though I knew who it was that watched. I disregarded the feeling, but after a few minutes it clicked. I felt as though my mom were watching me.

I could see her, at home in her recliner, her chihuahua-terrier Nelson laying alongside her legs on the kicked-up footrest. She watched from there, a smile on her face, Nelson's eyes fighting sleep, his chin resting on her shin. It was a very clear image, one that made me chuckle. The feeling persisted for about twenty minutes longer, then abruptly vanished. Not long after, I found State Highway 28.

● ● ●

The paved segment was only 5 miles long, but there was a rest stop along it; I sheltered from the afternoon heat there. I refilled my water and cooked some noodles. There were various information boards and a few maps. The road I had just traversed was known as the Lander Cutoff, part of the Oregon trail. Another board was topped by a quote: "When you start over these wide plains, let no one leave dependent on his best friend for any thing." I smiled at the quote. It fit into the theme of my trip, the theme of self-reliance and self-motivation.

Curious glances came from all the highway travelers that stopped, but no one asked. One young man did offer me water, which I had to turn down, having plenty already. I left, still feeling well, and hoped to ride another 25 miles. The landscape was much the same as it had been all day, with one exception. The route took me through South Pass City, an old mining town. I stopped at the mercantile there to find ice cream, but it was closed. Maybe I would have had more luck less than 5 miles down the road in Atlantic City.

I descended the steep hill into Atlantic City. It was similar to South Pass City in that both were small. Like Polebridge, neither had a population listed on the map. As I dropped into town, it was clear that it wasn't as big as it looked. Several of the businesses were closed, shut down. I rode up to the mercantile still hopeful for ice cream, but it wasn't open, nor was the bar next door. I pursed my lips as I read the business hours posted on the door. Next time.

I turned my bike around and headed back for the route. It was only 10 more miles to the river where I planned to camp; the river would be the last water source before I entered the Great Divide Basin, a 3,600 square mile region where water didn't drain. Rather, it evaporated or collected in small temporary lakes. This was one of the driest stretches along the entire trail, and its barrenness had earned it an air of infamy. At least I wouldn't need to worry about rain while I crossed it.

On the way back through town, I passed a shop I thought had been closed. Now the door was open. Not only that, but someone sat outside lighting a camping stove to cook some noodles. I couldn't imagine a local using a camping stove, so I pulled over. Dan confirmed my suspicion. He was also a cyclist. He and his wife Emily were northbound riders. They had started in Colorado and had just crossed the Basin. They were also in search of ice cream when they found the store we were now in front of. Dan explained that the owner, Yvonne, had invited them to stay there for the night. They had been talking when they saw me ride by.

"Yvonne looked at me and said, 'He'll be back. Make sure he knows he can stay here tonight too.' And look at that, you're back."

"Yeah, I thought this place was closed when I first rode by. There isn't any ice cream inside is there?"

"Actually, there is," Dan said.

We went inside. The front half of the one room building was a small store. The back was a small computer lab where a dozen computers lined either wall. Dan and Emily had brought their bikes inside and had gotten settled. I still felt good, good enough to ride the last 10 miles of the day. But a storm was developing to the south, and it was headed north. Was 10 miles really that important? I had already done 85, a respectable mileage by my standards, so I stayed.

I had to battle temptation, being in a place full of food, most of which was candy and assorted fudges. But that didn't stop me from surveying the various jars of flavors while I kept Dan company. He had kept the store open for Yvonne.

"I figured if we are here, might as well keep the store open. I'm sure she could use the business."

And sure enough, people came in while it was just us there. Dan, with no retail experience, manned the cash register Yvonne had left unlocked for him right after they met. It's hard not to be taken in by the charm of a small town. But neither of us knew how to use the register, so Dan resorted to good old fashion paper-and-pencil addition to calculate prices.

Yvonne was sweet enough to bring the three of us water. The store had no plumbing, but the few gallons of warm water Yvonne delivered were more than enough to bathe with and to wash the sand and desert dirt from my legs. After we closed the store, we took turns dousing ourselves with water behind the building. After, we sat around the table to talk.

Dan and Emily were a few years older than me. They were both teachers, but Dan had originally studied biology and held a few research positions out of school before he became a teacher. We unfolded our maps and exchanged trail notes with each other. Dan and Emily also told me they had passed Allison's group.

Dan said, "It sounded as though they planned on camping at the reservoir tonight."

"Yeah? I was thinking of camping there tomorrow. Was there water?"

"Yeah, but that was the only place. All the other streams shown on the map are all dry. That was the only place there was shade too. There's an old wooden cart of some kind there. I convinced Emily that we should take a nap under it. It was really nice to find shade."

So Allison was a full day ahead of me. That was more than I had anticipated, but I was still confident I would catch them … soon.

Chapter 24

"ARE YOU GUYS CARRYING PROTECTION? Bear mace or anything?"

"No, actually," she said. "And he's still coming."

I glanced back over my shoulder, "I'll take care of it."

• • •

I parted ways with Dan and Emily that next morning. We pointed each other in the right direction and gave our last waves and wishes of good luck as we separated. I climbed out of Atlantic City; the hill's steepness forced me to hike. On top of the hill, the landscape stretched out for an eternity. The only things to obscure the view were the atmosphere and the curve of the earth. There were no distinguished geologic features at all, and even worse, there were no trees. Just sage and sage and sage.

Before I reached the Sweetwater River, the last water source until I made camp that night, I encountered two people. I was confused to see the two walking along the road. In the two or three minutes it took me to ride to them, I couldn't figure out what they were doing. When I got closer though, it clicked. Large-brimmed hats, trekking poles, hiking boots, and large backpacks: Continental Divide Trail hikers.

"Hi, I'm Yukon. This is Litter Box."

"Yukon? Oh man, there's another Yukon out here somewhere on a bike."

"Really?" he said as he cracked a smile.

Yukon and Litter Box were headed for Atlantic City. It had taken them almost a week to cross a desert I hoped to say goodbye to the next morning and several months to traverse ground I hoped to cover in a couple of weeks. They had several questions about Atlantic City, most in regard to what kind of greasy food they could find there.

While we swapped tales of the trail, a critter of some kind started to sneak up behind us. My back was to it, but Litter Box saw him coming.

"Do you guys see that?" she said.

"Yeah. There's something coming at us," Yukon said.

I turned. The flat landscape allowed us to see the animal a long way off and, sure enough, he was coming at us. He skirted along the edge of the road to keep himself halfway concealed in the small ditch there. We continued to talk since we were in no immediate danger, but we all three kept an eye on him.

"Is that… is that a badger?" Litter Box said.

Yukon and I both agreed with her identification.

"Are you guys carrying protection?"

They weren't. I turned my bike around and rode back toward the badger. When I got closer I started to yell at him to let him know his cover was blown. I stood up, both to make myself look bigger and to pedal harder, driving right toward him. It had the desired effect. He halted for a second to make sure it was him I approached, and then he turned and sprinted as fast as he could. He went back down the road about fifteen yards before he tore off into the sage, still running as fast as he could. I returned to the hikers who thanked me and, because the land was so flat, we watched the badger still, this time running away from us. That badger was a great sprinter.

The hikers continued toward their greasy reward in Atlantic City, while I headed to top off my water. On my way, I passed the marker for the intersection of the Oregon Trail and Pony Express. My bike lay on the ground while I took a few pictures of the scenery. How many people had travelled through that area? The California and Mormon Trails weren't far off either, a fascinating fact when you consider the barren landscape. How could anyone survive out here? Why would anyone route a settler's trail through here? Why would anyone ride a bike out here?

The riparian vegetation along the Sweetwater River would be the last green for a few days. I was slow to fill my water containers, my mind wandering as I stared at the channel filled with the cool relief I would be deprived of the whole day.

I pedaled away from the river and my gaze left its track for the new set of tracks in front of me. The road lost its hard-packed quality and was covered now in fine gravel. It made biking hard work, but it also captured and held the signatures of the bikes that had been there before me, illegible, twisted back and forth across the road by the rider that had been searching for the hardest surface. I followed the tracks all day; there were five sets of tires in some places, fewer in others. These must have been the tracks of Allison's group. Somewhere below them were Dan and Emily's tracks as well.

Yukon and Litter Box had cut cross-country and only found the road just before they met me. I saw the appeal of traversing the sage, of chancing an encounter with the wild horses that wandered the area, or even the pronghorns. I was lucky enough to see a herd of the horses, a dozen or so outlined by the sky where they stood on top of a small ridge. They kept tabs on me, tried to assess if I was a threat or not as I came up the road towards them. They held their ground, but once I stopped to take a few pictures they moved on and disappeared over the ridge. I saw a single pronghorn too, our encounter similar to that with the horses.

One other chance encounter I had was with some shade. At mile 36, the road crossed West Alkali Creek. Just as Dan and Emily had promised, it was dry. That meant the culvert that funneled the water under the road was dry as well. Its four-foot diameter was large enough for me to sit in and take a break from the sun. The shade it offered was worth the corrugations that made it difficult to get comfortable. That is until I unpacked my sleeping pad and took a nap in the culvert. Just like the day before, the hour of light sleep worked wonders on my body and my attitude, and when I woke, I had lunch. I left a package of noodles to cook in the sun while I slept. They were steaming when I ate them.

I crossed the Continental Divide again that afternoon and then crossed through the bed of Arapahoe Creek. The map described it as a good water source all through the summer and into the fall, unless it was a dry year. The creek bed was as dusty as the road.

* * *

Clouds had been building all day. It was to be expected in such an arid landscape. But among the cumulus clouds, there was one that did not belong, the black sheep of the herd. Its darkness was reflected on the ground below as its shadow ambled along and approached me from my right. It was hard not to ignore the blacks and grays of the cloud in an environment bleached to a uniform white by the sun.

"No way. It's not going to rain on me."

Just as I ruled out the possibility of rain in one the driest stretches of the route, fall streaks painted their strokes below the cloud. An immense wind hit me from the side as the storm began. Whatever. It wasn't a headwind, and I was riding away from the rain. Less than half a mile down the road, I made a broad right turn. The storm was now in front of me. I battled the wind while its direction alternated between a crosswind and a headwind. We fought for several minutes before the storm won and centered over me, almost in a cartoon fashion given the small size of the system.

"No way. It's raining on me."

A smile crossed my face as the drops started to accumulate. I laughed as water began to drip off of me. Given all the rain I had already encountered, it only made sense to find more on the driest stretch of the route. Five miles was all I covered before I made it through the rain; the wind now pushed me away and helped my bike along. My tailwind was short-lived though. The road made another extreme turn, to the left this time, and I was thrown back into the crosswind. The storm and I travelled in parallel for 10 miles while the dark hues slowly dissipated and the frequency of the thunderclaps decreased. The wind gusts consistently tried to force me off the road.

It was a surreal experience, a paradox of sorts: a raining desert. The wind was warm on my face, but carried the unexpected smell of water along with the fragrance of sage strengthened by the moisture. Those last 20 miles were incredible, me engaged with this solitary rain cloud. The two of us spun around each other, and I experienced wind from every direction as the fall streaks blended with the sun streaks to create our own spotlights: it was my own version of a rain dance.

I ended the day at A&M Reservoir, a small pond of water sunken below the plane of the landscape. It was not the oasis I had imagined (hoped, more like). The water did not sustain any tree or brush growth, and the grasses along the rock and sand banks of the reservoir were minimal. Fish had been stocked, though, and the occasional splash produced by the fish brave enough to jump had me track ripples across the pond. I had a large supply of water now, a relief after the hot and mostly dry day.

I met three more CDT hikers at the reservoir who were also drawn to the water. Physically, they looked more the worse for wear than me. But if there is one thing that didn't mean crap on the trail, it was appearances. I enjoyed my conversation with the hikers and felt inspired to hike both the PCT and CDT after I listened to their stories. I also felt somewhat embarrassed and flattered at the same time.

"Yeah, you're the first Divide biker we've actually had a conversation with. We crossed paths with the racers a couple of weeks ago and all they ever said was 'hi' or 'bye.' They never had time to talk," Gnar (another trail name) told me.

"That's partly why I didn't want to race, even though I wouldn't have been competitive. I rode with a guy from the Netherlands for a few days, and he turned out to be awesome, and we became pretty good friends. But he rode slower than me. If I was racing, I probably wouldn't have said more than a few words to him." I smiled at the memory of Cefas. "The people I meet seem to be the best part of the trip."

"That's why you're so much cooler than the racers. We are actually talking to you."

I held a lot of respect for the racers. It took a lot of balls to do what they did. But I had to wonder if they missed out on something else.

The hikers finished their meals and left. They aimed to hike a few more miles before they set up camp. I pitched my own grizzly-bear-snack-sack, its bright orange matched only by the desert sunset. It was satisfying to sit in the sand in front of my bivy and watch the sun disappear. The breeze had persisted and pushed across the water to bring cool air to my face and to dance along the fabric of my bivy. Later that night, when I woke to answer nature's call, I would sample the desert's other splendor: the stars.

Chapter 25

it is much more difficult to judge oneself than to judge others

Hmm. Interesting.

• • •

The flat expanse of desert continued the next morning. Within 20 miles though, I was back on pavement and moved at a brisk pace towards Rawlins. The last 15 miles into town would be on US Highway 287. That meant traffic. As I approached the turn onto the highway, I crested a slight rise that let me see all the way to the highway. The road was perfectly straight and at the end was a massive hill. That was going to be a burden on the legs. But as I covered the distance, the hill shrunk. By the time I reached the highway, the hill was gone. That straight stretch had been nearly 5 miles long, which made a relatively small change in the slope of the road look like a massive change: an optical illusion. I laughed. It was an appropriate similitude for my trip. The perceived challenge was immense before I began, but once I started toward my goal, the opposition gradually diminished.

At the turn, though, the hill in front of me was very real. I found it on my map's elevation profile; the top was another Continental Divide crossing, and the shoulder was wide, but of no comfort. I waited next to a large orange sign weighted down by sandbags and watched the pilot car guide a line of traffic down the single open lane on the hill. Construction zone. A half-mile to my left, I saw the huge train of cars and trucks that waited to take their turn going up the hill. I doubted I would get to lead this column as I had in Canada.

As the last car passed, I began to pedal with all my might, my head on a swivel. This could have ended badly. I kept pedaling and reached the place where the road narrowed, then the trucks of gravel and dirt, then the graders and loaders that reworked the bank along the road. The column of cars gained on me, but the low speed limit allowed me to get halfway through before I needed to pull off and let the column pass. After the last car, I continued. At first sight of the oncoming column, I pulled off again. It took one more cycle of traffic to get through the construction zone. I reached the uphill flagger just as the pilot car caught back up to me the second time. That was not the kind of traffic I had expected.

Back on the wide shoulder, the cars still passed in waves, mediated by the pilot car. In front of me, near the top of the hill, I saw the silhouette of two cyclists. Members of Allison's group? I caught them on the downhill side and rode with them just long enough to find out they were on the TransAmerican route and that they, too, were from the Netherlands. I didn't even think to ask if they had heard of Cefas. The fact that he was an Olympic athlete and a reality show winner had slipped my mind. He was just an everyday, down-to-earth guy in my eyes.

Riding two-wide on the shoulder was awkward and not that safe, so I pushed on ahead. I was thrilled with how easy it was to leave the road cyclists behind, their bald tires unable to keep up with my knobby tires and mountain biker legs. In town, I stepped into line at the largest Subway I'd ever seen. I drew some interested stares from the lunch crowd with my wet clothes crusted with salt, my legs covered in dirt, and with the few muddy drips of sweat that clung to my face.

I followed Dan's advice and found a cheap motel for the night. For dinner, I stepped across the street to a Chinese restaurant. I had been craving Chinese for a long time, and because I had been sick, I missed my chance in Pinedale. Not now though. I was hungry. I devoured my almond chicken and received the customary fortune cookie. I cracked it open and ate the first half before I looked at my fortune. I pulled the slip of paper from the remaining half.

it is much more difficult to judge oneself than to judge others

I read the fortune a few times before I transferred its bit of wisdom to my journal. It made me think. I had been working so hard to catch Allison and her group, but why? Now I wasn't sure I would want to ride with them if I had caught up. A big group would have taken away that solo element, the battle with myself, the internal struggle. If I was in a group, I would have the support of others, the encouragement and motivation that I was trying to find within myself. Even if I still rode my own bike, carried my own gear, found my own water and food, the group would take away the one thing I was most trying to develop on this trip: self-reliance. I knew everyday would be an internal struggle, one that only I could win or lose. A group would dissolve that conflict. How could I win a battle I wasn't fighting?

I ate the second half of my cookie. It was not as sweet as the first half. I was unsure what I would do if I caught the group, but I wouldn't need to know before then anyway. I settled my bill and left.

● ● ●

The next morning, I straddled my bike on the edge of town, reading a construction sign on the side of the road. Possible four hour delays? The clerk at a gas station had told me the road I planned on taking would be closed. After we tried for a few minutes to confirm that we were talking about the same road, I shrugged off her insistence. There were no convenient alternates visible on my map, so I risked it. Now, on the edge of town I stood with my phone to my ear in search of more details. An answering machine? It wasn't that early.

I stood for several minutes while I weighed my options. The clerk had said the construction was more than 20 miles out of town. If my gamble didn't pay off and I had to turn around, that would be more than half a day wasted. But who was to say I couldn't pass through the construction zone? I could camp and sneak through at night if I needed to. The sun climbed higher as I ran through the possible scenarios. Time was wasted with indecision.

Lightbulb: Ralph.

As far as I knew, Yukon was still ahead of me. I pulled up his race progress on my phone. He had passed through the day before, on route. If he could do it, so could I. The sign did indicate work would be halted for a lunch break, so my goal was to get to the construction zone by noon. That would leave me with a whole hour to pass through. Thanks Yukon!

The ride was nice as I left Rawlins, my bike a little lighter. I had mailed home an assortment of gear I could live without. That included my mp3 player, which I still couldn't get to work. Dead weight. I left the pavement behind and rode onto a hard packed surface, some kind of chemically treated dirt and gravel combination that was just as hard as pavement. The terrain was rolling, as Dan and Emily had said, but I didn't mind. Every mile bought me closer to a tree line near the Wyoming-Colorado border.

Then the wind picked up.

To that point, I had been fortunate enough to escape the notorious winds of Wyoming. If Billy Rice had had problems with the Wyoming winds, how could I possibly handle them? The answer: with a ducked head. Of course it was a perfect headwind I experienced, and it left me in want of a more aerodynamic set up. But I kept at it. I had to make the construction zone before noon.

As I crested the last hill before the end of the "pavement," I expected to see another construction zone. Instead, I saw another CDT hiker down the road. Two Hats was his name, after his hat, which he had custom made from two separate hats. While we talked, a pickup pulled up next to us and the driver leaned out of his window and his passenger leaned forward to see us.

"Hey! It is hot out here! Do you guys need some water?"

Two Hats and I looked at each other. "You never turn down water on the trail."

The two got out of the pick up to find the water cooler in the bed of their truck. They were biologists, based out of Dubois, in the area to survey the wildlife as part of the pre-construction study for a wind turbine array.

"Yeah, can you believe they plan to build the largest land based array of wind turbines in the world right here?"

I smirked. "Yeah. That's pretty easy to believe after the morning I've had."

Two Hats chimed in too. "I've had some pretty strong winds the last few days, too."

The biologists were nice and a convenient source of water. They had all sorts of questions and stories about previous encounters they had had with racers in the past. They soon left though to return to work. Two Hats and I followed suit soon after, putting our own noses back to our own unique grindstones.

Where the hard pack ended, the construction did not start. But the climb to the next Divide crossing did. The hill was steep, not the steepest I had seen, but still intimidating. Throw the strong wind into the mix, though, and I was left to push my bike up the hill. Surveyors had planted stakes with ribboned ends along the road, markers for the construction. Every ribbon was stretched to its full extent and pointed in the direction opposite that of my travel. Every hundred yards there was a stake and piece of ribbon to remind me of the wind, as if I could forget.

Nearly 5 miles of climbing, all on foot, because the wind was too powerful to allow me to ride. Noon came and went, and I still hadn't found the construction site. But I was close. I started to pass excavators and graders parked on the side of the road next to stacks of large, corrugated tubes, future culverts for drainage. My clock approached 1 and I didn't want to be caught in a four-hour delay. That was when I heard a hiss. My back tire squirted green slime from my inner tube. All the way through the rubber? The tread was worn thin, almost gone. I would need to find a new tire in Steamboat Springs. In the meantime, I pumped the tire back up to pressure. It held air, so I went with it.

A few hundred yards from the top, I found the massive construction project the gas station clerk had told me about. It was only three hundred yards long. The gravel road was reduced to a single lane where the lone steamroller operated. Each end was manned by a single flagger. No pilot car. No vehicles. No delay. Massive? I crossed the Divide as I passed through the construction and found the flagger at the other end sitting down on the job. Possible four hour delay?

Chapter 26

April 2012

"WAIT, NATHAN. Can you run that part by me again? What comes after the petroleum ether?"

"After we add the petroleum ether, we let the solution fractionate and use a separatory funnel to keep the bottom layer. To that we add the ethyl acetate to wash the solution and use the sep funnel to keep the top fraction that time. The ethyl acetate part we do three times total."

"Got it."

"Ok. After that we'll take five 50-milliliter samples in separate flasks and add 2 milliliters of our ytterbium acetate to each one. From there, it's easy. We just refrigerate the solutions overnight and do a series of centrifugations and chloroform washes the next day, and we'll eventually have a dry pellet."

"And the pellet is the purified condensed tannins?"

"Yup."

"All right, I got it. So how do we purify the phenolic glycosides?"

Justin and I were at it again. Crayfish were a thing of the past. Now we had another ambitious research project that revolved around a strange problem on our national wildlife refuge. On opening day of elk season every year, hundreds of elk would flock to the refuge where no hunting was permitted. Clever. The problem was the foliage of the refuge could not support that many elk, and it took its toll on the refuge. Our research focused on how overgrazing altered the concentrations of certain chemicals in the trees. Justin and I had entered the world of biochemical ecology.

We were a group of three that quarter, and there was a lot to figure out. I was in charge of the chemistry aspect of the project. I volunteered. It was a dense subject, but I liked biochemistry. I spent hours pouring over chemical ecology journals trying to decipher the methodologies vaguely described in research papers. I highlighted, took notes, cross referenced papers to make sure we had a complete and up-to-date procedure. The end product was a set of detailed flow charts. As far as the chemistry went, that was the easy part.

Just like with our crayfish, our chemical analysis was all about seeing past the surface, looking deeper inside, trying to understand how external stressors were influencing internal processes.

The rest of the research wasn't as tedious; it was awesome. Our first week of class, our group of three went for a long hike around the refuge. We were looking for suitable aspen stands for our research. We were awfully particular, removed from the classroom, enjoying our time outside. Our second week, we retraced our steps and collected soil samples. There was no rush; our research depended on leaf samples and our stands had not budded out yet.

The other aspect of our project had to do with the health of the stands. This meant we dabbled in dendrochronology, a fancy term for analyzing tree rings. Essentially, we were looking for growth. Larger tree rings meant more annual growth—growth was equated to health. So we spent a few weekends on the refuge, our pockets loaded with McDonald's straws to store our tree cores in. We spent a lot of time with our aspen stands that quarter.

I knew this project would be difficult. Justin and I developed it for our Field Ecology class, but were both approved to earn extra credits, because of the amount of work it would require. That was fine by me. I still preferred to be busy.

* * *

"The symposium?" My shoulders dropped under the weight of my backpack. Who had time for the symposium?

I stood in one of the long hallways of the science building with my senior capstone group. I had not thought about our crayfish project in weeks, a project we finished four months before.

"I know we're all insanely busy, but I think if we all contribute we can get it done in time."

Our university had a student symposium every spring where

students could present projects they had worked on throughout the year. It was an interdepartmental event, so presentations ranged from statistics lectures to musical performances. I once attended a presentation on zombies. For us, it was a platform to show off our capstone project. It was also a great resume entry.

"Yeah, I'm in," I said, a slight shrug in my shoulders.

"Me too."

"Yeah, let's do it."

More work. What we needed was a polished abstract, approved by our project advisor, to submit to the symposium committee. We met a couple of weeks later, a few days before the submission deadline. We revised, reworked, and rewrote our abstract to a higher level of professionalism. Justin took it to our advisor; she made a few edits, but was pleased overall. That was good because her name would be on it as well.

Justin pushed the keyboard away and leaned back in his chair. "All right, guys. I think we are ready to submit."

"Let's do it," Jake said.

I halted the submission. "Listen guys, I've been thinking. There's one more name that needs to be on this abstract."

"Yeah."

"I was thinking that too."

"Good. It wouldn't be right to not put his name on it, whether he was our official advisor or not. But I don't think we should throw his name on without asking first. Who knows, maybe he doesn't want his name associated with the crayfish." We laughed. The project had been stressful for all of us, Dr. Hancock included. "Justin, can you print me a copy? I'll run down to his office and ask if we can publish his name too."

● ● ●

"Nathan. Come in."

I stepped into Dr. Hancock's office and sat down. It was removed from the other biology professor offices, stuck in the lower floor of the building, at the end of a short, narrow, windowless hallway. Dr. Hancock's windows opened to the building's courtyard and flooded his office with light, light that slipped beneath his door and into the hallway. I always watched for shadows in that light whenever I walked up to his door and tried to guess if he was in his office or not before I even knocked. Today I guessed wrong.

"Hey Doctor Hancock, I just have a quick question for you."

"About the tannin assay?"

Dr. Hancock was helping Justin and me again, this time on our aspen tree project. His lab had equipment we needed. He allowed us to use his lab space too.

"Actually no. This is about the crayfish project we did back in Fall Quarter."

I explained my group's position. Dr. Hancock had really been our project advisor. It was his lab we used, his advice on protein assays we listened to, and his help and guidance we always sought first. Without him, our project would have been a complete failure. That's what I told him before I asked permission to publish his name on our project. He agreed. We talked about the abstract and the results we received, how we ran our statistics. Then the conversation turned.

"So, Nathan, what are your plans for the future?"

"Well, I'm thinking graduate school."

"You aren't one of these young, married guys are you?"

I laughed. "Definitely not. I don't even have a girlfriend to speak of."

"That's good. It seems like all of you young guys are getting married and having kids before you even leave school."

I knew exactly what Dr. Hancock meant. I had classes with a few guys that were married, a few more than that were engaged. One had a baby on the way.

We talked about where I wanted to go, what I wanted to study. That lead to talk about outdoor recreation. I was a rock climber. Dr. Hancock was a mountain biker and whitewater kayaker.

"Yeah, Nathan, if you end up in Colorado, just get a crappy pickup to haul all your gear around in and just have a ball. That's what I did, a lot of mountain biking and kayaking. My wife and I both had those adventures, then after we met we were able to have those adventures together. We waited to have kids and I'm glad we did. Doing those things together was important for our relationship. Now I'm at an age where I totally appreciate and enjoy my kids. I think these young couples see their kids as keeping them from adventuring. But for my wife and I, our kids are the adventure now."

I went to get Dr. Hancock's permission to publish his name on our presentation. I left his office after twenty minutes, my mind churning. I had thought graduate school was just the next step, the thing that people did once they got a degree, the next destination on the red line. At least, the construct I had been adhering to operated that way. But listening to Dr. Hancock talk about his life, about the way he did things, it was nothing like my current model, the red line model. His model was more appealing. He really made me think about life, about what I wanted to do with it.

At the time, that was a pretty big inconvenience. I had a lot of work to do and graduation was only a few weeks away. It wasn't the time to question my life decisions. I had come too far and worked too hard for the biology degree to let it go to waste. In retrospect though, his timing was perfect. He caught me right at a transitional point—in multiple aspects of my life.

Chapter 27

THE WIND WAS CEASELESS. It filled the sails of the boat and pushed me further out to sea. It raised bumps on my skin as well, but the sun was bright and the sky clear. I breathed the ocean salt and bid farewell to land as it retreated over the horizon. I turned to face the ocean ahead of me and said goodbye to a love lost. Laurie. We had been in love. She had been a fairy tale.

I met her before I started college and only knew her briefly. We lived far away from each other and fell out of touch. It wasn't until after my first novel was published that we reconnected. I had been traveling around the country to promote my book when I landed near her home. She came to a book signing. I recognized her instantly, but I didn't let it show on my face. She walked up to the table and handed me her copy.

I can't remember what I said, but it made her laugh. Her laugh was the greatest and sounded just how I remembered. She scanned my face for any sign of recognition, but I played it off like she was another person in the crowd. I handed her book back, and her face fell.

She was halfway to the door when I called out her name and told her to read the inscription.

Laurie-

You are even more beautiful than I remember, which was

already more than I thought possible. Please have lunch with me.

That was the beginning of our relationship. We were together for several months, but the distance made it hard. She flew cross-country to visit me for a weekend. She broke it off. She went back east; I went further west and refused to stop at the ocean. The wind carried me away from all of that pain. Or so I thought. What if I hadn't gone west? What if I had followed Laurie east? What if I had tried to make it work? What was it about tragedy that I found so appealing?

Wait.

I didn't get on that sailboat. I didn't have a relationship with Laurie. I never wrote an inscription in her book.

I never wrote a book.

I never left my bike.

But the wind was ceaseless.

● ● ●

I understood why Billy Rice had struggled in Wyoming. It was 15 miles from the construction zone to the tree line. I had already pedaled enough to cover twice that distance and still no tree line. The wind held me back. The terrain was hilly, and the wind forced me to walk up every slope and to pedal down the other side; yes, coasting was impossible. I stopped once to refill my water at a location Two Hats had told me about. It was the last sign of construction, a few heavy loaders parked near a new culvert already buried and conducting water under the road. The gas station clerk telling me about the closed road was a distant memory. Was it really just that morning? The memory had been caught by the wind too and carried far away, far from that stream. And it was at that stream I saw them again. Tire tracks. Five sets.

I still hadn't given much thought to the fortune cookie and what I would do if I caught up to Allison's group. Instead, my time was filled with endless conversations. What had started as a friendly conversation with my buddy Shane back in Montana had grown, spread through my mind. I had conversations with a lot of friends. Then I had conversations with friends I had fallen out of contact with. That grew into conversations with friends of friends, acquaintances, and strangers. No person or topic was off limits. Everyone was an actor and I, the director. I played out scenario after scenario. Again, I was reminded of a movie: *Inception*. I had built an alternate reality. Was this a bad thing? I wasn't sure. It wasn't until I realized the emotions generated by the various scenarios I created were real enough that I thought it was a little off. I didn't stop though. It was a great way to pass the time. And in Wyoming, when the wind blows, time moves slowly.

"Just give it a week, Nathan."

I pushed up another hill, leaning on my aerobars to cut the wind better. At the top, the color composition of the landscape had changed. In the distance, on the horizon, there was a band of green. Not the dull, silvery green of sage, but a dark band of green that extended from the foothills all the way to the top of the ridge. Trees. I was close to leaving this soon-to-be-wind-farm behind. I used my cell phone to listen to music the last few miles to the trees, the wind constantly trying to drown the music from my ears, to hold me back, to keep me from leaving behind the vast stretches of sun-drenched sand and sage.

My grin reached ear-to-ear as I started up a small hill. The white bark with its characteristic dark scars was more than familiar. Closer and closer I got. One tree there. Four there. A whole stand. Closer and closer I drew, and the thicker and thicker the aspens grew. I climbed up to them, and their shelter pushed the wind back, held it at bay, and allowed me to continue uncontested. The wind blew harder, angered, and reached down through the gap in the canopy above the road, stretching its arm toward me, its shoulder pressed against the treetops, its fingertips just short of me. The branches recoiled under its weight and flung him off.

It was a welcoming feeling, my old friends protecting me, my aspen trees I had spent so much time studying, had spent so much time getting to know. They were different here though. I studied stands separated by ponderosa pines and basaltic outcrops. Here they grew as a forest; it was a whole landscape calling me in. The leaves danced to the music in my ears—a celebration for having crossed the desert. A childlike wonder took hold of me as I saw the trees for what felt like the first time and watched the sway of every leaf, the bending of every branch, the chorus of trees moving in sync to the chorus of my music.

I spent very little time looking at the road over the next miles. I peered into the forest, trying to see just how far the white trunks extended, to guess how long the leaves could tremble, to feel just how long the trees had anticipated my arrival. Riding here was a whole new experience. Seeing the trees, it was in a whole new light. It was liberating.

I soared as I climbed through the trees toward Aspen Alley. The old growth aspens towered over me on the single lane of gravel, the green skylights letting just enough light through to illuminate the history the trees contained. In every trunk were initials, dates, names, some enclosed in hearts and pierced by arrows. Some scars were fresh, others stretched and distorted by time and growth. And all the while, the leaves danced, the leaves celebrated.

The growth thinned as I neared the top of the climb, where I stopped to eat dinner. It was strange, my mood being so affected by the environment. It was one of those mystical experiences we had lost all understanding of. It was sublime to rediscover part of that connection.

My belly full, I continued down the road, paved now. The sun started to fall from the sky, and the bright sphere was filtered through the treetops that threw me into intermittent shadow. From my vantage point, I could see into Colorado, the landscape I would soon begin to ride across. It was a serrated surface that sliced into the sky. The mountains were green and gray and several shades of spectacular. I set up camp a few miles from the Colorado border, already having forgotten the barrenness and sage and wind of Wyoming. My attention was directed forward.

Chapter 28

I WOKE UP to drops of moisture suspended by my bivy like little chandeliers that threatened to crash down at any movement. It had rained during the night. Wyoming wasn't going to let me go that easily. But the weather couldn't hold me back on the paved descent to Colorado; the mountains' gravity pulled me in as the Earth's gravity pulled me down the hill. I decided on an alternate that would shave a few miles off the route and avoid a rocky climb. I was anxious to get to Steamboat Springs and get a new tire on my rear wheel.

Colorado was beautiful. The road snaked up a river valley where the scenery alternated between ranches and groves of aspens. The long gradual climb started to wear on me, though. I finished off the remainder of my snacks, drawing every bit of energy I could to finish the climb. Near the top, a pickup pulled up to next me, matching my speed as the passenger hung out of his window.

"Hey, are you riding that route?"

"Yup."

"Nice man. Do you want us to take your bags to the top for you?"

"No thanks."

"Well, how far are you headed?"

"Steamboat, hopefully."

Our conversation was pretty one-sided. I offered short answers through strained breathing. But I was told I was close to the top and that it was all downhill to Steamboat Springs from there. He had been right.

On the descent, I realized I had felt good while eating my trail mix. It wasn't until half an hour or so after I finished it that I felt fatigued. At A&M Reservoir, I talked to one of the CDT hikers about her eating habits. They were simple: snack all day and eat a decent meal at night. I would try that too. Not only would it save on time, but on stove fuel as well.

I pulled into Steamboat Springs in the early afternoon and began to make my way through town on the Yampa River Core Path. There was a lot of traffic. It was a beautiful Friday afternoon, and the whole population was out in force. I hadn't been in the vicinity of so many people for some time. I was disconcerted by the number of pedestrians and bicycles on the path—it was the first time I had to weave through traffic.

The path brought me to my next planned stop: the Orange Peel Bicycle Shop. It sat on a corner, across the street from the bike path, next to a park. Its outside had a carousel of bicycles, all waiting to be rented and taken through the streets. The building itself caught the eye with an architectural style reminiscent of art nouveau. I spoke to a salesman and got my bike in the mechanic's lineup. The wait would be a couple of hours. As I finished talking to the salesman, a group of three guys walked up to the shop from the street.

"Hey, you look like you are riding the divide?"

"Yeah. I'm trying anyway," I said.

"So are we," he said pointing to his friends.

"Oh, nice. How's it been going for you three?"

The talkative one told me about the trouble he had had and how he had to hitchhike into Steamboat the day before to get his bike fixed. The other two had come in earlier that day and had dropped their bikes off to get some work done too. They had come down to see if their bikes would be ready the next morning.

"You guys haven't run into another group by any chance, have you?" I asked.

"No. You're the only other mountain biker we've seen in a while."

"Really?" I thought for sure they would have known of Allison's group. "Yeah, I only ask because I've been following a group of five for a few days now."

"Yeah, that's us."

"Oh. Are you guys riding with a couple of girls?"

"Yeah, they're back at the hotel"

"Is one of them named Allison?"

"Yeah. How'd you know that?

"I've been working hard to catch you guys."

I explained about Oliver and the North Fork Hostel. That was an eternity ago now. At about that time, the weather started to turn and dark clouds topped the mountains and began to make their way down into Steamboat's valley. I wanted to ride a few more miles, but I had finally caught Allison and her group. The late hour and bad weather made me wonder if I should stay in Steamboat for the night. Even the salesman tried to persuade me to stay.

"Steamboat isn't a bad place for a rest day. It is a pretty neat town," he said.

I considered it. What if I had stayed for the night and set out the next day with that group? I had worked hard to catch them, and I finally had. A day or two of riding with them wouldn't have hurt. It's not as though I would have been committed to them. Sleeping inside and out of the rain would have been nice too.

it is much more difficult to judge oneself than to judge others

I turned to the trio. "I'm actually going to head out and get a few more miles tonight."

"All right man. Well, maybe we'll see you out there on the trail over the next week or so and get a chance to talk."

"Yeah, that sounds good." I nodded my head as though we had made plans. It wouldn't happen. There was a good chance I would never see these guys again. They said they had been averaging 60 miles a day. I said I was doing the same. I lied. Really, I had been averaging closer to 75 or 80. I had caught them twice already. I was confident the gap between us would only grow, as long as I didn't get sick again.

My bike came back from the mechanic with a new tire and tube for my rear wheel, new brake pads, freshly adjusted derailleurs, and a clean drivetrain. My backpack came out of the store with a new jar of chamois cream. I did some shopping and left town to continue my solo journey. It was almost 7 p.m. already, and the rain began to fall.

I was dead tired when I stopped to set up camp. The route had cut through a lot of private land, all agricultural. The high exposure made camping in a stealthy fashion difficult. So I rode past 9 that night, the only occasion I rode in the dark, just to reach a swath of BLM land a half-mile wide.

In contrast to the surrounding area, the BLM land was covered in vegetation. As I scanned the roadside for a decent spot, I scared a fox that prowled on the road. I set up camp in the dark a few yards off the road and tried to make lots of noise during the process to establish my territory for the critters I was sure were just out of sight. I crawled into my sleeping bag. It was hard work to catch Allison, and the three guys I had met were nice, but I was happy with my decision.

Chapter 29

I FOLLOWED THE ROUTE ALONG the edge of the Yampa River the next morning. It was a dirt road, speckled with pies and the cows that had left them. As I started up a hill, a racer coasted down, cheering me on.

"Hey buddy! I've been watching you on the race tracker. Keep it up!"

"That couldn't be me. I'm not even racing." Why would he think I was? "Thank you though!" Ralph. I must have been very close to Ralph now, and the racer thought I was Ralph.

The rest of the morning took me past the Stagecoach Reservoir and to a 15-mile climb up to Lynx Pass. Instead of finding a descent on the other side, the mountain plateaued, and the route carried me through wonderful alpine scenery and past the Rock Creek Stage Station, a Wells Fargo mailing station from the 1880s.

Around the bend from the old log structure was Rock Creek itself. What was not at Rock Creek was a bridge. Luckily, it had been a warm day, so I looked forward to getting wet. I wish I could say the same for the gentleman that got there before me. The GDMBR wasn't just followed by mountain bikers. The route was also popular with motorcycle tourists, so it was no surprise when I saw two touring motorcycles on the near side of the creek. Things did begin to look curious as I drew closer though.

"Hey, how are you doing?" I asked.

"Well, my bike is running. That's good."

His bike certainly was running, at an idle, in the middle of the road. The dirt surface below the motorcycle was smoother than the rest of the road and a few shades darker. Fluids had been lost from the bike where it sat.

"Were you having some engine problems?"

"You could say that."

The man and his wife came up on the creek from the far side, riding the route northward. Instead of stopping to inspect the crossing, he just went for it. The stream was almost thirty-yards wide at the crossing, stretched out by the low grade of the road, and he almost made it the whole way. Unfortunately, there was a deep trench just before he made it out. He hit it, lost control, and dumped his bike over in the creek. It had been completely submerged. His wife, on her own motorcycle, rode the long way around and helped him get his bike out. In the meantime, all of his gear boxes filled with water. So his bike did lose a lot fluid on the road, it just all happened to be creek water. If only I had been twenty minutes faster.

"You know, we passed another mountain biker today."

"Yeah? Do you know his name?" I had a suspicion that I did.

"I can't remember. But he was a college professor, I think he said."

"Does the name Ralph ring a bell?"

"Yeah! That's what it was."

"Awesome. I've been trying to catch him for almost a week now. Any idea how far ahead of me he is?"

"It's only been an hour or two since we spoke to him. I bet you catch him by tonight."

I was close to Yukon. My legs went back into competition mode. I thanked the motorcyclist for the underwater topography lecture he gave me and then forded the creek myself.

A few miles further, I missed a turn and accidentally found the highway. I lost fifteen minutes as I tried to rectify another navigational error that the map's addendum would have cleared up. At least it wasn't as catastrophic as Fleecer Ridge had been. Back on route, I began what the map referred to as "one of the most dramatic dives" on the route and, when I lost nearly 2,000 feet over a couple of miles, it was hard not to agree.

To get to the top though, I traversed a lot of rolling terrain that seemed endless. I began to curse the route, the constant up and down, or rather the too-steep-to-ride-up and too-steep-to-ride-down. On the last hill before the true descent, I ran into another northbound cyclist, Stephen. He had spent four hours on the climb, which meant mostly hiking his bike. Stephen also told me I was only about an hour behind Ralph, and after we exchanged pep talks, I descended in about thirty-five minutes down a steep, exposed road. I understood how it would take four hours to climb. I also understood the maps warning of "dangerous, sharp corners" when I almost collided with a car on its way up the hill. The timing with which we both came around the blind corner was amazing. I braked and began to turn to the inside, but once I realized the turn was too sharp, I bailed to the outside of the curve, going around the car on the wrong side, dangerously close to going off the road and down the incredibly steep hill. That incident made me laugh.

Previous to the car encounter, I was pretty upset. I had to fight another strong headwind that came up from the Colorado River valley. It was strong enough to hold me back. After meeting the car, I realized just how much of an influence my expectations had on the quality of the experience. Even though I was coasting at 18 mph, I was upset because the wind slowed me down. Eighteen is faster than a decent clip. It only took a near miss to slap me across the face and make me realize how ridiculous my attitude was. After the near miss with the car and a good laugh, the descent was a blast.

At the bottom, I passed through the town of Radium and was wrangled into a house by the calls of "ice cream" from a rafting company employee. The day was too hot to turn down ice cream. Again, I heard I was only an hour behind Ralph. But now that I had descended down to the river, it was time to climb back out of the valley. The first climb was 2 miles. The second was 4. Both were steep. Both left me feeling accomplished and satisfied with my effort. The second also left me with a long, straight descent. My brakes went untouched. It was at the bottom, where the dirt road met the highway, where things got interesting.

The wind I had fought on my way down to Radium still howled. As I sat at the pavement waiting for a break in the highway traffic, my contact lens slipped on my eyeball. I had worn contacts long enough to just close my eye in response. If my contact fell out now, I could kiss it goodbye. Operating with only my left eye open, I dismounted my bike and leaned it against a signpost. I cupped my hands over my right eye to shield it from the wind and tried to blink my contact back into place. A few blinks and its position was corrected. My hands dropped, and I took a look around to make sure I still had it. I did. The very next blink, it fell out.

The scene unfolded in slow motion, half of it in focus. My contact dropped almost a foot before the wind caught it and blew it off the side of the road into the sand. The narrow band of blue visible on the edge of the contact stood in such stark contrast to the bleached sand, I could see it ten feet away with my one good eye. I ran over to it before the wind could grab it again. I cupped the contact between my palms as I tried to determine the best course of action. These contacts could be worn for a month without needing to be removed. To cut weight, I had not packed any contact solution. So I rinsed the lens with water; naturally, it was transferred from my water bladder to my palm via my mouth. Clearly, sanitation was a concern as I rinsed the contact I had just picked up off the ground with saliva-laced water.

While I rinsed, the intersection became even more busy. Cars waited to turn onto the highway, two or three at a time. Of course, there I stood in the sand, spitting into my hand and poking myself in the eye. What a sight that must have been. It took multiple tries to get my contact back in. The wind wanted to blow it away every time it approached my face. Twenty feet away was a broad sign, low to the ground. I ducked behind it. I think that was what drew the attention of the police car that pulled over on the dirt road. I'm sure it looked like I was trying to duck out of sight. I even considered walking over to see if I could climb in his car and use his visor mirror. To protect and serve right?

A few more attempts, though, and I got the contact back in. It didn't sit right, and it burned like hell, but it was back in. My right eye still closed, I wandered back to my bike and picked it up from the ground. The wind had knocked it over. As I threw my leg over it and got ready to ride again, I saw two road cyclists coming down the pavement and gave them a wave, the right side of my face scrunched up, holding my contact in place. They didn't even wave back!

I decided to ride to the town of Kremmling, just 2 miles away, and hopefully sort things out there. So with one eye and no depth perception, I turned onto the mildly busy highway. Of course, after a half-mile, the shoulder disappeared. I did my best to ride the white line, one eye open, cars brushing my shoulder. The last mile into town was pretty tense, but I made it unscathed. And of course, as soon as I made it to the broad streets of the town, I was able to open my eye. My contact was secure, and I could see, but only through the burning sensation.

Chapter 30

"A CONTACT FIASCO. Man, that was hilarious."

The previous day was one of my lowest mileage days, but the intensity of both climbs and the unexpected difficulty of the descent that came between made it one of the most rewarding and satisfying. In Kremmling, I found a hostel (over a hundred years old), and managed to escape another night of rain. The two road cyclists I had waved to also stayed there. They didn't acknowledge me there either, not even when we pulled our bikes out of the same garage at the same time that morning.

I returned to the route and left the pavement behind for my beloved dirt and gravel. The night's rain made a beautiful blue sky for the morning that had me feeling great. I replayed in my mind what I had dubbed the "contact fiasco" and had a good laugh about it as I peddled up toward Williams Fork Reservoir. I wished I could have seen the whole thing from an outside perspective.

The reservoir water was placid, as if the birds of prey in every nest on top of every pole were related to the halcyon and carried its mythical powers. The sky was immense already, but above the lake it grew further, reflected back so that one on the lake might feel suspended in an eternal free fall, unable to discern which way was up. I skirted along the banks, the fisherman and kayakers my only company. It was quiet enough to hear a kayaker's paddle cut through the surface of the water as it dropped, then create the back eddy as it withdrew again. My drivetrain rattled on.

At the far end of the reservoir, I missed a turn, and instead of guessing where, I spotted three fly fisherman and pulled up to them to ask. They were packing up their gear and breaking down their poles having finished fishing a small stretch of river right above its mouth to the lake.

"Excuse me, do you guys have a second?" The oldest of the three stepped forward.

"Sure, what do you need?" He rested one arm on the truck bed, his voice calm and inviting.

"Well, I'm headed up to the pass and missed a turn somewhere. I'm just wondering if you can get me back on track."

"Well, which pass are you headed for?"

I couldn't remember. I unfolded my map and found the name: Ute Pass. They knew of it and were a little surprised I was headed up it on a bike. After we all examined my map and a road atlas of theirs, we got my navigation all straightened out.

"So how far are you headed?"

"Well, I'd like to make Breckenridge today, but the long term goal is the Mexican border."

"Mexico! Oh man! That's a long ways from here. You must have started in Denver?"

"Oh no. I started up in Banff, up in Alberta."

"Banff! We know Banff pretty well; there's great fly fishing up there. My son here played hockey in Calgary," he said as he indicated one of the younger men. "You started in Banff?" They all became a lot more intrigued. "So you've been riding for a while."

"Yeah, this is the last day of my fourth week. I'm hoping to make Mexico in the next two."

I told them a bit more about the trip and what I had done and seen so far. They too were impressed with my light load and had all kinds of questions about food and cooking.

"Well, where is your fly rod?"

"Oh man, I don't have one. Next time though. I've seen a lot of fly fisherman and a lot of streams that looked like fun to fish."

After some talk about good fly fishing spots between Banff and Colorado, we parted ways. I backtracked a quarter-mile, to the turn I missed, up a small, steep hill. The red pickup with the family of fisherman came up the hill as I made the turn, and the father stuck his arm out of the window to give an enthusiastic wave. I returned it, a large smile on my face. A few weeks prior, I had been too stubborn and proud to want to ask for directions. Now, because of interactions like that one, it had become a favorite activity.

* * *

Back on track, I followed a wide dirt road while the whine of small engines gained on me quickly. Three motorcycle tourists flew by me. All three waved. I waved back, envious of the speed they traveled at, but also proud of my own bike. Ernest Hemingway once described how a bicycle allows you to form accurate memories of the country you ride through. Anything with an engine, though, leaves you unimpressed, and you only remember the large hills. Would my memories be clearer than theirs at the end of the ride? Would I have even more memories, each hill being distinct? Would I feel more satisfied, having covered the ground under my own power?

I wasn't feeling satisfied as I climbed up Ute Pass. It was a steep climb on pavement that cut past a marred landscape, the victim of mining. The climb was definitely one that I could not forget, as was the descent. Five miles of paved downhill with an outstanding view out across the valley and up to the Gore Range mountains. Stunning.

It was 13 more miles to Silverthorne on the same highway I had lost my contact alongside of the day before. The rain began to fall as I pulled into town, so I found a sandwich shop to take shelter in and eat some lunch. Ralph's race page told me I had already passed him. I hadn't seen him though. He must have gotten a late start from the campground back at the reservoir. I set my phone down and quietly munched on my sandwich, the thrill of catching Ralph extinguished. It would have been nice to see a familiar face, to swap more tales of the trail with someone that understood. I finished up my massive sandwich and massive soda and returned to my bike to set out into sunshine once again.

* * *

"Hi there. You look like you're headed somewhere."

I had left Silverthorne and was riding alongside the Dillon Reservoir on the Blue River trail system when another cyclist pulled alongside me. He was without bags, but towed a trailer loaded with, of all things, another bike. The path we were on traversed the most urban area of the entire route and was never further than a few hundred yards from the nearest building. It hadn't occurred to me that other people might use the path too. I hope the surprise of seeing him didn't show on my face.

"Sure am. I'm riding the Great Divide and am headed for Mexico."

"Wow. How far are you headed today?"

"Breckenridge at least. I'd like to get farther though."

"I'm riding to Breck too. Mind if I join you?"

Paul wasn't a local either. He was from Maryland, but he and his wife liked Breckenridge enough to buy a condo and spend their summers there. Paul was also a mountain biker and had lots of questions about the tour, never having done one himself. Paul was an excellent guide and directed me through the confusing bits of the bike route while he gave me some of the local history along the way. It was 17 miles to Breckenridge and Paul's company kept me at the cranks through the last 5, my energy depleted. As the bike path came into Breck, we were gaining on another pair of cyclists. Huh, those panniers looked familiar. Hadn't I seen them before? Paul and I caught up to them, and as I had suspected, it was the couple from the Netherlands I had met outside of Rawlins. We all chatted a bit before Paul and I passed them and left the path behind. Paul guided me down main street, pointing out the best restaurants, shops, and grocery stores along the road.

"Listen Nathan, here's my cell number in case you need help while you're in the area."

"Thanks Paul. I really can't thank you enough. You've been an excellent guide."

"Well, good luck on your trip. I hope you make it to Mexico."

"And I hope you make it to Costa Rica for your bike race."

Paul headed home, while I headed for a restaurant. The sky had clouded up on our way into Breck, and rain looked inevitable. I had hoped to start the climb up to Boreas Pass, but Ute Pass had taken a lot out of me. Boreas would have to wait. I called a few places to see if they had any room and, as Paul had thought, the two bike races in town that weekend had filled everything up. I rode down to a city park that Paul had suggested I camp in. It was the finish line for one of the races, crowded with people and drowned in loud music and sporadic cheers as racers crossed the line.

"Well, I'll just start climbing and stop at the first decent spot."

I didn't make it out of Breckenridge. I was back on the main route for a half-mile when I noticed a small pull out. I stopped to look around and found the pull out dropped down a bank to a small, flat piece of ground, next to a small brook. It was below the level of the ground, so I wouldn't be noticed from the pull out. I was sold. My bivy's bright orange color made me wait to set up camp though. I was sure I was on private property and didn't want to draw attention to myself. From my clearing, I could see cars and their drivers on the road just downhill from the pull out. If I could see them, they could probably see a bright orange piece of fabric. I ate, journaled, and poured over my maps until the sky started to darken, then I set up camp.

Chapter 31

THE SERPENTINE PAVEMENT carried me up and away from Breckenridge and to stunning views of the sleepy-eyed town. The cloudy sky cast a soft light on the valley and left only a single slice of blue sky to be seen on the horizon, sandwiched between the mountain peaks and gray clouds. Trees dominated the town and concealed the many houses below; it was a forest punctuated by the paced stripes of streets and the occasional brick building taller than the trees. Moving up the far ridge, gray was replaced with green and the stripes of the light grassy ski slopes separated the dark, thick evergreens. These were the stripes easiest to see and the last bit of the town to vanish as I climbed away.

The clouds began to burn off, and my sweat cooled me while the sun warmed me, relieving the sting of the morning's cool air from my arms and legs. The road followed the old railroad grade that descended into Breckenridge, meaning the climb was at a very low grade and cut through rock outcrops the color of brick and through tunnels of aspen. The sky had almost cleared, but one cloud was stuck on a solitary peak. It poured from the heavens and flowed down over the peak, the flood disappearing before it could wash me away. I passed the historic Bakers tank, a cistern used to refill the water reservoir of steam locomotives, and was soon delivered to the top where the old mail building and train depot still stood, the wood aged to a dark brown that still held the panes of leaded glass behind which sat a "closed" sign.

The peak's vegetation petered out, and trees gave way to shrubs, shrubs gave way to grasses, and grass vanished between the rocks. The lack of vegetation told me this was a high pass. My map told me it was the second highest on the route. I hoped the tallest pass would go as easy on me as this one had.

The road bumped and bucked, jarred and jostled me on my way down. The view was strikingly different from any previous to my sixteenth Divide crossing. Instead of lush forests capped by the barrenness of rocky peaks, I looked over an arid, martian land: South Park. I crossed the wide basin on gravel roads intended for development, development that never happened. Grids were left unfilled, cul-de-sacs forgotten. I passed countless roads that led to nowhere, their signs coated in dust. It was a strange sight that became eerie when I passed the South Park sports center. The abandoned baseball diamond was overgrown, save for a wide circle in center field that had been fenced—a temporary corral perhaps? The basketball court's slab of concrete was still clean, missing the streaks of shoe soles and bike tires and the blood stains of over zealous children, yet it cracked, weary with age, its feeble chain-link fence leaning to one side. Bathroom doors stood open, sinks and toilets filled with all matters of garbage and waste, while the jungle gym still gleamed yellow, not having had any hands to climb and polish it to its metallic core.

This park was a paradox, an ancient structure that was still brand new, but its use had been repeatedly postponed until it was reclassified as abandoned. Someone had put a lot of time and effort into seeing that park built, but nothing into seeing it used. This was a pattern I recognized in my own life. How often had I put time and effort into the development of a dream, but never saw those dreams become goals, never saw them come to fruition?

The park was still on my mind as the rain swept toward me across the basin. It gave me only enough time to pull on my rain gear before it washed away my tracks, before it erased the record of someone else having been there. The rain was heavy, but it was only a few miles to the pavement, and 5 more into the town of Hartsel where I found shelter in a diner.

● ● ●

"I'll take a dollar for that stuff."

I glanced down at my hands. Was something hidden? No,

nothing was.

"A dollar? Are you sure?"

"Yeah," she said, one eye still on her ancient tube television set.

"But this candy bar alone is a dollar. This has to be worth three or four all together."

"Well, I am the owner of this mercantile, and I set the prices, not you. I say it's a dollar."

"Really?"

"Of course. I like my Divide riders."

It was still raining when I finished my lunch at the diner. I crossed the street and entered the mercantile to kill some time, hoping the rain would let up before I had to set out again. Like any mercantile, what was on the shelves said a lot about business. No fresh fruit meant business was infrequent. The markup on milk and eggs said they usually spoiled before being purchased. The lack of boxed dinners and canned goods said business was slower than it once was. In fact, the lack of food in the mercantile was surprising. It also carried the air of an antique shop. Furniture laid in an adjacent room; walls were covered in trinkets; and shelves were stacked with maps and brochures. I spent more time browsing through the merc than I had intended, more than I had thought possible. When I snapped out of my daze, I grabbed a candy bar and bag of banana chips.

"A dollar?"

"Of course. I like my Divide riders."

My cyclist status was no secret. I had walked around the store in my backpack, gloves, and helmet. My bike laid against the bench outside the large front windows of the store, propped up on one of the panniers.

"Well thank you. I appreciate it."

"Let me give you some advice too," she said as she turned away from the TV to fix both eyes on me. "You are going to head out of town, take a right, then ride about 2 miles before you turn onto 53. That's the road you're going to follow all the way to Salida. Now, in the past few weeks we've been hearing about a bear out along 53. He's a black bear, but he isn't scared of people, just curious by the sounds of it. And he's been causing some problems. So keep an eye open for him and don't bother trying to scare him off."

That stretch of road was almost 45 miles long. It really was the one road I would follow for the rest of the day.

"Is there any place in particular he's been seen? I was thinking I might camp out there, so is there any place I shouldn't sleep."

She raised an eyebrow. "You don't plan on going to Salida tonight?

"Well, I hope I make it that far. But it's getting later, and my legs are starting to get tired, so I'm not sure if I'll make it."

She glanced at an ancient clock on the wall. "It's only 3. You'll make it just fine."

She was so certain, I believed her. I thanked her again, both for the food and the advice, and emerged from the store. The rain had let up, but still encouraged me to pull my rain gear back on. I put on some music. The next stretch would be similar to the previous: lots of abandoned developments and not much else. Now with the clouds in the sky, there wasn't much for scenery either.

The rain hung in limbo all afternoon, unable to decide if it should fall or not. Individual drops made their own decisions, sometimes hitting me and other times not. But the wind had no indecision about its strength and direction. I'd found myself another headwind. It was cold, one that had me keep my layers on, but surprisingly, I wasn't bothered by it. I was crossing a flat landscape, one that I could still traverse despite the wind. I lowered my head and listened to my music while I wandered around that headspace, that alternate reality where I talked with whoever I wanted and said whatever came to mind, where I could even edit and replay conversations if necessary. This wind could not compete with that reality, not like the wind in Wyoming where I had to pedal hard to get down a hill.

My eyes were peeled for the friendly bear. I hadn't had a bear encounter since Montana. Maybe those two grizzlies had spread the word about me. Maybe I had earned a reputation. Yeah, that must have been why I hadn't seen any bears. What I did see a lot of though was mud. The road became soft enough for my tires to sink in. Mine were the only tracks that led up to another creek ford the mercantile owner had warned me about. The creek wasn't too fast to cross like she thought it might be, but the water was a caramel brown. I crossed barefoot, my rain pants pulled up to my knees, just above the water after I sunk ankle deep into the mud that felt like caramel. It was warm between my toes and even the water felt warmer than the air as I rinsed my feet.

After the ford, the road started to mimic the creek bottom. Mud flowed through the tread and clung to my tires. Several times my front fork was plugged with mud. I learned to ride around the worst spots, but it wasn't much better off the road than it was on it.

I continued to fight the mud as I climbed; its dead weight pulled me down and clogged my drive train, refusing to let me leave the wide basin. But I topped out and crossed into the adjacent county where the road became instantly less muddy. My map had promised an incredible view from the top, but it was missing. The ridge I had just topped was adjacent to the Sawatch Range, home of the famous "Fourteeners," a number of peaks exceeding 14,000 feet that marked the Continental Divide. They were hidden. The view was now a canvas white-washed by the low hanging clouds.

Stephen, the cyclist I met on my way down to Radium, had talked about the "red line," the line that traversed our maps, pointed our direction, told us where to go. It was the line we had to follow. It was a purist attitude really. Stephen had broken that attitude, strayed from the line so that he might look upon something more beautiful. He had circumnavigated South Park and Breckenridge and followed the Sawatch Range instead. It had been spectacular, and he recommended it. I had even considered it. But then I had met Paul. Our conversation was too nice to pass up on, and as he escorted me to Breckenridge, he escorted me right past the critical junction that separated the two valleys. I didn't regret my decision to ride through Breck and South Park, but I did start to question my desire to follow that red line. What was so important about it anyway?

I coasted down past rocky outcrops covered in juniper and piñon toward the Arkansas River and town of Salida. Daylight had started to fade, and the descent chilled the sweat I had generated on the climb. My hands took on a blue tinge, but I still smiled. Back in Hartsel, I hadn't been sure I would make Salida. When I encountered the strong head wind, I was almost certain I wouldn't make it. The owner of the mercantile knew though and didn't hesitate to tell me. I rode into town as my odometer marked another 100-mile day.

Chapter 32

Early December 2012

"COME HERE, Ozzy. Come on. You can do it."

He stood at the doorway, his eyes fixed on me from the safety of a floor that had a thread count. But his bed, his place of comfort and safety, laid next to my feet, five feet away from him and across a hardwood floor. Jared and Whitne had adopted Ozzy when he was 2 years old. He was an Australian Shepard with the telltale mismatched irises. He was quite charming. But he wasn't fond of hardwood floors. With a bit more encouragement, he tested the floor with a single paw, then the next, only his hind legs remaining on the carpet. The next step was pivotal and his first hind leg left behind the carpet for the hardwood. Once it hit the floor, Ozzy was committed and went for it. His legs wobbled and his pupils dilated as he spotted each step he took to cross to his bed. He crawled into it and turned around before he sat. He gave a sigh as he looked back at the floor. Then he jumped up into the chair next to me and laid down; his chin rested on the armrest of my chair, his wet nose pressed against my arm. The two of us spent a lot of nights like that; Ozzy asleep, while I held a book beneath a small lamp, my feet kicked up.

I had graduated in June, and for the first time, had not returned home immediately to work on the farm. I would go back for harvest, but not until then. I wanted time off, time to relax, time to let the issues of the last year dissolve away. I wanted time to think about my life, what I wanted to do with it. I didn't know how, but I felt this all somehow related to the graduation card Amber had given me. What did it mean to be a "man"? These questions had bothered me since graduation, and I began to search for answers.

I spent my last free weekend that August with Shane. We skipped the usual beer at the ale house and chose instead to go rock climbing. We spent the night beneath the stars during a meteor shower, and then woke up the next morning to do a few multi-pitch, alpine climbs. I always appreciated the massive gravity of the rocks I climbed. They pulled me in. They focused my mind. They gave me clarity. When you're fully exposed on a rock wall, it's difficult to hide—even from your fears. I returned home after that trip and worked harvest and continued to help through the fall. When work began to slow down, I began to study writing.

Books had a newfound presence in my life. I had always been too busy during school to read more than one or two books every several months. With the constant barrage of work, it was hard to justify reading for pleasure. Now that school was over, I read to my heart's content. After I reflected on the aspirations of my younger self, a substantial number of the books I read focused on writing. I soon became fascinated with story structure and the elements that made a story great.

This pursuit carried over when I moved to Montana to live with Jared and Whit. As I had learned with Brandon, living with my brother was a great way to strengthen our relationship. Ozzy was a great companion during that time when I spent almost all of my wakeful hours with a book in my hands. I read a lot of nonfiction, but fiction dominated my diet. At my peak, I read a book per day. I surrounded myself with notecards to create scene-by-scene breakdowns of the books I liked most. I read and analyzed, and then did it again. Many nights I would stay up to finish a book and laugh, cringe, sneer, or even cry, the whole time with Ozzy's wet nose pressed against my arm and his chin on my armrest.

The content on writing started simple, as guides or pamphlets from writing blogs. This became books more dense than I thought I could handle. And as I learned and examined, I expanded the content I learned from. I branched out into mythology, then to philosophy, and even to psychology. I not only learned about writing, but about living. It was during this educational period that I felt I was getting closer to the answer of the question Amber had inspired me to ask.

Apart from that progress, my reading shook the foundations of my personal philosophy. I had always had respect for science, enough to pursue it in school. The appeal was in the search for truth, while consciously trying to avoid bias and subjectivity. Then I read books that exposed the framework I couldn't see while I was in school, books that showed me a point of view not taught at traditional schools, books that exposed the bias. I saw the parochialisms and my perception of the scientific community changed. I placed my five-year education under scrutiny, and all of a sudden, my entire personal philosophy began to crumble.

There was one good thing in regard to my crumbling philosophy though: I was the one tearing down the walls. That meant that I got to be the one who rebuilt them.

Chapter 33

ONE MONTH.

A full thirty days.

That was how long I had been on the route. Was that all? Not longer? My first day, the day I broke my panniers within the first 2 miles, was an eternity ago. Back then, I was sure I wouldn't get through Canada. But now I was in Colorado. I had come a long way and had crossed a lot of bumps along the road that led there.

I left Salida that morning after a rest day and headed for Marshall Pass. It was a 26.5-mile climb from my hotel to the summit of the pass. Sun rays pierced the landscape as I wound up through the Sawatch Range, past the occasional dispersed campsite occupied by the fly fishermen and mountain bikers of the area. The road cut above O'Haver Lake, a small fish pond when compared to the mountains, but a looking glass for the clouds that lingered above, a mirror that produced reflections clear enough to discern individual limbs and cones of the pines anchored along its banks.

"Good morning! You look like you're a racer."

I smiled. "No, just riding for the enjoyment, for views like this one." I had begun to take pride in my non-racer status. There is something to be said about riding the route solo because you chose to, not because it was a stipulation of qualification.

"Yeah, it is pretty spectacular isn't it?" he said as he leaned out of his pickup window, his silver hair catching the light just like the lake. I had stopped to take a few pictures when the driver had come up behind me.

"How has the climb been?"

"Excellent! It's been one of my favorite climbs so far."

"How far is it from Salida to the top?"

"About 26 miles. Have you ever done it?"

"No," he shook his head. "I'm not such a purist. I just throw my bike in the back of the pickup and drive to the top. I ride the trails up there."

He asked about my trip and said he was considering doing it someday. I encouraged him to commit to it.

"Well, I'll let you get back to it. Hopefully it doesn't get much hotter than this. I wouldn't want to climb in this heat."

"Actually, it's not bad at all. I would take this heat over rain any day."

He laughed. "Well, if I don't see you at the top, good luck with the rest of your trip."

He pulled away, the road's light brown dust stirred by his tires. I rode past the overlook and into some shade where I snacked and cooled down for a few minutes. It was another hour before I reached the top, where the familiar pickup was parked and unoccupied. It wasn't the only one; there were quite a few more cars there than I had imagined there would be. But this was a special place. Marshall Pass was the intersection of the Great Divide Route, the Continental Divide Trail, and the Colorado Trail. I pulled up to the sign that marked the boundary between opposite sides of the range, between the two different national forests, between the Atlantic and Pacific. I snapped a picture to commemorate my seventeenth crossing. Cefas would be in that same spot very soon, accompanying his girlfriend on the Colorado Trail. How many like-minded people must pass through there in a year, doing something similar to what I was doing? The number I imagined was considerable given the remoteness of where I stood.

Just as the climb to Marshall Pass had been one of my favorites, so was the descent. It was another true descent, and I coasted more than 15 miles before I reached the bottom. The road passed under more pine and aspen, and I caught the glare off Marshall Creek, which wandered intermittently up to the road before it vanished again in the tall grass and shrubbery of the small drainages the road traced. The last 2 miles in particular were picturesque. The road cut along the hillside of a narrow valley, the floor a perfect plane with the most curvaceous meanders of the stream punctuated by the occasional oxbow half concealed by the grass that had grown to be several feet tall. A lone fly fisherman had braved the sea of blades to stand on the banks of that stream beneath the Sawatch sea.

Sargents, a town barely more than its gas and service station, ended the descent, and I stopped there for lunch. It had been a great day so far. What had made it so great? I had spent four hours on a climb, and it had actually been enjoyable. What! While I ate my BLT, I realized I hadn't had any expectations about the climb.

I took a rest day in Salida the day before and had been sick again; not bad like in Pinedale, but enough to be preoccupied and not think about the route. Without any expectations about the climb, it was hard to be disappointed. The lack of disappointment coupled with the satisfaction of being on the bike again and making progress made the day great (and the fact it wasn't raining). Despite the benefit of rest days, I always felt the day was wasted. I would torture myself trying to guess how far I could have made it if I had kept going.

Still savoring the success of the morning, I continued on. The day's heat had built afternoon thunderstorms that began to flank me as I rode along a desolate dirt road. The rain started to fall a few miles off, smearing the horizon as I looked across Cochetopa Canyon, in awe at the storm where its dark front met blue sky and revealed the true immensity of the overlying clouds.

I camped that night at Upper Dome Reservoir, where several insect hatches were occurring. Ralph wasn't there. He had passed me again while I rested in Salida, and I thought I might catch him there. Maybe tomorrow.

* * *

The lake was shrouded with fog when I woke up. Wait. That wasn't fog. It was insects. The hatches of the night before were nothing compared to this. The fish must have been in a frenzy at the sight, the fly fisherman too. I packed quickly and pedaled out of there with my mouth closed and head lowered.

The reservoir was at the bottom of my first climb, which I would summit in the first 10 miles of the day. My eyes scanned the dust for tracks, and they found a fresh set. Ralph's? Halfway up the pass, another cyclist came coasting back down, no gear, no water bottle. A day-biker. I had to remind myself again that Great Divide riders were not the only mountain bikers in the world, a fact I forgot again and again. At the top of the pass, three motorcycles passed me. I had to remind myself again that mountain bikers were not the only people that rode the Great Divide.

The day grew hot and the vegetation more sparse. There was little shade, but I managed to find cover beneath a tree before I started up the second pass of the day, Carnero Pass. The heat increased its intensity as I climbed up the canyon, the occasional grove of aspens to keep me company. The road was steep, except for a half-mile stretch that skirted along the side of a narrow meadow, the opposite side claimed by a dilapidated log cabin, its roof sagged with the rot of age and weight of time.

The descent was as unpleasant as the climb. There was a strong wind, and the road dropped into a canyon, which funneled the wind. It was deafening. The wind was so strong and constant, all meaningful sound was lost, my ears bathed in the white noise of air waves. It was sensory deprivation, and after half an hour, it was torturous. It died down as I passed between the "gates of the canyon," a large rock outcrop of columnar basalt metamorphosed into a slight curve. The curve resembled that of a hillside tree's trunk, the bend a product of several years worth of erosion and upward growth. The basalt itself seemed to be growing from the hills.

I emerged from the windy canyon and approached the next turn onto a county road. The turn was sharp, almost hairpin, so that you actually seemed to backtrack parallel to the road you just turned off of.

"I know that green shirt!"

Ralph had made the turn and had passed the backwards section to where the road veered off. He was ahead of me on my right; I was behind him on his right. His bright neon green, long-sleeved shirt stood out in the desert. I pedaled faster.

At the turn, there was a small information board that created a sliver of shade, the first I had seen since the top of Carnero Pass. I lay in the shadow that was barely wide enough to fit my shoulders and too short to fit my legs, even when bent. I snacked and hydrated, but my water was uncomfortably low. There was a town a half-mile off-route where I could refill, but I wanted to catch Ralph. Maybe I could find water in one of the streams shown on the map—even though they flowed through the desert? I continued on route and my gamble paid off. I filtered water at the first stream I crossed, which had a fair-sized beaver dam just feet off of the road. Then it was back on the bike to catch Yukon.

"Hey Ralph!"

"Well Nathan, I didn't expect to run into you."

"Yeah, I wasn't sure I was going to see you again. I've been following you for a couple of weeks now, and you are a hard man to catch. Did I see you were up riding past midnight a few nights ago?"

Ralph laughed. "Yeah, I wanted to get Marshall Pass over with. I actually lost my light on the way up; the batteries died. So I rode to the top in the dark."

I explained to Ralph how I had gotten sick and had to take a few days to rest, which was when he passed me. I didn't bother to mention I had already passed him again and then taken another rest day to let him pass me. He still had not taken a single rest day; I didn't want him to think I was belittling his effort. The fact that he had ridden every day for more than a month was an impressive feat in itself.

Our ride together was short lived, less than a mile. I took a side trip a few miles off route to see a natural rock arch. If Ralph had started the day more than 15 miles ahead of me, I would probably catch him again by the end of the day. We said a very loose goodbye with the assumption we would see each other later. I rode to the arch by myself. It was a let down. It was still an incredible natural feature, but to call it an arch was misleading. When I thought of a rock arch, an image from Arches National Park was called to mind. What I looked at was more like a hole in the wall. It was another experience tainted by my expectations.

I returned to the route and found the obscure "road" that would lead me to Del Norte. It was a double track across the desert. It had never been graded, just worn into the landscape by the ATVs and motorcycles that followed its path. It was sandy and soft and rocky and rough and cut by drainage divides that left large divots and even puddles in places. It was a hell of a ride. It climbed between two rocky outcrops and near the top, the road vanished. The route followed the eroded drainage down the other side, a dry creek bed that was predominately sand. It was a blast to ride down. As the wash bottom leveled off and the cut in the landscape tapered down, another road appeared, gravel. It circumnavigated an air field with large right angle turns and led me to the pavement that carried me across the Rio Grande and into Del Norte. No sign of Ralph yet.

My first stop in town was the town hall to speak with the police. They allowed campers in the city park, but permission had to be granted first. Once I got the go ahead, I set off to find some food.

• • •

"Does this table work?" the waitress asked.

It looked like all the others. "Yes, it's perfect." She sat the menu on the table as I sat down. I didn't even open it. "Are you still serving breakfast by any chance?"

"I'm sorry, we don't serve breakfast all day."

"Oh that's ok. I've just been craving breakfast for a few days and haven't had any luck finding any."

"I'll tell you what, let me talk to the cook. We aren't very busy right now, so maybe he won't mind."

"Really? Thank you, I appreciate it."

She left. I picked up the menu. It wasn't a bad menu, but I really had been craving breakfast for several weeks. I had breakfast both mornings I was in Salida. I also had breakfast after saying goodbye to Paul in Breckenridge. It must have been all the carbs that I craved.

"I talked to the cook," she said as she set a water in front of me, "and he wants to know what you would order before he says yes."

"Well, I'm kind of craving a ham and cheese omelet with hash browns, but really any breakfast he is willing to cook would be fine with me."

"Ok, I'll let him know. Anything else to drink?"

"An orange juice if it's not too much trouble?"

"Coming right up."

• • •

I spread my map across the table. Both my orange juice and water glasses were empty and the plate that had held my omelette and hash browns was clean. I leaned back in my chair, my feet kicked out in front of me.

"Anything else I can get you, hon?" she said as she filled my water back up.

"Two things actually, if it's not a problem. First, can you tell me what day it is?"

"Sure, it's the eighteenth of July."

"Yeah," this wasn't the answer I was looking for, "but what day of the week?"

She paused and looked at me, brow furrowed. She measured me up as if it was some kind of trick question.

"Well, it's Thursday."

"Oh, thank you. I just didn't know. I've been on the trail for a while and that's the kind of thing I just don't keep track of."

"I see. Well, what was the second thing you needed?"

I sat back up and leaned forward, my arms on the table. "I'm wondering what kind of pie you have?"

• • •

I left the restaurant satisfied and made my way to the grocery store. I stocked up and headed for the city park as bolts of lightning lit up the sky. It began to rain when I was a block from the park. When I got there, the best covered structure was the stage, an elevated platform about four feet above the ground. I stashed my bike beneath it right as the rain began to pour.

I made a few phone calls to some family that night, just to check in and confirm that I was still alive. We talked about the trip, but it was difficult to explain my experiences to them. It wasn't for a lack of trying, it was just that they didn't have the right frame of reference. It's hard to understand the difficulty of a rain storm when you've always had a roof to shelter under. It's hard to relate to riding a bike 100 miles through a barren landscape and arid climate when you've never ridden a bike more than 20 miles, in any conditions. From the moment I decided to ride the route, I knew it would be a solo trip. But the farther I went, the more I realized what the "solo" classification entailed.

I met two more riders in the park that night. They traveled much lighter and much faster than me. They also asked if I was Yukon.

"No, but I did see him earlier today. He said he was staying in town tonight too, but I haven't see him since I got here."

I set up my bivy under the stage, glad to have the added protection from the rain, but I lay awake in my bag. Tomorrow was going to be a big day. Indiana Pass, the tallest pass on the whole route. It was also one of the hardest climbs on the whole route.

The corners of my mouth lifted. "Give it a week, Nathan." The motto had metamorphosed: originally, it bore an air of tolerance that had now been replaced with perseverance. Instead of saying, "Just hold on for one more week," I was now saying, "I can handle anything, because I know I'll still be riding a week from now."

"Yeah, give it a week."

The patter of rain on the stage's corrugated roof sang me to sleep.

Chapter 34

WHAT CRAPPY WEATHER.
What a weird day.
Wonder where I'll be in a few hours.
Hmmm; where's my journal?

Just had this thought: you never know where you're going to be in the future. I was just thinking about where I would be a few hours from now, and I realized that, this morning, I would have never foreseen sitting in the driver's seat of a blue F-250. It's futile to wonder where exactly I'll be in the future. All I can really do is look at the map and hope I'm making progress along the correct road. I can only see the miles I've already covered, those yet to be traveled are a complete mystery.

I looked up from my journal, the pages filled with the ink of my pen and the crumbs of my Pop-Tarts. What a weird day it had been. Weird was fortunate, much better than the disastrous day it had almost become. But I guess the day was still young; I had another 20 miles to cover before nightfall. Maybe it had been so weird because it started with me waking up under a stage. Yeah, that in itself was pretty weird. Perhaps that had set the tone for the whole day.

* * *

"Good morning, Nathan."

"Hey, good morning guys. Did your stuff dry out?" The night before, the two other cyclists had been under another picnic table covering, sheltered from the rain. The roof wasn't effective against the park sprinklers though, which turned on after we had all gone to sleep. We had a short conversation in the dark; they asked if it was ok with me if they slept on the stage above me. I had no problem. I understood being cold and wet.

"Yeah, it seems to have dried out for the most part. So are you ready for Indiana Pass?"

"I hope so. I'd be lying if I said I wasn't a little intimidated though."

"Us too. Well, good luck. Maybe we'll see you out there."

The two headed off to find breakfast. I ate in the park as I packed up. My gear sat on the edge of the stage in the bright sunshine. It was going to be a beautiful day.

It was just over 23 miles to the top of Indiana Pass, and the climb started immediately outside of Del Norte. Granted, it was gradual at first and slowly built in severity. The map's elevation profile looked like an exponential growth curve. I was thankful to get a warm-up on a low grade over the first 10 miles of pavement. The first 10 miles of every day were the worst; I had to entice blood to flow to my legs and my heart to pump it there. After I warmed up, the riding got better. Today was different though. After the first 10 miles, the pavement ended and the road became gravel. Where the gravel started, so did the first hill. My route climbed up the hillside and out of a sight around a corner.

Great.

It was steep to say the least. The road was also wet with the night's rain, which made some segments muddy. My tires left behind the impression of their tread to mark the way for cyclists that would come after. I also left behind my footprints, further consolation for the cyclists who had to push their bikes up the steeper hills, just like I did. And that was how it went for several more miles: lots of hard pedaling interrupted with some pushing.

The two cyclists from the park passed me. I wished I had their light loads, their almost non-existent gear, a true racer setup. I already regretted having stocked up on food for the next few days as the guidebook had suggested. I was also weighed down by an abundance of water. The subalpine setting the route was headed for had been the target of mining for a long time and, as a result, all the surface water had been contaminated with heavy metals. The one-time miner town of Summitville had since been abandoned and then reclaimed by the EPA as a Superfund site.

Less than 5 miles from the crest, the sky darkened. Less than 4, the rain fell. I pushed my bike off the road and under a tree, the branches' needles inefficiently shedding the water. I may as well have been under a leaky roof in a monsoon while I pulled on my rain gear. But I was still determined. And this rain wasn't as bad as the Canadian rain. Three miles from the top, the rain became a torrent and tried to push me back down the hill, refusing to let me top the highest elevation along the entire route. The clouds started to break, but beyond the mountain. The blue sky and cumuli were so near. I was so high on the mountain top I almost touched them. But they were out of reach. Puddles that had appeared in a few minutes reflected the blue light from below me as well. I was trapped, in a bubble, between two hemispheres, one blue and beautiful, the other gray and gloomy. I couldn't move from my trapped position. I looked away from the puddles and started back up the hill again, still covered with the ugly gray I had learned to detest.

The road began to level off as I neared the top. Trees thinned and the rain, defeated, retreated to a sprinkle. Forests gave way to the subalpine meadows and rocky outcrops. I crossed a large creek that flowed both under and over the road at the mileage where my map marked an "intermittent stream." The rain should have been no surprise; it fit the trip's weather trend. Exhausted, I reached the top. Indiana Pass: 11,910 feet above sea level. I was soaked, both from the rain and sweat, and the wind worked to cool me as I took a few pictures—as if I would have any trouble remembering the climb.

As it turned out, the descent was much more memorable. A half-mile down from the summit, the rain picked back up. It was Canada all over again, but 10,000 feet higher. A few hundred yards through the rain was enough to soak me through, and a few hundred yards of rain was all I saw. Beyond that, it was a mix of snow and hail.

The backside of Indiana Pass was as steep as the front, so I pedaled very little. This means I wasn't generating any heat, a big problem when wet and experiencing a lot of wind. On top of that, I was pelted with hail and covered in snow. My only physical activity was steering to avoid the ruts created by the runoff, now filled with hail that tried to swallow my tires. The road was still wet below the snow and hail, which made it dangerously slick. Any abrupt turn, and I might have ended up on the ground. Despite the difficulty of navigating the roads, the task was largely mental and left my muscles unstrained and underworked. I lost heat quickly.

I scanned the side of the road for any suitable place to set up my bivy. I ran through a checklist of activities I would need to do as soon as I stopped. Set up bivy. Get sleeping bag, sleeping pad, and food inside. Strip out of wet clothes. Do best to dry off. Get into bag. Eat, eat, eat. But to my dismay, I couldn't find a suitable place. The road cut across the steep hillside. The only feature close to flat was the road itself, now a small tributary of the contaminated streams below. Every turn brought hope for a place to bed down; every turn let me down. My shivering was out of control at that point, and the descent had just gone up a few degrees in danger when I realized my hands had problems operating the brake levers.

This is bad Nathan.

This is really bad.

I stopped and looked to my map for help. Summitville was less than half a mile away. An old ghost mining town had to have something that resembled level ground if not an old shack of some kind to shelter either under or behind. I continued on my bike trying to consistently brake and keep my speed in check. I doubted my hands' ability to brake hard should the need arise. The snow and hail subsided. Even the rain it left behind was just a mist in comparison to the earlier downpour. But the damage had been done. My core temperature had plummeted.

I kept an eye on my odometer and ran a mileage countdown in my head. I hit the mark just as I rounded a corner, the only one that didn't let me down. There were a few ramshackle structures on the hills, the remainder of a bygone era. But it was the Superfund facility that dominated the view. It was large and gray, a portion made of large blocks, while the remainder was covered in aluminum and glass. It sat on top of a small incline fronted by a man made pond. The runoff from the hills drained there, and it was clearly filling up like some kind of moat in front of its EPA castle. But what stood out more than all of this was a shop door, open. The lights were on inside. It beckoned.

"Why not? Worst case, Nathan, they tell you to 'get the hell out of here.'"

I rode along the moat and blatantly ignored the bright orange signs that said "No Trespassing" and "Authorized Personnel Only." The large stones of the road turned and slipped under my tires, teasing my exhaustion. The last small hill that lead up to the shop (I mean tiny) was one of the most difficult of the day—I had to push up it. On the flat plane, I leaned on my bike for support as I walked it onto the slab of concrete that led into the shop.

I poked my head inside. No one was there, no noise. I leaned my bike inside against a cement post and called out. No answer.

"What the hell?"

I turned at the crunch of gravel and purr of an engine that came around the corner of the building. I walked outside. The driver did a double take when he saw me and brought his pickup to a stop. I mimed for him to roll his window down. He mimed for me to open the door. I struggled with the handle, but pulled it open and stuck my head in his pickup.

"Hey, I just got caught in a storm coming over the pass. I'm wondering if I can step inside and change my clothes and hang out for a bit while I warm up."

The driver's jaw went slack and his eyes opened wider. "Yeah, of course. Let me park this, and I'll show you inside."

He showed me to the company locker room.

"You can change in here. Don't drink the water though. If you need some there's a small cafeteria upstairs. It's just me and two other employees here today. I'm going to head up to the control room and just let them know you are here."

"Thank you so much. I can't tell you how much I appreciate this. I'm Nathan by the way."

"Skip." He extended his hand.

I tried to shake it. It didn't go so well. My hands were still frozen, and it was difficult to move my fingers. Forget a firm handshake. I returned to the bike and unpacked the dry bags holding my clothes. Back in the locker room, I slowly removed my clothes. For as big of a hurry as I was in to undress, it sure took a long time. It was impossible to pinch zipper pulls; I had to use both hands. I was thankful for the Velcro on my shoes and shorts.

"Hey Nathan, you still in here?"

"Yeah, Skip."

"Our building is pretty cold, so when you're done I brought around a pickup with the heater running. It's just outside the doors here."

My wet clothes finally removed, I pulled on all of my dry layers. I hung the wet stuff and headed back towards my bike. Outside I found a blue F-250 idling. It looked familiar. I grabbed my backpack and hopped in the driver seat. Cold air came from the vents. Engine was still warming up. I pulled food from my backpack. Eating would help warm me up. I started with Pop-Tarts and a bag of licorice that had been a compulsive buy in Del Norte. It turned out to be a good purchase. I ate a lot and drank a lot while I sat in the pickup; my puffy down jacket managed to catch all the crumbs.

It continued to rain while I sat there. The cab warm, I killed the engine. The dashboard was familiar too. An F-250? Oh yeah, we had the same pickup back home on the farm. It was a different color, though, and this one was in better condition.

What a weird day.

Hmmm; where's my journal?

I closed my eyes to let them rest. I opened them, the cab of the pickup cooler all of a sudden. Crap, I didn't mean to fall asleep. How long had I been at the Summitville Superfund facility? Too long. It was time to go. The rain was a sprinkle now, and my body had returned to a rosy temperature. I still had 20 more miles to go if I wanted to make Platoro, my goal destination. I returned to the locker room and gathered my wet clothes.

"Hey Skip."

"Hey, you're awake."

"Yeah, I didn't mean to fall asleep. But thank you for all that you've done."

"Hey, I'm just glad I was here to help. You were pretty cold when you showed up."

We talked a bit about my trip before I started asking questions about the facility. The environmental science student in me couldn't pass up what may as well have been a field trip to an EPA Superfund site. It was one of the most interesting side trips.

I set out again, Skip's mailing address copied down in my journal with the others I had collected along the way. Skip had seen another cyclist pass when I was sleeping. Ralph. Maybe I could catch him again. Or maybe I should just hope to stay dry.

* * *

"Damn, that is some red rock."

The route traversed a beautiful subalpine environment of pine trees and meadows. It would have been more beautiful if bathed in sunlight instead of rain. I was biased, though. On the other hand, the rain did nothing to conceal the color of the sister peaks Little Red Mountain and Big Red Mountain. Each were heavily eroded, which exposed the iron oxides and other metal oxides that dominated the soil of the mountains. Both slopes were a dark red with streaks of rich orange. Incredible.

I passed the base of the peaks and crossed the Alamosa River to begin up the second pass of the day. It was only 3 miles to the top of Stunner Pass, but my body was finished. I had to hike intermittently on the first half of the climb. I hiked the entire second half. From the top, I saw the small settlement of Platoro, another economy based on tourism. I intended to contribute to that economy. I coasted the last few miles into town and staggered into the first tourist lodge I saw.

"Hi there. How can I help you?"

"Well, I'd take a warm bed and hot meal if you got it," I said between deep breaths.

"We can help with the meal, but I'm afraid we don't have any beds available."

Happy to take what I could get, I wandered into the dining room. A large stone fireplace dominated the room. I sat at one of tables closest to it. I was hypnotized by the silent dance of the flames, the subtle crack of the wood. I hadn't watched a fire since my first night on the ride. Anytime I tried to have a fire since, whatever wood was available was too wet. I laid my jacket and outer layer on the hearth to dry. I considered the steam that came off of the clothes, then unfolded my map and laid it on the hearth as well. I demoted my "weatherproof map" to "mostly weatherproof." It had had a hard time on Indiana Pass as well.

I was finishing dinner when the older gentleman I had talked to on the way in came up to my table.

"Hi there. Sorry to interrupt your meal, but is there any chance you are still interested in a room?"

"Yeah, I'd love to get out of the weather tonight."

"Good, because I called down to the other lodge to see if they have any rooms, and they have one left. If you'd like, I could call and get it reserved for you."

"Really? That would be great."

I was always surprised when people went out of their way to help me, no matter how often it happened. It wasn't that I had never experienced it before, it was that these people were perfect strangers. All of these people I had never heard of, never met, never even seen before. And they helped me, even though it was likely I would never hear of them, never meet them, never even see them again. It stirred a warmth in me no fire could compete with. Humans are truly social creatures, and the bonds we share have great potential to be powerful.

I finished my meal and was given instructions to the neighboring lodge. The air was cold when I stepped back outside, clouds still lingered overhead, and puddles still lay underneath, but I still felt warm.

Chapter 35

BEST. ADVICE. EVER.

I'm not sure exactly what Mike meant.

I'm not sure he had intended any meaning. Really, it sounded like an offhand comment.

But the whole trip was worth that single moment of insight, of discovery, when after several weeks of effort and countless hours of searching I would see if the question I asked would be answered.

● ● ●

The sky was a thousand shades of blue that morning. Directly up was the darkest hue, and it was like staring into the Caribbean's blue wells that fall forever through shallow waters. Further to the horizon, the saturation began to fall until the color was almost white-washed where the peaks ended, the light from the surrounding valleys overflowing into this one still halfway concealed by shade. It made the mountains glow. I glowed too at the perfectly clean sky, one that had washed itself all through the night.

"It won't last all day," she said.

"No?" I replied through my pumpkin bread.

"No. We are getting afternoon rains now, so it will get cloudier through the day and start raining sometime in the early afternoon."

In my month on the bike, I had experienced the differences of regional weather and learned that residents of those regions were always the best forecasters. When a local gave me their opinion on the weather, I trusted it.

"Thanks for the heads up."

It was 23 miles from Platoro to Horca where the route returned to pavement. It was there I would need to make some decisions.

I traced the Conejos River down the valley, in and out of the shade, in and out of the sun, in the moment. Evergreens dominated the mountain slopes, but grasses and groves of aspen filled the valley floor. I had been warned about the washboarding on the road, but I was in too good of a mood to worry about it. The valley and weather were both so beautiful, it became one of my favorite stretches of the route.

● ● ●

Pop-Tarts were a good snack. They didn't have an exterior that melted like many candy bars, but they still had a sufficient amount of sugar. The S'mores flavor was the best, not just because Blueberry was bland and Strawberry got old, but because of the chocolate and marshmallow. The S'mores had an interior susceptible to melting. That was the key. They could stand the heat, but if they were jostled around and began to break, as was inevitable, the gooey middle held them together. Those Pop-Tarts could have been run over, but as long as they were in the package when it happened, they would come out in one piece—the interior would hold the exterior together. Any other flavor would just crumble and make eating them a chore. Yes, S'mores was the way to go.

The pastry I held above my map looked like a jigsaw puzzle, the pieces all put in the correct order but left unassembled. But it held together and only a few crumbs dropped onto the map spread out across my handlebars and aerobars. I straddled my bike at the intersection with the pavement, unsure of where I should go. My next junction was 11 miles down the road. A left turn would take me back onto dirt that would wander into the Tusas Mountains; no turn would keep me on the pavement and take me to Chama.

I recognized the whine that came down the road. Two-strokes. A few. Sure enough, around the bend came four motorcycles. They turned onto the road, and the leader stopped next to me and removed his helmet. He was an older guy, maybe mid-fifties. I was surprised by his age but was glad to see he was still living young.

"Hey, you look like a Divide rider."

"Sure am. You guys must be heading out to ride? Any idea what the roads are like up top?"

"They're a little rutted, not bad yet though."

"Yeah, I'm just trying to avoid getting caught in the mud. I was told it was going to rain this afternoon and really don't want to have to wait it out."

"We've had rain the past few afternoons, so the roads are already a little wet. We still get through though."

Said the guy on a two-stroke.

It turned out he had done part of the route, on his motorcycle of course. He wanted to do the whole thing, and I gave him all the reasons why he should. Our conversation was cut short by the other guys, though. They didn't want to get caught in the rain either, so they were anxious to get their ride started and finished.

They disappeared up the valley I came down. Their subtle whine echoed back down to me long after I lost sight of them. Back to my map. The roads were still a little wet according to them, but passable. I should have been more specific about where they had been. My map and guidebook both warned about the soil that would leave you stuck. I had seen pictures of people caught in the mud, bikes standing up by themselves and abandoned by their owners until the mud could dry. I looked up. My perfect blue sky had already grown clouds, and the enormous cumuli that dominated revealed updrafts that recycled the daily storms.

Two SUVs turned off the pavement onto the gravel road as I examined the sky. The second one honked. The first one responded by stopping. The driver got out and walked back to the second SUV. He climbed into the passenger seat and the pair turned back out toward the pavement. They pulled up next to me, the passenger window down. An older guy leaned out.

"Hey, how's it going?"

"Pretty good. Hey, would you happen to know how far it is between Chama and Abiquiu?"

"Yeah! We just hiked that the other day. I'm Mike. This is my wife, Maggie. Our trail name is M&M."

CDT hikers. These were the first hikers I had met hiking the route piecemeal, chasing the good weather up and down the country. They had given up the purist mentality to seek the most enjoyable experience. Granted, they had put in their time as the hardcore through-hikers. M&M were pretty well known in the hiking world, an impressive feat given how much time its members spend off the grid. We talked about our journeys, and I gave them the long version of my journey over Indiana Pass down to Summitville.

"That sounds terrible," Maggie said, leaning forward to look past Mike.

"Yeah, I'm pretty sick of the rain."

Mike said, "You need to get out of the rain. You should do the alternate you're thinking about. You've earned some time on the pavement. And besides, Maggie and I got caught out in the rain two days ago. It was pretty heavy rain, and the mud was awful. We didn't even have time to set up the tent; we just had to rig a makeshift shelter with it."

Maggie: "Yeah, it was horrible."

"Don't feel like you can't go your own way, you know?"

The comment called Stephen to mind and the Fourteeners I had missed. I looked down at my map, at that red line. What was so important about the line anyway?

"Yeah, hearing what you two had to say I'm gonna head to Chama. Avoid the rain if I can."

"Good for you," they said together, the many years of the marriage showing.

Mike took the lead again. "So what made you want to do this anyway?"

"Well, I had recently finished school and just wasn't sure what I wanted to do with my life. I didn't really want to start a career. I wanted to do something big, something adventurous. I had seen the documentary about the race and thought the route looked awesome, so I decided to do it. I thought it would be a pretty cool item for the life resume, a good challenge. I thought I'd come out here and try to find myself."

At that last statement, Mike chuckled and said, "Yeah, get that out of your system."

I thought I saw Maggie turn her head just slightly to Mike and give a look of incredulity at what he had just said. Then again, maybe I was the incredulous one and had just imagined Maggie was on my side.

"Well that's great, Nathan," Maggie said. "Has it been a good experience so far?"

I thought about it before I answered. "Yeah, it has."

We talked a few more minutes before I let them go. They would be hiking back to get the car, so we would see each other in the next few miles. Decided on my course, I started on the 6 miles of pavement up toward La Manga Pass.

Mike had said, "Get that out of your system." I couldn't get that out of my head. I didn't take offense to what he said. I wasn't insulted. In a weird way, I was inspired. But why?

The road was steep and curvy with the occasional switchback that made the inside of the turn even steeper. It was hot, and clouds continued to build. I tasted something strange. It was my sweat that dripped down my face from the effort of the climb; it wasn't salty like sweat. The taste was putrid, not at all like it should have been. Why?

I stood to put more force on the pedals. A drip fell from my chin and landed on my map, on the dot labeled Platoro. The map said the water in Platoro may not be suitable to drink, tap water included. The addendum had said otherwise, but it was the only variable I could isolate. I felt fine, but was convinced I had ingested contaminants in Platoro that my body was now trying to get rid of.

Great.

"At least I'm sweating it out. I just need to drink a lot of water and sweat a lot, get it out of my system."

Out of my system!

What Mike said had clicked. Being inspired by his statement didn't seem strange any more, rather it made perfect sense. I had said the trip was, in part, an attempt to "find myself." Well, where did I go? Did I lose myself? Was my body just mindlessly wandering around without me? No! So what the hell was I looking for!

In my study of philosophy, I had read about switching our energy from action to contemplation. This made no sense to me when I read it. Wasn't that counterproductive? But Plato, he defined contemplation as "knowing and being." We should switch our energy from "seeking and becoming" to "knowing and being." Switch your energy from seeking to knowing. What was it I sought?

I had been suffering from the illusion of an internal separateness. I had thought there were two versions of me: the person I was and the person I wanted to be. I was searching for that other person, as if there were a secret that other person had, as if he knew what I wanted and needed, what was best for me, what I should do. What a bunch of bullshit. Mike was right, I needed to get that kind of thinking out of my system.

To constantly seek and become was to constantly try, to constantly accept my faults, to constantly make excuses for the behaviors that I abhorred; it was a strengthening of my conscience, which was really the weakening of my character. To know and become, on the other hand, would be the unification of my two self-perceptions.

I could have spent more time preparing for this journey. I knew nothing about bicycle touring, but when push came to shove, I decided to be a tourist and not waste any more time trying to become one. Maybe I wasn't very skilled at first (I still cringe at the thought of the possible newspaper headlines about the suffocated cyclist), but that was the difference. Instead of constantly preparing for the future, I chose to live in the present. I stopped trying to become a cyclist and just started being one.

The hill started to plateau as I neared the top of the climb. Up in front of me were two familiar faces hiking down the shoulder. We stopped and talked for just a few seconds.

Maggie: "Nathan, do you mind if I take your picture? We keep a website that we use to document our travels and the people we meet."

"Of course I don't mind."

"It will probably be a few weeks before it gets updated, but you'll be on there."

"Well, I'm honored. It was a real pleasure meeting you two."

Mike: "Good luck, Nathan."

"Thank you, Mike." More than you know.

• • •

I stuck to the pavement and passed the old Cumbres and Toltec train that blew black smoke from its ancient engine. I crossed into New Mexico, took lunch in Chama, and headed south, only stopping once for about forty-five minutes to wait out an afternoon thunderstorm. My bike lay at my feet, both of us beneath some roadside brush, my bivy unpacked and ready to be set up if needed. I watched the lightning, heard the thunder, and smelled moisture on the air, but the rain never came; it missed me, but only just. When I set out again, I travelled less than a hundred yards before the road became wet, the rumble strip divots filled with water, and the ditches full of runoff and mud. I was happy with my route choice.

I made it to Abiquiu Reservoir by the end of the day, just like M&M said I would. I had planned to stay at a campground on the reservoir, but Maggie had recommended a place called Ghost Ranch. I stopped at the end of its long drive.

"Well, I guess a recommendation is only valuable if you take it."

I rode up the drive, a rolling road that cut through the dry desert more stereotypical of New Mexico than the greenery I had seen all day. The ranch was a large complex of buildings. It was the location of religious-based retreats as well as other tourist activities. I found the office just a few minutes before it closed.

Nineteen dollars for a tent site with access to a bathhouse? I almost walked out. But Mike and Maggie had insisted it was a great place. I was too tired to leave anyway; my odometer read 98 miles as I pulled in. I started to fill out the paperwork for the secretary when a second woman that had been in the office left.

The secretary spoke freely. "Ok, Nathan. The woman who just left is one of the owners. I didn't want to say anything in front of her, but we give Continental Divide hikers and bikers a complimentary night."

"Really?" I said, more chipper than I was a second before. Mike and Maggie were right.

"Yeah, she's not a big fan of that policy. So I'll keep your paperwork, and here is a map of the ranch." We traded the documents. The overview schematic showed the ranch was much bigger than it looked. "Here is the campground right here. Just go ahead and find a tent spot, and put this slip on the campsite marker." She circled the campsite on the map with a highlighter as she spoke. "And this is a meal ticket for breakfast. Here is the dining hall, and breakfast is served between 8 and 10." She took the campsite slip and meal ticket and folded it up inside the highlighted map.

"Well, thank you so much."

"It's our pleasure. You know, a lot of hikers and cyclists stay here an extra day. It really is a great place to rest. And the church group that was here this week is leaving tomorrow, so your rest day would be nice and quiet."

"I'll think about it. Thank you again."

I walked out of the office and back down the sidewalk to where I left my bike. My leg was halfway over the bike when I heard my name.

"Nathan! Nathan!" It was the secretary again. She ran down the sidewalk to where I sat on my bike. "I just realized that the campground hosts are gone for the weekend, so you could stay tomorrow night for free, too. No one would know. I can't get you any more meal tickets, though, so you'll need to buy those. And if you want to stay Monday night you'll need to pretend that you just got here and pay, because I'm going to shred your paperwork."

I was stunned. How did nineteen dollars for a single night turn into two free nights and a free meal? "That's incredible. Thank you so much."

She walked back up the sidewalk toward the office, and I headed for the campground.

"M&M were right. This place is awesome."

Chapter 36

Late December 2012

"HEY NATHAN. HOW ARE YOU? It's been a long time. What are you up to these days?"

"I'm good. I just spent a few weeks in Montana at Jared's place. I got back earlier today actually."

"Montana huh? Let's see, you graduated from college right?"

"Yeah, back in June."

"Great to hear it. How's the market looking? Having any trouble finding a job?"

I was at my home community's annual Alumni Basketball Game. It took advantage of the fact that most people were home for Christmas, so all of the old high school basketball stars would come together and play a game. Ticket and raffle sales went to a college scholarship that would be awarded to a high school basketball player. It was a great event, a reunion of sorts. But when you were like me, with a degree but without a job, it generated a lot of awkward conversations.

"I'm not even looking for a job."

"Oh really? Why's that?"

I had the same conversation multiple times. I wanted to tell all of those people that I didn't want a job because the thought wasn't appealing, that it sounded like a prison sentence, that even just the sight of a job application killed a piece of my soul. But this was a community of farmers. Hard work was in the blood. No job equated to laziness.

When the game started, I took a stationary position in the stands with some friends to buffer myself from any unnecessary conversations. I didn't want to have to justify my decisions to anyone.

After the game, I was back at the farm, staying with my brother Brandon. After a six-hour drive from Montana and the awkward questions at the basketball game, I just wanted to relax. I went to my brother's bookshelf. While I tried to choose a book, I couldn't get my mind off all of those questions. Why wasn't I looking for a job? Why wasn't I studying for the GRE and applying to graduate school? Was I really going to try to be a writer?

"What the hell am I doing? What am I going to do with my life?"

I had avoided all those questions. I had avoided the conversations where those questions would come up, because I didn't want to have to justify my answers. Justify my answers? Did I even have answers to justify? That was the real reason I avoided the questions: I didn't have the answers.

My eyes scanned the spines of several books. None grabbed my attention. I had read a lot of them already, and the rest just weren't interesting at the moment. Then my eyes fell on a shelf that held some of my own books. Two adjacent books there did catch my eye. Both were GRE prep books, study guides for one of the graduate school entrance exams. One of them focused only on the math section, a book recommended to me by Justin. From crayfish to aspens to the GRE, I trusted the guy.

I reached for the books and pinched both spines with one hand, but I never pulled them off the shelf. I paused as soon as I touched them. Another book had screamed for my attention as soon as I had reached out. It was missing its dust cover and was just a plain black book, the title and author written in small gold letters on the spine. It was a familiar book, one I had read two years before. I pulled it off the shelf and opened the front cover. There was an inscription.

Nathan,

Thanks for being a part of my story... I'm glad we're friends!

-Amber

Amber. She had given the book to me as a gift before we had become a couple. It was Donald Miller's *A Million Miles in a Thousand Years*. The idea of the book was simple: the purpose of story is to document how and why a character changes; life is also centered around change, so if we recognize our life is really just a story, we can accept the responsibility of being the writer.

It was such a simple idea, romantic and idealistic. How had I forgotten this book? I read it again over the next few days and saw it in a whole new light, a benefit of having studied the elements of story for the past few months.

Convenient? Or sign? I know what Megan would have said.

What wasn't so convenient was the one writer's credo that had always stuck out in my mind the best: murder your darlings. A story always starts at a moment of change in the main character's life, and if the protagonist is going to change for the better, he must be put into uncomfortable, challenging, difficult situations. But there was one flaw with Miller's philosophy: when you are the writer and the protagonist, you have a conflict of interests. That conflict is the first obstacle to overcome when writing your own story.

Less than three weeks later, Shane and I took a trip to Leavenworth to see a couple of our good friends. We had just finished our dinner of homemade lasagna and sat around the kitchen table with a few beers. I waited for a small break in the conversation.

"So, I have a question for everyone. I've decided I'm going to ride my mountain bike from Canada to Mexico. I'm just curious what you guys think about that?"

Chapter 37

"HELLO? WHO IS THIS?"

I wasn't a fan of phones—my cell phone in particular. It made it too easy for people to get ahold of me. I looked for reasons to not answer my phone. So rarely did I answer numbers I didn't recognize. Something told me I should answer this one though.

"Hey Nathan, it's Collin. I know it's been a while, but I just wanted to see how you were doing."

"Wow. Collin. It *has* been a while."

"Yeah." I could almost see his eyes fall at my comment. "How are you man?"

"I'm alright. Pretty surprised to hear from you, though. I thought if we were ever going to talk again it would have happened more than a year ago, you know, when I was having a pretty rough time."

"Yeah, I meant to call, I just didn't get around to it."

"Just like you didn't get around to telling me you had moved back? You were in the area the whole time, practically my backyard, and you never told me? We were good friends man. What the hell happened?"

"I don't know," he said. "I'm sorry."

"Well, don't worry about it. Listen, man, I need to go. I'm riding a pretty rough road right now, and it needs my full attention. Bye."

● ● ●

Ghost Ranch had been good to me, but I wasn't ready for another rest day. I had said goodbye to the place after breakfast and got a late start. I stuck to the pavement to avoid more afternoon rain and followed a detour that the racers had taken. It wasn't the greatest road: rolling terrain, narrow to non-existent shoulder, and pavement patchwork that should have cost someone his job. It drove me back into my alternate reality. There, my imagination conjured up a phone call from a long lost friend. Actually, I had imagined several conversations with him: some phone calls, some in-person, but all centered around the same topic, centered around my anger towards him. We really hadn't spoken in years, but I thought about him every day on my trip. When we were roommates, he had bought me a small notebook to write in. It was this notebook that now served as my journal.

At mile 20, thoughts of Collin were forced from my head as I came to a small market. I needed a drink and snack. There were two guys inside, both Hispanic, one behind the counter, leaning on it, and one in front. We talked about the day's heat and how they had been seeing cyclists since the racers came through.

"Yeah man, where is the rest of your group?"

"Oh it's just me. I'm riding solo." The two raised their eyebrows and glanced at each other. The guy behind the counter stood up. My brow furrowed in response to their movement. "What?"

"Well, it's just that this isn't the best road for bicycles. Not a lot of people around here care enough to share the road, you know? And on top of that you're alone. This isn't the best road for a white boy to be alone. You know what I'm saying?"

"Yeah, I hear you. Thanks for the heads up."

"Yeah, when you get back on your bike, I wouldn't stop until you get to Cuba. That's another 40 miles down the road."

"What's the road like? Flat at all?"

The clerk's friend spoke up while he shook his head. "No, it's all up and down. It's not even the best road to drive because of all the hills. It's probably worse on a bike."

Awesome.

I was riding a prejudice, non-cyclist friendly road. Great detour. I finished my snack and grabbed another sports drink.

"Good luck out their, man."

"Hey, thanks guys. I appreciate it."

I did what they said and just kept riding. I stopped once more at another gas station 15 miles outside of Cuba. I stayed there a while and talked to Kathleen, the station's clerk. She had watched all the racers come through over the past few weeks and was excited to see another cyclist. She was very supportive and put into perspective what I had accomplished so far. My fatigue had grown over the past few days, and I had started to anticipate the finish; I had tunnel vision and just kept looking forward without a thought of all the miles I had already covered. Kathleen was right. Even if I stopped right there, it was still quite the accomplishment. Rejuvenated from our talk, I set out for Cuba once again, back on safer roads according to Kathleen.

I was 10 miles from Cuba when the monsoonal rain began. It was pointless to put on my rain gear, it fell so heavy, but I did anyway. I considered stopping to shelter, but the rain wasn't cold as it had been on Indiana Pass, so I pressed on. The rain continued to fall the whole way there, and when I got to town, I pulled under the eve of a UPS distribution center. Flanked by the vans, I turned on my phone to find a place to stay. While I searched, two native guys walked over towards me off the street.

"What's up man? It's raining, huh?" Both guys were massive, NFL lineman size—ok, maybe college football-sized. And both were soaked just like me. Their wet jeans and t-shirts couldn't have been comfortable.

"No shit it is," I said casually. "You guys got caught out in it too?"

"Yeah, man. We were a mile or two out of town when it started. We were trying to hitch a ride back to the res, but got back here as fast as we could once it started."

Only one of them spoke. That put me a bit on edge. I started to glance around, as nonchalantly as I could, and planned an exit strategy. "Yeah, I was about 10 miles out of town when it started. I had to ride almost an hour to get here. Is the rain always like this here?"

"Yeah, man. It's monsoon season now. It's going to rain like this pretty much every day. What are you doing anyway? Traveling or something?"

"Yeah, I've been riding my bike for a few weeks now. I started up in Canada. I've seen the craziest rain on this trip. I haven't been able to get away from it. That's why I'm looking for a place to stay in town. I need to find some food too." I had managed to put my phone away, secure my map, and close all my bags.

"Food, huh? Why don't you take us with you, man? We could use some food too. You know what I'm saying, a burger or something? Even just money. We could use some cash, you know?"

My heart rate quickened. It wasn't because he asked for money per se, but the way in which he did it. He had gotten closer and closer to me during our conversation. Now he extended his hand toward me. It was time to go.

"Listen man, I'm broke. I'd love to treat you guys to a burger, but I don't even know if I have enough money to get home." I jumped back in before he could reply. "I've got to get going guys." I pedaled from under the roof and called back over my shoulder, "Good luck getting home." The second guy had not said a word the whole time.

I found a cheap motel for the night and taped to the wall of my room was a map of New Mexico. It had the route of the CDT drawn on it and a message scrawled in pink highlighter that said, "150 miles left to Colorado! Woohoo! CDT baby." What were the odds of staying in the same room as a CDT hiker? Maybe the map had been left behind by a hiker I had met. I loved CDT hikers.

● ● ●

The next morning, my shadow was stretched out, incredibly long, the up and down of my legs exaggerated on the pavement to create a caricature's negative. The sun had just risen over the eastern rim of the basin, and the light washed any pre-dawn color from the environment and my constricted pupils. I turned off my light, shed a layer, and put on my sunglasses. I had set out early that morning with the hope of reaching Grants. With the monsoonal rain fresh in my mind and the forecast, I stuck to the paved alternate.

I had covered the first 30 miles by 9 and stopped at a gas station, the only structure I had seen since I left Cuba. I sat outside in the shade with my sports drink and breakfast sandwich when a guy started talking to me. We recognized each other. It was the quiet native guy I had seen the night before. He had hitched that far, alone. He didn't have the best things to say about his friend.

I left the gas station, and the desert swallowed me. It was a desolate stretch of road, with only the occasional house (sometimes abandoned) to occupy my attention. Each mile marker was torture. They revealed how slow progress was and dragged the ride on and on and on, pedal stroke after pedal stroke. The wet sand and puddles on the side of the road were a reminder of what I was trying to outrun. The sand was endless and rocky outcrops were rare. Even the vegetation wasn't enthused by its home, the short branches bland and colorless, the waxy leaves waning as the day progressed. No shade anywhere.

More than 80 miles into the day, the route crossed through a tunnel forty-yards long. It was a product of the nearby mine. The road had been covered and crushed rock piled on top to create a bridge for the large mining equipment that constantly went back and forth, while I rested in the shade. On the opposite side of the tunnel was a security checkpoint guarding the road that led to the mine. I rode right up to the checkpoint and asked if they had any water to spare. That led to me trying to persuade the security guard to move to Washington.

As slow as the day had gone, it went quickly for how hot and uninteresting the landscape was. Even the rolling terrain didn't bring me down, and it was impossible to tell when I crossed the Continental Divide, even though it happened five or six times. The count had become unimportant anyway. What Kathleen had said the day before had really stuck: it was already an amazing accomplishment.

The sky grayed, and as I made the last major turn of the day at mile 100, it was dark with moisture. Two storms lay ahead of me; the route cut down between them. I looked on from the porch of a shut-down bar to see what the storms would do, to see what my course of action would be. Another century ride was respectable, and the bar would be a good place to camp for the night. But Grants was only another 20 miles.

I bit my lip and went for it, mentally prepared to get wet. The converging storms produced an intense headwind, and the closer I got to town, the busier the traffic became. I stopped several times to ingest more sugar, more fuel to get me into town. It worked. I covered the 120 miles from Cuba to Grants, where I stayed for the night, and without getting rained on.

● ● ●

"Is that pahoehoe? Or is it aa? Man, I can't remember which is which."

The next morning, the route carried me south of Grants through the El Malpais National Conservation Area, the "badlands." Native

American myths from the area spoke of fire rock that covered the land.

"I'm pretty sure it's pahoehoe."

The dark, basaltic crust that had been laid down as lava over the landscape like a blanket was slowly processed by the local vegetation that worked to break it down into soil. Some ripples and currents that had formed during the lava flow were still visible in the hard rock, but time showed its face where the flow had fractured. Plants poked through the dark shield in numerous places, their roots doing hidden damage to the basalt.

"Badlands" was an appropriate name for the sight. My attitude fit right in with the landscape. After 15 miles, I realized how hard the day before had been on my body. I wanted to turn back to Grants and take a rest day. That would have been a 30 mile ride though. Thirty miles to get nowhere? What a waste of effort. I kept going.

The route turned onto County Road 41 and headed south toward Pie Town, the day's destination. I was excited to get there, not just to rest, but to get a piece of pie (what else?). The first hundred yards of the road took the idea of Pie Town and burned it, just like the pahoehoe had burned the landscape. The washboards on the road were awful, to the point that I threw a temper tantrum and cussed the road and yelled at the washboards. I told them they were an "abomination."

Progress was slow on the texturally rhythmic road. The grade was low enough that it should have been enjoyable, but thousands and thousands of successive speed bumps took the fun out of it. The most terrible washboarding only lasted a few miles, but it continued, not bad in places, worse in others; it was one of those factors beyond control.

About the time the washboards stopped, the terrain began to roll and gave me the roller coaster experience only a cyclist can understand. The recognizable clicks that occur on the uphill in the theme park only sound during the downhill on the bicycle. There were several more miles of the up and down marked by the backward clicks that were brief in comparison to the climb, the difficult pedaling that took so long to cover less ground than the easy pedaling. My mood improved after I got off that very backwards roller coaster in that very cruel amusement park. It was time for some food.

My legs were lifeless as I climbed up the last small hill to the Daily Pie Cafe. I stumbled into the small place, but was immediately taken in by its quaintness. An old cast iron stove sat in the corner on top of a hardwood floor, gray with a dignified character. Booths lined a wall of wood paneling covered with bumper sticker wisdom: "That was Zen and this is Tao," "My karma just ran over your dogma," and "The truth will set you free, but first it will make you angry" were among my favorites. And most importantly, the pie case opposite the door was the first thing I saw when I walked in. On the glass was a whiteboard titled "The World's Only True Pie Chart" and it displayed the cafe's current pie selection, in the form of a pie chart of course.

I sat down in a booth, surprised with the bench's springiness. My backside had suffered from the horrible washboarding all day, and being on the booth bench took me to a younger age when I would bounce on such a chair and swing my feet back and forth while I waited for dessert to come. Maybe I was too tired to bounce and too tall to swing my feet, but I was still excited to eat a meal, especially the dessert. The waitress came over.

"You know, you're the first rider we've seen come through this summer."

"Really?" I was beyond surprised. Not even a racer? Maybe they had been in too much of a hurry to stop. I had started just a couple days after them and had only been passed by two cyclists so far. There were two cafes in town, so I guess it was possible. But what about northbound riders?

I talked with a few people in the cafe, an older couple that didn't know about the route. I told them all about it with the help of the waitress and cook. They had seen quite a few riders since the route's development. Then I devoured a massive burger dripping with cheese. Then came the pie: a piece of chocolate cream and a piece of blueberry. Delicious.

"Can I get you more water or root beer?"

I leaned back in the booth, maybe bouncing a little bit now. "No thanks. I don't think my stomach can hold any more."

"Well, I'm glad we got you fed. Are you staying in town tonight?"

"That's the plan. My map says there is free camping at Jackson Park, so I'll probably head there."

A few wrinkles appeared on her forehead. "Well, why don't you just stay at the Toaster House?"

"The Toaster House? I've never heard of it."

She turned to face me. "It's the local hostel. All the hikers and bike riders stay there."

"Is it expensive?"

"No, it's donation based."

"Oh," I sat up a bit straighter. "Where is it exactly?"

"Go back down the hill to where you turned and just keep following the route. You can't miss it."

I couldn't miss it? I was so exhausted, I was sure I could. I left the restaurant and coasted back down the small hill to where the route cut across the pavement. I made the turn back onto the gravel road that sliced through Pie Town. Sure enough, a couple of blocks uphill and I was at the Toaster House. She was right. I wouldn't have been able to miss it. There wasn't any kind of sign or other obvious indication that it was a hostel. The only clue I needed was the only one I had: its name.

The front fence was centered on the main walkway of large flat stones where a metal archway and open gate stood guard. The rest of the fence was wood—twisted branches and stump remnants of repurposed trees—around which were twisted electrical cords that anchored their toasters, all bright and shiny. The majority of the kitchen appliances decorated that gate, the slots oriented downwards as though they were to look upon all who entered with their slotted eyes. Beyond the fence was a log home where potted plants grew on a covered porch, where a deck wrapped around the far end of the house, furnished with couches and lounge chairs and the rescued pilot seats of SUVs, all illuminated by the strings of lights wrapped around the roof's timber supports.

I laid my bike down and walked up the back steps onto the covered deck. Notes. Notes everywhere. Read a note that says go inside. Go inside. Read a note that says where the beds are. Find a bed. Read a note that says take a Pie Town bumper sticker. Take a sticker. Read a note about laundry. Read a note about the pizza in the freezer and the beer in the fridge. Read a note about the extra back-country gear you can help yourself to. Notes everywhere. Gear everywhere. Comfort everywhere. Read a note that says to sign the guest book. Open the guestbook.

I read countless entries. All expressed their gratitude for having such a wonderful place to stay, for excellent conversations that went late into the night, for the warm beds and sturdy roof, and for the brief relief from the trials of the trail. On the kitchen table, behind the guestbook, was a small tin can with a flimsy red plastic lid. The lid was slotted. There was no note.

I removed the panniers from my bike and carried them inside. It was late afternoon, and the heat had died down to a comfortable temperature. I lay down on one of the porch couches.

"Aloha. You must be the bike rider I heard about in town."

My eyes snapped open, and I jumped up. "I sure am."

"Oh, I'm sorry, did I wake you up?"

"Oh no, I was just resting my eyes."

It was Nita, the owner. She had lived in the Toaster House for years and had raised her kids there. She had since moved outside of town, but left the house open for all Continental Divide travelers. She was born in Hawaii and showed up to the house in a flowery sun dress. She had fresh peas with her too, still in the pod, which she offered to me.

"You know, peas remind me of home."

"Peas? Why's that?"

"I grew up on a farm. In a month, I'll be home trying to cut down over six hundred acres of peas."

Nita cracked a wide grin. "I love peas, but I can't even imagine six hundred acres."

We both laughed as I tried to explain what a whole field of peas looked like. Nita pointed out the various odds and ends of the house, reminded me about the beer and pizza, and told me which bed was the most comfortable.

"Well Nathan, I need to go. Do you think you'll leave tomorrow?"

"Yeah, I'll head out in the morning."

"Well, I don't have my camera right now, so I'll come by in the morning to get a picture with you," she said as she started to move toward the door. "And don't forget to sign the guest book!"

I made a pizza and drank a beer, my first since dinner with Jared, Whitney, and Cefas almost four weeks before. I ate my second dinner on the second floor deck as I watched the sun set on "a little slice of heaven."

Chapter 38

"IS THERE ANYTHING ALONG THIS ROAD? Any place I'll be able to stop?"

"Yeah. Mile marker 43."

"What's at mile marker 43?"

• • •

The morning in Pie Town choked out the sunlight. It was the first morning in several that I didn't wake up to a perfect blue sky. My daily rain anxiety set in early. I ate breakfast back at the Daily Pie Cafe where I talked to the owner more and delighted in his Blueberry Belgian Waffles and Cafe Scramble. It was the breakfast I had been searching for.

The island greeting announced Nita's arrival, her stride fluent as another bright flowery sundress danced around her ankles. "Aloha, Nathan. Did you sleep well?"

"Aloha, Nita," I said as I smiled at her charisma, "I slept great. I think the beer I drank helped with that."

"Well, I'm glad to hear it. Do you mind if I steal you away from your breakfast to get that picture?"

We walked outside to where my bike rested against the building and took a few pictures. The sky was darker.

"Nita, can I ask you for some advice? I'm worried about getting rained on and am just curious what you think the weather is going to do?"

"It's definitely going to rain today. And it will probably be a lot. We got a half-inch of rain the day before yesterday, and you can see the sky is already clouded up."

We talked about the road conditions I could expect and what other cyclists had done in the past. I told her my idea to not take the map's suggested alternate, but rather to follow the route down to the next highway.

"That's a good idea, Nathan. You should be able to make the pavement before it starts to rain."

"I hope so. I really don't want to be stuck in the mud."

With a final "aloha" and hug, Nita went her way and I went back to my breakfast, eyeing the sky with some apprehension.

● ● ●

The Toaster House was dark and empty as I loaded my panniers onto the bike. The log home awaited its next guest while the sky darkened further to show just how full it was. My tires didn't kick up any dust from the washboards as I rode farther from Pie Town. The road was a repeat of the previous day: rolling terrain with scattered vegetation.

Thunder.

"Crap."

The clap came from behind me. Or was it above me? There was a fractured blue sky toward the horizon in front of me, and I knew my only chance was to outrun the storm. And so it went for the next 20 miles: the storm tried to drift over the top of me, while the sounds of thunder emanated from behind me. I did manage to outrun the storm, and I found bluer skies and whiter clouds when I entered the Gila National Forest. I found the heat too.

I crossed the Continental Divide again after I pushed the last stretch to the top despite the encouragement I got from the forest rangers that drove by. The weather had improved a lot by the time I crossed. Was the detour still the best idea? Maybe the weather would hold long enough for me to cross the Gila. I stopped 5 miles from the pavement and sheltered in the shade beneath a large piñon tree to take a nap. I lay there for two hours, but couldn't sleep; the air was too hot and the ground too rocky.

My rested legs carried me to the downhill where the road overlooked the San Agustin Plains, an expanse of flat land covered in sage and short grasses that made the area look like a desert filled with the wrong colors. The route continued south down the ancient lakebed, and on the horizon were more misplaced colors of burnt blue, steel gray, and falling ash. More rain. The paved alternate looked more feasible again, but I was low on water and didn't know what opportunity I would have to refill along the pavement. Worst case, I could follow the route 5 miles further to a water source and backtrack to the pavement. I deepened the creases of the map to stow it away and lost more ink where the creases intersected.

Along the pavement, a small squeak developed and grew with each crank of the pedals. I pulled off onto a wide shoulder, where a gravel drive led into a small complex of buildings. As I dug for my chain lubricant, I heard a car door close and its engine start from behind the buildings. Maybe I could find out what the road held from the driver. My bike's seat leaned against my head, my knee in the dirt, one hand squirting a stream of lubricant while the other hand cranked the pedals backwards when the gate behind me opened. I stood up as a green sedan pulled up next to me.

"Are you broke down," the driver asked. He wore a blue plaid shirt under a set of red Carhartt suspenders, white hair blended into gray sideburns that faded back to snow white on his chin.

"Oh no, I'm just lubing the chain." I arched my back into a stretch.

"You must be doing that bike race."

"Well, I'm not racing, but I am riding the route."

A woman had locked the gate and walked back to the car. We all talked a bit about the route and the documentary that had a scene filmed at the church we stood outside of.

"Do you two know this road pretty well?"

"Sure do."

"Good. I'm trying to avoid the rain and mud and am thinking of following this road to get to Silver City. Is there anything on this road? Any place I'll be able to stop?"

Without a look to his passenger, the driver said, "Yeah. Mile marker 43."

Mile marker 43? Now here's a man that knew how to give directions. These directions were much more precise than "you can't miss it." I laughed with his specificity. "What's at mile marker 43?"

With a quick glance at his wife this time, "Well, we are."

I glanced around for a mile marker. "You mean we're at 43 right here?"

"No. I mean us," he said pointing to himself and his wife. "Our home is at mile marker 43. Why don't you stop by. We'll feed you and let you used the spare bed, get a good night of sleep. How does that sound?"

Too good to be true. "Well, how far is it from here?"

"I'd say about 25 miles."

"Well, that sounds wonderful then," I said, not sure what to make of the situation. We hadn't even introduced ourselves, but I had accepted an invitation to dinner. Strange? Maybe a little. But I wouldn't have to stay if I felt at all uncomfortable.

"All right. What would you like for dinner?"

Like? I must have looked ridiculous, slack-jawed and sweat-stained. I was still so surprised at having been invited to dinner that I couldn't comprehend deciding what dinner would be. "I'm not a picky eater, especially these days."

"All right. Can we take your bags for you and lighten your load?"

"Oh no, I'll hold on to those." I didn't have any suspicion of foul play. To give up the bags was another step toward an easy ride that I didn't want to take. An easier route to avoid weather was one thing; pawning my gear off onto somebody else was quite different. "Mile maker 43, right? I think it will be a couple of hours before I get there."

"We'll be there. You'll see this car in the driveway. Just ride on in."

"Ok. I'll see you soon."

I tried not to watch the car as it drove down the long flat stretch of pavement in front of me; an object like that put the road in perspective and revealed just how much longer it was than it looked. Another 25 miles of riding? Sounded like a challenge. I had grown more and more tired since the 120-mile day and now I had no idea what kind of terrain lay ahead of me. I hoped there wouldn't be much climbing.

• • •

Mile marker 43. Into the driveway. There was a cluster of outbuildings on the lot, the most interesting an old wood shed, the plank walls faded to a dull brown matched by the rust on the corrugated tin roof. The exterior walls were decorated with all manner of odd and ends, a bulletin board of history: old logging saws, circular saw blades, a mechanical sickle, elk antlers, glass bottles, various shafts and sprockets, a bed frame, old stirrups, and even a pair of cowboy boots. The collection continued next to the building: old wash basins, a gas pump, a child's wagon, and various metal tractor wheels. The metal objects tried to blend into the wood beneath their rust, but the sun's rays gave them away, the bright orange iron oxides aglow.

My brakes squeaked as I applied enough pressure to halt the rotation of the wheels. I stopped short of the end of the driveway and walked my bike the last twenty yards past the green sedan and up the walk way that led to the house.

From inside the house: "Oh honey, look who's here."

The sound of foot steps preceded his arrival in the door way. "Heck, you made it a lot faster than we thought you would," he said as he descended the few steps to the ground.

"Yeah me too. After I crossed the Continental Divide there was a slight downhill grade almost the whole way here. I'm Nathan by the way."

"Nathan, I'm David." We shook hands, mine smooth and white, his wrinkled and tanned. We both had callused hands, though, textured hands.

"Is there somewhere I should leave my bike?"

"We can move some of these chairs and lean it under the porch here."

We worked together to rearrange the patio furniture. Before I had the chance to give it any thought, I removed my panniers, already comfortable enough to stay.

"Let me give you a hand with those, Nathan," David said as he reached for one of the panniers, "and I'll show you your room."

We stashed my things in the spare bedroom, and David showed me to the kitchen where he introduced his wife, Sherry. Then David was out the door and at the barbecue to start the steaks and potatoes.

"Well, Nathan," Sherry said as she started to make a salad, "it sounds like you've come quite a long ways. You must have been invited in to quite a few homes along the way."

"Actually, no," she looked up from the salad bowl, "this is the first time anyone has invited me in."

"Really?" She turned and faced me at the kitchen table as one hand dropped out of the bowl and to her side, "Well that's surprising. We are the first, and you're already almost done?"

"Yeah. Granted, I haven't run into a lot of people. The route is pretty desolate in places."

She went back to the salad. "That's still a bit surprising."

Before long, David returned with the potatoes and steak, mine cooked to a perfect medium rare. In between mouthfuls, I answered their questions about the trip as best as I could, sometimes having to dig for answers. My trip timer had six weeks in its sights, and my journey had morphed into an alternative lifestyle. It was difficult to recall everything that had happened.

As we finished dinner (mine could have qualified as two dinners), people started to show up to David and Sherry's for a bible study. I was given the option by my hosts to opt out, but I wanted to be a good guest so I decided to participate. I'm not a religious person, so it wasn't the easy route. After I agreed, David made me wonder about my choice when he warned me about the pastor that led the bible study, saying he was "intense."

This should be interesting.

And it was. I was the target of a series of questions fired by the "intense" pastor. I answered them as best as I could, trying to maintain my anonymity among this group of strangers. But with his infinite sensitivity, our study leader asked if I was ready to receive Christ as my personal savior.

A dozen pair of eyes were fixed on me. A few sets among them belonged to some very young children. My heart wasn't in it. I couldn't answer in the affirmative—that would be a lie. But I didn't want to be a bad influence on these kids; a bad reflection on my hosts; an ungracious guest that insults the personal beliefs of those kind enough to take me in.

With the color rising in my face and the answer timer winding down, I said, "No... not here. That seems like too personal a thing to do in front of a group of strangers."

I played my hand well. The pastor played his better and called my bluff.

"Well, we can go into the kitchen," he fired back. "Just the two of us."

Fine. He wanted a straight answer. That's what he would get.

"No," I said. "My heart wouldn't be in it."

Given the conversation to that point, I knew it was pointless to explain what I was doing. To be saved by Christ? My whole trip was about salvation—but I was trying to save myself. I was searching for my inner strength. I was searching for my own answers, not someone else's.

After everyone left, I looked to David. "Did I do ok?"

"Yeah, you handled yourself well. Lee has a way of coming on a bit strong, but you held your own against him."

We spent the rest of the night in the living room where David and I folded, unfolded, and refolded my maps as we inspected the bike route.

David: "So do you think you'll leave in the morning?"

"I'm not sure. I might, but if I wake up to rain, I won't be in any hurry to get out of here."

"Well, you are more than welcome to stay another day or two, Nathan. It seems like you could use the rest, and this would be a great place to get it."

"Yeah, I might do that. But let's wait and see how I feel in the morning."

The conversation wandered until we somehow got to conservation biology and its ties to ecology. It was a late night, the latest hour I had seen in several weeks, but I did not feel guilty about it. The more I talked with David and Sherry, the more sure I was that I would take a rest day there, my last rest day before the finish.

• • •

"Well good morning, Nathan."

I stumbled into the kitchen, my arms raised above my head in a full body stretch and my mouth wide open in mid-yawn. "Oh, excuse me. Good morning to you too, Sherry."

"I hope you're hungry. I've got breakfast cooking for you." All this talk about morning and breakfast was misleading. I had slept in, and it was after 11. "David should be home for lunch soon. If you're still hungry, I'll cook you up some lunch then too."

It had been four weeks since I last saw someone that I knew. There had been lots of human interactions since then, but you can only go so deep with a stranger. David and Sherry though, they made me feel right at home. They treated me like one of their own. My stay with them was restful in a way that was more than just physical, but emotional. I felt safe.

"So Nathan, I've been wondering why you decided to take this trip," Sherry said as she stood over a cast iron skillet at the range.

"Well, I graduated from school and just wasn't sure what I wanted to do. I had known before, had felt good about the direction of my life, but some things changed before graduation. So I decided to do something big, and this was the adventure that sounded most appealing."

"What does your family think about this trip?"

"I don't know. Some of my extended family seemed pretty negative about the trip. They were worried I would get hurt or something, which I get. But it was like they couldn't see the good in it. Only the negative."

"What about your parents?"

"My dad and stepdad were both supportive."

"And your mom?" she said, eyes on the skillet to turn its contents.

"She's actually a big reason I'm out here."

Sherry looked up from the skillet. "Really? Why's that?"

"Because almost two years ago, she died."

Chapter 39

The Beginning

ONE SEPTEMBER DAY in particular marks the beginning of this story.

I was home for harvest on the family wheat farm.

It had been a long summer. A few weeks before I finished my fourth year of school, Amber and I had broken up. It hadn't been my doing. A few days later, in true Amber fashion, she sent me a letter. It elaborated on our final discussion and addressed the biggest problems with our relationship. What she had meant by sending the letter or what effect she anticipated it having, I never found out. It wasn't ten minutes after I finished the letter that my mom called. She had been battling cancer for several years, a metastasized form that had been playing hide-and-seek among her various organs. This time, three tumors had been found in her brain. Amber's letter was set aside. Less than a week later, mom called again.

"Morning, Nathan. I'm sorry I called so early. Were you sleeping?"

"Yeah, but my alarm was about to go off anyway," I said. My fatigue faded away faster than usual. Apprehension built in my chest. Mom was pretty good at calling at an appropriate hour. Never early in the morning. "What's going on?"

"I just need to talk to you is all. Do you have time to drive into Spokane this morning?"

"This morning?" That wasn't a good sign. "I guess. I have a rock climbing class to teach at 11."

"You can be back by 11. Brandon is coming up now, so can you be here in half an hour or so?"

"Yeah, of course. I'll see you soon."

My mom and stepdad lived in Spokane and were only a 20-mile drive away from me. They had moved from the small farming community where I had grown up to be closer to her doctors. I was sure the cancer would be the topic of discussion. Mom had made the brain tumors out to be nothing when we had spoken on the phone, but that was what she always did. Despite my disapproval of being called "the baby" of the family, that was always how mom thought of me. She thought she was protecting me by painting her condition in a kinder light.

I walked into her house, greeted by Nelson's barks and found everyone sitting around the dining table. The table was bare; no dishes or food, no decks of cards or board games. Nothing that normally drew the family around it was on the table. Not even a tablecloth to hide the grain of the darkly stained wood. It had been left exposed.

Mom's liver, after years of chemotherapy treatments, had started to fail. Her doctor said that at best, she had a year. I had watched my mom battle cancer since before I graduated high school, and never had I seen her scared of it. Not until that morning. Not until every option had been exhausted and every last shred of hope consumed.

We had a discussion about the coming months, what would happen. The conversation was slow, held back by silent tears and suppressed sobs. Just a few hours earlier, I had been stressed out about school. Perspective.

I detached myself from the family to make a call. I ended up in the basement, cold cement underfoot and irises dilated in the dim light. The ring of the phone in my ear was slow, distant.

"Hey bud, what's up?"

"Hey Shane. Listen man, I need a big favor. Can you cover my rock climbing class this morning?"

"Which class? What are you guys doing?"

"It's an intro class and it's our last day. Can you just take attendance and quiz them on the terminology?"

"Of course, man." I had called Shane for a reason. He was one of the most dependable guys I knew. I didn't have the composure to talk to several people to search for a substitute teacher. I had managed to sound fine, maybe business like when I talked to Shane. Until: "Too hungover to make it or something?"

He chuckled his nonchalant chuckle. I held the phone away as I withheld my burst of tears. A short moment of concentration and the phone was back to my ear and mouth. "No man, nothing like that. I just ... I can't make it. Can you just tell my class I'm sorry I couldn't be there?"

Now he knew something was wrong. "Yeah man, of course."

"Good, I owe you," I said, my breathing back under control. "Shane?"

"Yeah?"

"Thanks, man."

• • •

Two weeks later, school ended, and I returned to the farm. It was against my own wishes but in accordance with my mom's. While I was there, I lived with my brother Brandon for the first time in a decade. I took a class in Spokane that summer, so once a week I sat through a three-hour lecture and afterwards went to visit my mom. The class wasn't for my biology degree. It was a requirement for my second major, Environmental Science, a major I had declared casually because it hadn't seemed like much more work than I would already be doing. Why not make my resume more appealing? It was this second major that had prevented me from graduating that June and had shifted my schedule in such a way that I couldn't graduate before the following June.

Mom had always been proud of my academic accomplishments. She once wrote a letter to the president of the university to suggest a different form of recognition be given to student's that made the Dean's list multiple times. When I made the list as a freshman, I was sent a congratulatory letter through the mail. By my senior year, I just got an email with the same letter attached. The president was nice enough to write my mom a reply.

Mom was excited to see me graduate. The ceremony would be just over a year from us learning about her liver. Her goal was to be healthy enough to see me walk across the stage and receive my degree. The doctor's most optimistic estimate for her was a year. She wanted so badly to see me graduate. If I hadn't declared that second major a year earlier, she would have seen me graduate that June. Now, she would have to wait. Now, it would be a battle.

The summer passed, and then September came. Harvest. Axel.

"Tim, you copy?!"

"Yeah, I got you Brandon, go ahead."

"I need to know where your gun is right now!"

"… What… what do you need my gun for?"

"I got Axel. It's not good."

I sat in my combine by myself, surrounded by hundreds of acres of pea stubble, dried to a crisp yellow cover over the brown earth. I cried. Axel had lain on that road alone and afraid. I wasn't able to be by his side at the end. It wasn't more than three hours later I had the same fear about my mom.

Brandon drove up to my combine in the farm's service truck. All he said was, "We have to go. It doesn't sound good." That was all he had to say. We grabbed our things and left for Spokane.

• • •

"Am I scaring you?" Brandon said from the driver's seat. In twenty minutes, we had covered half the distance to Spokane, a drive that normally lasted an hour. Yes, I was scared. I nodded to confirm his suspicion, my vocal cords paralyzed by my effort to hold back the tears. "You want me to slow down?" My brow furrowed and I shook my head no. It wasn't his driving that scared me, but what it implied. He hadn't told me what was going on. His driving suggested time was short, maybe short enough that when we got to Spokane, Mom would already be gone. I still saw Axel on the road, still felt the guilt of not having been by his side. I could not have handled not being with my mom at her end.

Several illegal passes, three yellow lights, and one red later, we pulled up to the house and hurried in, still wearing our cowboy boots, our jeans stained with grease and oil, our shirts and faces smeared with dirt. We walked passed the dining room table into the living room where several family members had already gathered. A lethargic state gripped my mom, somewhere between sleep and comatose.

Aunt Lea greeted us. "Hey boys. She's ok for right now. She's been mostly sleeping since about 10 this morning. We'll try to wake her up so you can say hi, and you know, just … let her know you're here."

She sat in her chair, covered in a blanket, Nelson on her lap, his chin resting on her thigh. Brandon and I stood on either side of her chair while Lea prodded her awake. "Sharon, Sharon. Look who's here, sweetie."

Mom cracked her eyes open. She turned her head and when her eyes focused on me, she smiled. "Yes, sweetie, Nathan's here. And Brandon's here too." Her gaze with me broke and she rolled her head to the opposite shoulder to find Brandon. She smiled at him too and then lifted her fist, thumb and index finger extended to make a gun. Her thumb bent, the gun going off toward Brandon. I almost saw her wink as she did it. We all chuckled a bit at the gesture and her eyes closed again.

Brandon and I joined the circle of seating, and the family asked how the farm was, how harvest was going. Our eyes met across the circle. Then I watched my brother explain that Axel had died, how he had to put Axel down. Brandon was the toughest person I knew, and I had never seen him cry before. Never. His tears flowed now though, his silent gaze pointed to the ceiling as he shook his head at the memory.

Jared and Whitne made the drive from Bozeman and arrived a few hours after us. Mom was moved to her bed where she stayed the rest of the night. Aunt Lea was an experienced nurse and the only medical staff that was there. At 3 a.m., she told me it was almost time. I woke my brothers.

I held my mother's right hand for the next hour until I felt her give it a gentle squeeze. That was when I knew. I squeezed back and over the next few seconds, her light, quick breathing shallowed further, until she exhaled for the final time. My mom died at 4 a.m.; she was surrounded by her family.

The moon was bright, full above a perfect, clear sky. I sat outside on the porch steps staring at it. The occasional sound of sobs emanated from inside the house. She was gone. I wasn't ready for her to leave, but she was gone anyway. And that last squeeze of her hand, what had that meant? Was it fear? Was it encouragement meant for me? Was it nothing more than a pre-rigor mortis twitch? The possibilities frightened me. I didn't tell anyone about it, not until I relived that day with Megan, several months later. She had been in town for business and our reunion brought us to the driveway at 4 in the morning.

Two days later, Brandon and I were back at work. I thought I might take that quarter off from school, but I didn't know what else I would do. Staying busy was more appealing than having ample amounts of time to sit around and feel sorry for myself. I really didn't want to push my graduation back any further either. So six days after I returned to work, I was back at school and thinking about crayfish.

Chapter 40

THEIR FUR KNOCKED DEW FROM THE GRASS. Their feet threw dark, soft mud into the air. Their low profile and long, slender bodies let them turn rapidly and attempt to out maneuver each other. They ran between the shed and the trees, through the yard, and under the kitchen window where I ate breakfast with David and Sherry. The bunnies were a comedic relief for the meal.

I had woken early and packed my bike up, prepared to leave. It was hard to leave such a welcoming home, and neither David nor Sherry were ready to see me leave. After my last wave, I had to turn away to keep from shedding any tears.

It was 110 miles to Silver City along the paved alternate. The monsoonal rains had continued during my rest day, and David and Sherry couldn't believe I had been on my bike during some of those storms. With more rain in the forecast, I hoped to cover every mile to Silver City that day. By noon, I had completed 50 miles and crossed one pass. It was easy to tell I had taken a rest day. But the temperature and humidity made the ride more difficult as they both began to soar. I had to stop at a gas station in Glenwood where I ate my ice cream at a picnic table under the covered porch.

When I left, the road rolled and wound. I couldn't help but get frustrated at how inefficiently the road traversed the landscape. To the east, thunderstorms swelled above the Gila Wilderness. I would have been under them if I had stuck to the main route. Then clouds began to build above me as well. The terrain flattened as the storm began to release its payload. I was on the leading edge of the storm, fortunate to catch a tail wind and cruise at 25 mph, trying to outrun the storm.

For an hour I stayed ahead of it, driven by the thunder behind me and awed by the lightning to the east. Wait, was that a storm to the south too? My blue sky was running out. I stopped in the town of Cliff and sheltered on the covered porch of a closed down roadside bar, where I checked the weather on my phone. The storm to the south had several advisories associated with it: the most notable were wind gusts to 60 mph and quarter-inch hail. Sandwiched between three storms? I stayed on the porch to wait it out.

I occupied most of time with writing, reflecting on what I had done. Looking back, there were some instances where I had set myself up for failure. But then I had succeeded. It occurred to me that this was the only true success. How can you possibly succeed if there is no chance at failure? I had not taken enough risks in my life, I had not given myself the opportunity to succeed. I had not strayed from the red line I thought I was supposed to be following. Why was that?

I knew why. Cefas and I had had a whole conversation about it: fear. I had never noticed its prevalence in my life, though. Where had it been hiding? I used to think of my life as a timeline and that I was somewhere in between the two termini; I was always approaching the end of my life, but was never actually there. This mental image created the illusion that I would always have more time. That was where my fear had hid: in the promise of tomorrow. To do away with it, I had to recreate my perception of time. I still imagine a timeline, but now I am the terminus—I am always at the end of my life.

With this perception, there is no great battle of the ego. Instead of seeking and becoming, I can know and be. This new understanding was liberating.

This new understanding changed my perspective on life. But I had to acknowledge my fears to gain that understanding. That was where my alternate reality had come in. That strange world where I went to escape. I had interacted with people and had grand experiences. I thought it was just an illusion until I realized it had been a solipsistic existence. I was the only person in that reality. All of the discussions, all of the arguments, all of the encouragement, that was all with myself. I looked back on those conversations and saw myself communicate, grow, and confront issues I wouldn't have addressed otherwise.

• • •

I set out at 5, after more than an hour of waiting, and with a weather report that said there was no chance of rain now. Five miles later and it was raining. Not only that, but the storms had caused flash floods that inundated the land. Another 5 miles and a loud hiss startled me to attention. I pulled off the shoulder to inspect the noise. What! Fewer than 120 miles from the finish and I got my first flat tire. Damn. I pulled off the panniers and inverted my bike, setting to work on the repairs in the flooded New Mexican landscape.

I was drained on the last climb before Silver City. As I neared the Continental Divide once again, the light started to fade. The thick cover of clouds blotted out the sun and left me on a lonely highway where the traffic had disappeared with the light. My headphones gave me that last bit of motivation I needed; they allowed me to absorb the energy of the music and push it through my pedals. As the sun fell, it broke below the clouds and sent out shafts of light as if it were sunrise. The blue bulges of the lowest clouds grew pink with the warmth, and the color spread across the clouds until the sky looked like one massive bundle of cotton candy, fluff of blue and pink. It was an incredible sunset, but I needed a better view. I forgot my fatigue and found the energy to climb up to the Divide in search of the best vantage point to watch from. The highway didn't feel lonely during that sunset.

I coasted down a large hill through the dark into Silver City. My whoops and hollers a remnant of my sunset sugar high. I pulled into the first motel I saw, and while I checked in, I met another pair of cyclists riding the Divide. They invited me to their room. After I settled, I took them up on it. Robin and Kevin were northbound. They had checked into the hotel the day before, after their first day of riding and were taking a rest day.

"It's so weird, " Robin said, "to think you're finishing tomorrow when we have just started."

"Yeah it is. I've only seen a couple of northbound riders and that was on the first half or so of the ride. I've gotten used to the idea that every cyclist I run into has been at it for a while. Not you two, though."

"Yeah, have any tips, any advice for the ride?"

"Yeah. The best advice I can give you is to not let the red line dominate your ride. There are a lot of ways to get to Canada from here. Don't be afraid to go your own way. It won't make the journey any less extraordinary. You know, I haven't been on the official route a whole lot in New Mexico just because of the rain. And from what I've seen and what I've heard from the locals, monsoon season has begun, so unless you want to get stuck in the mud, I would recommend the paved alternates."

Kevin jumped in: "Yeah, there was a huge storm here today. I mean, it really poured."

"Yeah, I saw the storm on my way in. I waited it out for the most part, but I got to see all the flooding it caused."

We talked for more than an hour. I gave them a list of the best places to eat and the best places to stay, parts of the route I enjoyed the most and the least, which stretches were the most desolate and those that were the most urban.

"Wait, you chased the grizzly bear?"

"Yeah," I said through my laughter. "It wasn't the best decision but I was pretty tired at the time, and it worked out. Speaking of which, are you guys carrying bear spray?" They shook their heads no. "I never used mine, but there were times I was glad I had it. If you don't mind the extra weight you can have it."

"Yeah, that would be great."

I walked back to my room to retrieve the bear spray. It wasn't long ago I had talked to Billy Rice, had clung to every word he said, had tried to take every bit of knowledge he had about the route. It wasn't long ago that I had talked to Oliver at the North Fork Hostel, had listened to his touring stories, had gotten tips and tricks from him. It wasn't long ago that Cefas and I had ridden together, had coached each other. Now it was my word that mattered. I was the experienced bike tourist, just a single day away from finishing the longest mountain bike route in the world. When I had said goodbye to Megan, all the way back in Banff, I had set the wheel in motion; now it had come back around. I had come full circle. I went from learning to teaching; listening to speaking. I had started as somebody that wanted to do and had turned into somebody that had done. Instead of becoming, I was being.

• • •

I left Silver City the next morning and headed for Columbus. I took the pavement, having learned from Robin and Kevin that the main route had been washed out and awful when they came across it. Who knew what is was like after the large storm that had rolled through on their rest day. The next day, I would ride to El Paso, just 80 miles from the route's alternate terminus, where I would catch a train.

When I set out from Banff, I had hoped that my family or friends would pick me up from the end, had hoped they would be there to see me cross the finish line. I had imagined an emotional reunion, where I jumped off my bike and collapsed into their arms with physical and mental fatigue. But the further I rode from Banff, the more I realized that wouldn't happen. Fatigue? I would be mentally and physically stronger at the end than I had been at the beginning; there would be no collapsing. Besides, no one would be there. Not because they wouldn't come, but because I didn't want them to. It had been a solo journey, one that began long before I ever made it to Banff. No one that might pick me up could possibly understand what I would be experiencing, and I sure as hell wouldn't want to try to explain it.

"Hey, what are you doing!" I slapped the Mexican border patrolman's hand away from my bike.

He looked at me, eyes wide and body tensed. I guess he didn't get his hand batted away very often. "I need see inside," he said pointing to my frame bag. He had tried to open it by undoing the Velcro strap that secured it to the bike.

"Well that's not how you open it. It's going to fall off my bike if you do that. The zipper is here," I said to him, pointing to the side of the bike opposite of him. He walked around and looked at the zipper. He didn't even open it before he let me pass into Mexico.

I wasn't going far. I hadn't even planned on crossing into Mexico, but 2,700 miles was a long way to travel and not set foot over the finish line. I biked maybe 200 yards into Mexico before I turned around. It was late afternoon, and I still had 3 miles to ride back to the campground. It had been a long, extremely hot day. I was ready for rest.

I got in line with the cars to cross back onto US soil. A guy selling CDs tried to tell me I didn't need to wait in line with them, I could cross through the pedestrian check point with my bike. Of course, I don't speak Spanish, so it took a few minutes and a lot of miming before he got his point across. On my way back through the Mexican check point, a different patrolman stopped me and asked if I wanted to get my passport stamped.

"Hell yeah!"

We went inside the small office where he stamped my passport, shook my hand, and said, "Welcome to Mexico." Then he stamped it again, shook my hand, and said, "Thank you for visiting." Nice guy.

I crossed back over to the line of cars that waited to get into the US. The pickup ahead of me was pulled out of line, the driver and his passenger detained. I had to wait five minutes while they were secured and the pickup moved. Then a guard instructed me to the booth.

"Great Divide?" the guard asked.

"Yes, sir."

"How long did it take you?"

"This is day 41."

"How long were you in Mexico?"

"About 15 seconds."

He glanced at my passport. "All right, go ahead. Have a good day."

"That's it?"

"Yup."

A different guard had made me believe I would need to unpack all of my things. I guess not. And it really busted my chops that the guard who admitted me back into the country didn't even give a "congratulations" or "good job" or any acknowledgement of what I just finished.

I made it back to the campground to find it empty. My last night was another spent alone. It fit into the solo theme of my ride, a ride that had been the performance of a lifetime, one no one had been there to see.

A storm moved from the northwest and the sunset's light crept just below the clouds like the light beneath a closed door. The storm was the only one that celebrated my accomplishment with me. It produced one of the best light shows I had ever seen: a fiery display of blue-white lightning bolts set adjacent to an orange-red sunset.

Fade to black.

Epilogue

"HEY MAN, are you studying to be a doctor or something?"

"I'm sorry?"

"I just see you writing up a storm over there. You must be studying something, right?"

The landscape outside my window zipped by. I was on the train, catching up on my journal. The guys across the aisle started a conversation when the woman seated next to me left for the dining car.

"No, I'm not studying. This is just a journal. My last few days were pretty busy, and I didn't get a chance to write."

"What are you writing about?"

"Well, I just finished riding my bike from Canada to Mexico."

The two guys looked at each other. "For real?"

"Yup."

"Hey, man, I'm Paul. This is Mike."

They were blown away by my trip. Apart from my conversation with them, though, I didn't talk much on the train. I was too baffled by the speed that we moved with. I tried to capture the details of the landscape through my window, but it went by too quickly. It went by in a blur. The hills were hardly noticeable, too, and I felt guilty for covering so much ground with so much ease.

After three days of travel, my train slipped through Cheney, past my old university. And after midnight, it pulled into Spokane. For almost three weeks, the area had been experiencing a heat wave;

when I got off the train, it was raining.

"There really is no escaping this stuff."

Being home was strange. For six weeks, I had set daily goals. I had felt satisfaction every night when I went to sleep. At home, I didn't know what goals to set. I still calculated mileages wherever I went, and I always scouted for good roadside camping. I felt guilt driving, not having to earn any of the miles I covered. In the first few days of being home, I noticed myself muttering a single phrase.

"Give it a week, Nathan."

After another harvest, I started to work toward telling my story. It was difficult to convey to people what I had done, what I had been through. Everyone saw the trip as a journey of the summer. For me it was the trip of lifetime, a trip that had begun when my mom died and that lasted almost two years. It was a trip that all boiled down to that moment of insight, of discovery, when after several weeks of effort and countless hours reflecting on the experience, I would see if the question I asked would be answered and what that answer would be.

When I read Amber's graduation card now, I don't cringe—the intensity of the search made finding the answer so fulfilling. So do I know what makes a man? No. But I do know what it means for *me* to be a man — and that is a freedom that will help guide the rest of my life.

* * *

One last note: while writing this book, I made a serious effort to find the dust cover for *A Million Miles in a Thousand Years*. When I finally found it, I was surprised at the cover art. It was a bicycle wheel.

Sign?

About the Author

AFTER A RURAL UPBRINGING fostered his love for the outdoors, Doneen earned degrees in Biology and Environmental Science.

While in college, he fell in with a group of rock climbers who exposed him to the world of outdoor recreation and has since been addicted to adventure. He currently works as a clinical chemist while he studies the craft of writing.

Want to see more? For pictures of this trip and excerpts from Nathan's other books, visit NathanDoneen.com. Continue on to read the beginning of *An Adventure Across Peru: A Mototaxi Race.*

An Adventure Across Peru

Prologue

CINDY, "THE SLUT."

Cindy did not receive this title from me. Nor from my teammates. In fact, she had done nothing to warrant it. So it should be no surprise that, in this story, Cindy is the victim.

This is a difficult admission. You see, it was into our charge that Cindy was placed. It was us who were supposed to protect her. She had not volunteered to travel to the northwest coast of Peru, to a village of a few hundred people, where we were first acquainted. She had not requested we drive her a few hundred miles to the Sacred Valley in southeast Peru, which was our destination. And she certainly hadn't offered to be crammed into the back of a mototaxi. But that was exactly what she got, so Cindy's fate rested squarely on the shoulders of my team.

I don't mean to belittle her anguish, but Cindy was not in poor company. All of us had signed up for unbearable driving conditions, unpredictable mechanical failures, and unexpected cultural barriers at every step of the way. We were all looking for our own brand of misery. How else does one explain an international gathering with the purpose of elective suffering?

Besides her forced participation, what really set Cindy apart from the rest of us was her Barbie Doll proportions–which is to say her inhuman proportions. That's right: Cindy was a doll, imprisoned by plastic wrap on top of a quinceañera piñata. And even though she was inanimate, she had earned the title of Pink Fairy.

It was the Pink Fairy my team was awarded, and with it, the responsibility for Cindy. This was our additional task, our additional challenge.

Chapter 1

THE CELLS OF YOUR BODY routinely kill themselves. Stay calm—this is a good thing.

Old cells collect deficiencies, malfunction, and become diseased. To preserve the organism as a whole, they elect to die. Meanwhile, healthy cells divide in order to replace those lost. Given the varied stresses across cell types, different tissues are replaced at different rates. The lining of your small intestine will replace itself after just a few days; your stomach lining, after a week; your skin takes ten to thirty days; and the red blood cells circulating through your body will be replaced after four months–that's 100 million new red blood cells every minute.

How do we know these rates? During World War II, some very smart scientists developed the atomic bomb–you may have heard of it. After two detonations dropped the curtain on the Pacific theater, research was amped up, dragging the world into the Cold War and igniting an endless series of test detonations. Then came some very clever scientists who put these bombs to good, honest, morally undisputed use. Their research used the carbon-14 leftover from the nuclear explosions to determine the above tissue ages. The clever part: they didn't need more detonations.

Back to my point though: cells die. Not only do they die, but they're *supposed* to die. That most of us are ignorant of this process doesn't alter the outcome. In fact, I might argue that because it doesn't alter the outcome, most people would choose ignorance. That's not difficult to understand–that millions of these little pieces of me are dying every minute is not something I want to think about.

Perhaps that's why I wasn't fazed when Duncan, standing before the craziest group of people I've ever been a part of, made a case for ignorance.

At least when dealing with Peruvian Police.

"There's a phrase I want you all to memorize. I think you'll be surprised at how often it can get you out of trouble." When you've decided to race one of the worst pieces of machinery on the planet a few hundred miles across Peru, from Colan to Urubamba, a heaping pile of trouble is exactly what's waiting for you. "For all of you who don't speak Spanish—*and* for those who do—here it is: 'No fumar español'–" Duncan chuckled, the two or three Spanish speakers in our group joining him. "–which means, 'I don't smoke Spanish.'"

The group burst with laughter.

"Saying 'I don't speak Spanish' is one thing. It is quite another to demonstrate it. What police officer wants to have a mime argument over a petty traffic infraction? Yes, it makes you look like a stupid Westerner, but you'd be surprised how many people have gotten out of a tight spot with that phrase. So please, commit it to memory."

Duncan went on to explain the guidelines of the race, all of which centered on the theme of "Don't be an asshole." Then, after a few more anecdotes and some advice from our Peruvian liaisons, Duncan concluded the meeting.

I left, my mind already racing. Would we get lost? Stranded? Robbed? Would we spend a fortune to keep our engine running–all 150CCs? Would the desert permit us to cross it, or would we be desiccated? Would the mountains continue to stand tall, or would they prove to be a climbable divide? Would the jungle sprout our success, or would it leave us devoured in a humid and hasty decay?

My mind darted, but my body strolled. We made our way back to our hostel, not far from the hotel where the meeting had been. Nothing was far in Colan, a quiet beach town near the city of Piura. Sand buried the streets. Each step sunk into the road, cushioned and muted. There was no rush here; the sand wouldn't permit it.

At the hostel, a few teams had gathered on the oceanside deck. The table was covered with maps and beer bottles, the air filled with speculation on routes. The Scots paid extra attention–they hadn't even brought a map. That's because this wasn't a race in the traditional sense. The reason for speculating was because there was no course and, in fact, there was only one rule: "Get your mototaxi to the finish…no matter what." How we went about this was irrelevant. The whole purpose of using mototaxis was to make their second-rate quality, low dependability, and unpredictability contribute to the adventure.

The sun arced to the horizon, beer bottles emptied, and the tide came in, the extended surf polishing the stilts on which our hostel stood.

The next night we gathered again, and for a few minutes we all sat quiet. Not with fatigue from the last day of mototaxi test driving and tinkering or with the soreness from the soccer match against the locals. We were quiet in respect of what stood before us.

This stillness was a first for the group—a very diverse group. Possibly the only thing we all shared was the English language. The organization that hosted this race was a British charity, called The Adventurists. They have a unique approach to raising money. Organize a crazy event, draw in crazy participants, and have *them* raise the money.

I can't stress the crazy element enough—"Adventurists" is an apt name. With events like the Mongol Rally, the Rickshaw Run, and the Icarus Trophy, you can see how narrow a cross section of society this charity targets.

There were nearly fifty of us—about twenty teams—seated at a banquet table, the remnants of a feast laid before us. This was the Launch Party, the last opportunity we racers would have to bond before being thrown to the mercy of our taxis. Around the table were seated a number of Brits, the dominant demographic. Also represented were Australia, New Zealand, Romania, Scotland, South Africa, Switzerland, and the United States. But at that moment, we were engrossed with Peruvian culture.

After we had crammed our faces with the best Peruvian cuisine, to the groaning of stomachs and creaking of chair legs, and after everyone declined a fourth helping, a group of locals marched into the banquet room, wearing traditional clothing and carrying instruments. We fell silent for the performance.

Historically, the Spanish restructuring of the Incan culture had not been subtle. Since that colonial era, Peru's culture has been seen as a fusion of Incan and Spanish traditions. "Clash" may be a more appropriate descriptor though, as was demonstrated by the performers. The first dance was one of strict choreography, executed in time with plucked guitar strings that snapped out from strummed chords, paired with the clacking of the dancers' thick-soled shoes on the wood floor. Even the costumes were constrictive. That is not to say this dance wasn't beautiful or impressive, but it could not relate to the dance that followed. The indigenous customs flowed through the breathy music, through the loose and simple ornateness of the dress, and out through the dancers' relaxed and fluid limbs. The same musicians, the same dancers, the same small dance floor, all able to embody such disparate traditions. More impressive still was the performers' ability to transition between them without suffering the paradoxical nature of hosting both.

We were quiet. We were transfixed. We all sprung to our feet and beat our hands red at the conclusion, exchanging impressed glances and nods of approval. Many bows and toothy grins were returned before the dancers retreated out of the banquet room.

Duncan, less attractive and much less graceful, took the performers' place. As the company representative, Duncan was here to collect paperwork, hand out mototaxi keys, and see us off on our grand adventure. He gave us all the last-minute updates, the current standings in regards to money raised for charity, and then began the pre-race award ceremony.

These wouldn't be considered awards by most people—more like mockery. But in our group, mockery was a symbolic tip of the hat. If you weren't the punch line of any jokes, you were doing it wrong. So the awards were a good laugh before the race began.

Trophies included a toilet seat, a set of orange coveralls, and the Pink Fairy Award.

Awards were not random, but reflected the team's character. For instance, that toilet seat went to the team voted most likely to shit their pants while the coveralls went to the team voted most likely to attempt a roadside repair. So to understand the Pink Fairy Award, you need to understand my team.

I knew Scott from college. As an endurance runner, Scott had the following mentality: when in doubt, push through; if doubt persists, keep pushing. This is the kind of philosophy that translates to self-enabling. Not the type that leads to self-destruction, but to masochism. This might explain Scott's desire to become a polyglot. Our university was located in Washington state, but he had studied abroad in Morocco just to work on his French and Arabic. And after he registered for the race, he had turned his attention to Spanish. And that's not to mention the computer languages he knew as a programmer.

On campus, while Scott had been typing away in the computer lab, I had been in a formaldehyde-filled biology lab prodding the department's most treasured pickled specimen: a small shark with one side of its body cut away to reveal the internal organs. So how did Scott and I know each other? We had both worked at the campus rock climbing gym. But being on staff together still hadn't made us best friends. In fact, we never even saw each other after graduation.

So, surprise was the appropriate response when after two years of zero contact, I received an email from Scott. I clicked through the hyperlink he had sent and watched the three-minute video. My heart raced. I spent another two minutes on The Adventurist website before I sent Scott a reply.

Scott had asked several people to join this team before me. Almost all of them were enthusiastic, even eager to sign up. But, as is typical, all of them had an excuse. So Scott had changed tactics. Who was crazy enough to join him? Maybe the guy who pedaled a mountain bike more than 2500 miles from Canada to Mexico down the Continental Divide...alone.

The travel résumés of Scott and I stood in stark contrast to Andrew, a friend and coworker of Scott's. He had never been out-of-country. An Adventurist event seemed a difficult way to begin an experience abroad, so I had to hand it to the guy for signing up. And not just for signing up, but for driving the bandwagon straight into this race. Scott had mentioned the Mototaxi Junket to Andrew and after a little research, Andrew was ready to go, with or without Scott.

His gung-ho-ness and brilliance made Andrew a crucial member of the team and he was determined to be prepared. Months before the race, he and Scott had learned what engine would be powering our mototaxi. Andrew bought an old scooter with an equivalent engine and rebuilt it, just to get himself acquainted. Impressive. So was the toolkit he put together. And that's not to mention all the comforts of home Andrew installed on our mototaxi in the days leading up to the race: a GPS unit (complete with DC converter so we could run it off our mototaxi's battery), a throttle lock for those long straight stretches (think cruise control), and even extra padding for the driver's seat.

These things would be useful. But were they in the spirit of the race? The Adventurists organization encourages people to abandon modern comforts, to throw caution, and let the chips fall. We were supposed to get lost, be uncomfortable, and hate life. These luxuries would make reaching those objectives more difficult. It was because of this preparedness that we had won Cindy.

The Pink Fairy Award was the issuance of an additional challenge. Everyone thought we—team *Three Tired Travelers*—were most likely to cross the finish line with our limbs still attached, so we needed to be brought down a peg or two. As a result, Cindy was given to us with a task: deliver her to the finish line in pristine condition.

This would be difficult enough, but I was concerned about the hidden challenge lurking within our preparations. You can't be ready for the unknown, which was what waited for us outside the village of Colan. Would our preparedness give us a false sense of security? Would we be blind-sided by the unpredictability of the race?

There was only one way to find out.

The Packing List

Introduction

"WHAT THE HELL AM I DOING?"

Those words literally came out of my mouth, in that order, only 1.6 miles into this bike tour. At that point, I had no idea what I had gotten myself into. I had no idea just how far out of my depth I was. I had no idea what other challenges were to come. And that was when my panniers were barely clinging to my bicycle. Still, I stuck with it and finished the route.

For accomplishing this feat, I can only claim a small fraction of the credit. Much is owed to the people I ran into along the way: those willing to give me some advice, a meal, or even a bed; those who rode with me, camped with me, and struggled with me; even those who offered nothing more than a smile or a word of encouragement contributed to my success along the route. However, these are not the only people deserving of some acknowledgement.

A portion of credit needs to be allotted to those who went before me, to those who documented their own journey along the Great Divide Mountain Bike Route. These accounts exist in any number of forms: social media updates, blog posts, memoirs, or guide books—my research took me into all these different media and I gleaned whatever information I could, eager to suppress that air of inexperience and ignorance that certainly surrounded me at every step of the way.

Now, here is my own contribution to that body of information that might help others plan their own tour.

As you read through my packing list, there is something you should keep in mind. I was first introduced to the GDMBR by a documentary called *Ride the Divide*, a film following the racers of the Tour Divide. Many of these cyclists are world-class athletes and cover the distance of this route in a very short time, carrying a bear minimum of gear and supplies.

It was this documentary that first give me the idea of taking this tour. And even though I had no intention of racing, I had seized upon the notion that I would attempt to ride this route as fast as possible. Because of this desire, a part of my packing strategy was to cut weight. Also, because I was unemployed and approaching bankruptcy, another part of my packing strategy was to cut costs.

This list reflects those goals, so please alter or add to this list as you will. With the benefit of hindsight, I can say if I was to ride the route again, it would be at a more leisurely pace and with a few more comforts.

Also worth mentioning is that, along with my research, I tried to prepare physically by riding my bike...a lot. I was active in the years leading up to the tour, but never as a cyclist. So when March came calling, I began to take my bike out daily. I started with short rides of 5 to 10 miles and slowly worked up to my first century ride. I was riding old rail beds, country roads, and mountain bike trails. I did not follow any particular training regime, but I was consistent in my rides along with some weight training and dietary supplementation. Despite these physical preparations, the first few days of the route kicked my ass.

A better preparation—and a recommendation—would have been more practice runs. I embarked on only one overnight bikepacking trip with my intended bike set up. Of course, I packed accordingly for that one night, so did not have every single piece of gear I had intended to take down the Great Divide. My, how it all added up. My first day on the route, my bike had gained weight, my gear had doubled in size, and my lungs had shrunk. Can you believe I was actually surprised by my pannier problems?

"What the hell am I doing?"

A better question might be what are you doing?! I am not a professional cyclist. I am not a wise and seasoned tourist. I'm essentially a nobody in the world of cycling. So keep that in mind as you plan your trip. Pack according to your wants and needs and remember that I offer this list only as guidance, not as rule or recommendation. As such, I have included annotations to provide my thoughts and feelings about certain items or pieces of gear I brought along.

I hope you find this helpful and I wish you the best of luck on your journey. If you have any other questions feel free to reach out to me through my website or by email at nathan@nathandoneen.com

Bike Setup

- Trek Mamba, 17.5"

    The Trek Mamba is a hard tail 29 inch wheel mountain bike fitted with a Rock Shock front fork suspension system. I bought this bike specifically for this trip, so intentionally sought out a hard tail bike. My research had revealed that full suspension bikes can complicate the use of rear panniers, so I opted for the hard tail rather than using a full suspension bike that towed a trailer—this was the setup Cefas used and we both agreed that the hardtail with panniers and without trailer was better, especially on hard ascents and fast descents.

    I also opted for a 29er given their ability "to roll" which made descents faster and those long flat stretches go by a little easier. Cefas was on 26 inch wheels, and it was easy to pull away from him on descents with both our bikes under the power of gravity alone.

- Some other components worth mentioning came stock:
    - Hayes Hydraulic Disc Brakes with 160mm rotor

        I had some reservations about the hydraulics given the difficulties involved with repairing them. I originally wanted a cable set up, but a mechanic talked me into the hydraulics. I ended up having no problems with the hydraulics during the trip. On the other hand, larger rotors would have been helpful on some of the steeper descents. I still made it out alive with the 160mm though.

    - Shimano Alivio trigger shifters

        I only had one problem with these during the trip.

While in Montana, the front shifter would not adjust the derailleur from the middle to the large chain ring. I was able to get by with just using the middle chain ring until I made it Whitefish where the shifter was disassembled and cleaned. There were no problems after that.

- Non-stock and additional items:
  - Shimano SPD Pedal, PD-M424

    The clipless pedals were a no-brainer for this trip. Having the ability to utilize a different set of leg muscles was helpful on many ascents and on many flat stretches.

  - Profile Design Century Aerobars

    These also became essential on those flat stretches and some of the more mellow grades. This also allowed me to position my body differently throughout the day which helped combat the fatigue and discomfort my upper body suffered if immobilized. They also helped a lot with head winds.

  - Sigma bike computer

    This was the cheapest model I could find—it operated by tracking the revolutions of a magnet fixed to a spoke. I calibrated it once at the beginning of the trip, despite manufacturer recommendations to calibrate as tire tread wears down. It wasn't super accurate, but it kept a close enough count of my mileage to make following the ACA map directions and guidebook easy.

  - Topeak Explorer Rear Rack
  - Frame Bag (custom made)

    This bag stored the majority of the spare bike components and the bear mace.

  - Handlebar Bag (custom made)

    This held my bivy, sleeping pad, cookware, stove, fuel, and camp towel.

  - Handlebar Light

- Serfas E-Gel Hybrid Saddle with Cutout

  I definitely appreciated the extra cushion.

- Rear Panniers

  I began my trip with a pair of Seattle Sport Rear Panniers. Each had a cargo-rack clip break within the first 2 miles. Though not of the highest quality, I think my poor packing skills were mostly to blame. I crammed most of my gear into these panniers which caused them to slightly bow in the middle. Since they weren't flush with the rack, they were able to wobble, adding extra stress to the clips. I ended up using a length of cord to "secure" them until I arrived in Whitefish.

  My second pair of panniers were Hyalite Equipment. These clips were also plastic, but I elected for a larger volume pannier to avoid the bowing problem. I also bought a pair of bungee cords to hook around the panniers as extra support. This set up caused no problems for me and lasted the remainder of the trip.

- Osprey Backpack (Manta 28)

  My backpack held water, maps/guidebook, rain gear, sunscreen, and snacks. My motivation for the backpack was to hold my water bladder and to have a little extra space for packing. It worked well for me, but I think in the future I would forgo the backpack for a larger handlebar bag or front panniers and, instead of using a frame bag, fix water bottle cages to the down tube and seat tube.

Bike Supplies

- Kevlar spoke
- 1 spare tire

    I kept a Kevlar bead folding tire stuffed in the bottom of a pannier. My rear tire made it about halfway and was replaced in Steamboat Springs, Colorado. My front tire made the entire journey.

- 2 spare tubes

    I started the journey using two slime self-sealing tubes. I made it to New Mexico before either went flat. Then, on the day I made it to Mexico, I suffered a dozen or so punctures.

- 1 spare chain

    Swapped in at Steamboat.

- chain lube
- quick connect link
- spare derailleur arm
- spare brake pads
- tire levers
- air pump
- air pressure gauge
- patch kit and glue
- 1 spare shifter cable
- 10 cable ends
- spare bolts
- spare nuts
- super glue
- electrical tape
- rag
- brush
- 1 Crank Bros multi tool
- 1 Leatherman

Camp Supplies

- Optimus Crux stove w/ 4 oz fuel canister

  I didn't use all of the fuel for the duration of the trip, mostly due to my eating habits. See "Food" below.

- GSI Halulite Minimalist Cook set
- camp utensils and lighter
- camp towel
- headlamp
- cordage and carabineer

  I was a rock climber in college, so felt naked without some cordage and at least one carabineer. The cordage was intended to anchor the bivy if need be, and also to hang my food and other smelly possessions in a tree, well away from camp to keep the bears from calling. Of course, these came in handy when my panniers broke, and for several days the cordage/carabineer combo were the only thing keeping my panniers anchored to my bike.

- Marmot Home Alone Bivy

  Bringing a bivy, my goal was to cut weight. I thought I had struck a good compromise with this bivy since it had two poles that would create a little bit of room inside if I needed to bed down in bad weather. However, part of the reason it was so light was because it sacrificed ventilation. I knew this going in, but the continual wet weather I was subjected to was not expected. So I had a problem with condensation inside the bivy, and because it was so narrow, it was impossible for me to move without bumping the side of the bivy and having the condensation rain down on me. Many mornings, my sleeping bag was wet along with everything else inside the bivy. Not soaking, but fairly damp. I would opt for more ventilation in the future.

- Marmot Sawtooth 15F Sleeping Bag

  The only night I woke up cold was when Cefas and I were sleeping on cots in the tent cabin. The next night, I slept on top of my sleeping pad on the cot and stayed warm. This bag fill was down which loses insulation capability as it gets wet, a reason my bivy condensation was problematic. I stored this in a Sea to Summit eVent compression dry sack.

- Big Agnes insulated sleeping pad

  I tried to cut weight and save money with this item. The specific pad I purchased was mummy-shaped with dimensions 20x60x2.5. This may seem a bit thick, but I justified it by making it a bit short. I'm pushing 5'11", so this bag is nearly a foot shorter than me. I slept with my feet hanging off the end, or propped up on my backpack. This worked out, but again, next time I'd probably opt for an appropriately sized sleeping pad.

- 4L water reservoir

  I packed this specifically for two stretches of the route: the Great Divide Basin in Wyoming and the stretch between Del Norte and Platoro, Colorado. The Great Divide Basin is the driest stretch of the route and can take multiple days to cross. South of Del Norte, the route passes through Summitville, an old mining town and the current site of an EPA Superfund facility. Surface water on this stretch is contaminated with heavy metals. I carried extra water for these stretches, but found I didn't use the extra water. This was somewhat frustrating because water is so heavy. Granted, the weather played a large role in my lower water consumption on those stretches.

- Katadyn Hiker water filter
- Camelback bladder (100 oz.)
- Osprey bladder (100 oz.)

  Both bladders went into my backpack.

Food

Dialing in my diet was a challenge and I did see some weight fluctuations during the trip. Without consistent access to a scale though, it's hard to say how extreme those fluctuations were.

Typically, I tried to minimize cooking. I ate at a lot of restaurants, found treats at gas stations and mercantiles, and bought snacks at grocery stores. I always kept a supply of calories on the bike though. At any given moment, I was carrying:

- peanut butter

  This is calorie dense. I ate it plain by the spoonful.
- microwavable macaroni and cheese

  I made this on my stove with just water.
- tuna fish

  This went into my macaroni and cheese.
- Trail mix
- toaster pastries

  I found the S'mores variety held together better. The pastries were bound to get squished in their packaging and break apart. The S'mores filling would slightly melt in the heat of the day and hold the broken pieces together. This made eating easier.
- All manner of sugary treats

Clothing

- 1 bike helmet
- 1 pair of gloves
- 1 rain jack

  In the interest of saving money, I did not buy a cycling rain jacket. Instead, I opted for one I had used during several biology field classes. It's breathability was very low, and often caused me to get wet from the inside while shedding water from the outside. It was a major contributor to my rainy-day misery. Next time, I would take a more optimized jacket.
- 1 pair rain pants
- 2 pairs mountain biking shorts with built-in, padded liner

  One pair had a liner that didn't breathe well. The buildup of moisture led to saddle sores and the need to lather on chamois crème. This was only a problem on exceptionally hot days, after several hours. On cooler days, I had no problems with this pair. My other pair breathed much better and I had no problems with the shorts themselves.
- 2 jerseys
- 1 fleece vest

- 1 down jacket
- 1 wool cap
- 3 pairs socks
- 1 pair mountain bike shoes
- 1 pair Chacos sandals
- 1 pair boxers
- 1 pair convertible pants
- 1 t-shirt
- 2 Outdoor Products 5L dry stuff sack

> Rain gear was carried in my backpack. All other clothes went into the stuff sacks which I kept in the rear panniers. I ended up sending my Chacos home...they're very heavy.

Toiletries

- chamois crème
- sunscreen
- bug spray
- deodorant
- toothpaste
- floss
- extra contact lenses

> I used a 30-day lens that was approved for sleeping in. I slept in them when camping and removed and cleaned them when I was staying somewhere with a bathroom.

- contact case
- contact solution
- body wash (waterless)
- hand sanitizer
- sanitation trowel
- first aid kit

Miscellaneous

- Nikon AW 100
- Contour+2
- travel camera tripod
- journal/pen
- iPod/headphones
- cell phone
- SPOT Tracker
- passport
- cash/credit card
- guide book

  This wasn't necessary to follow the route, but it has some information that the ACA maps don't. At night, I typically read about the segment I would be covering the following day.

- route maps

  The ACA's maps are weatherproof and are in fact pretty tough. I still opted to keep mine under a piece of clear vinyl though for extra protection from the rain. Apart from some wearing where the creases intersected, they held up very well.

- bear spray

  I never used it, nor thought I would have to. It was still nice to have though.

Budget

Money always seems to be a major topic of interest when people are in the planning stages, whether trying to create a daily budget or get a rough estimate. I also searched for a ballpark figure during my research, but found it quite difficult to get any numbers of any kind. That being said, I'll divulge what little information and wisdom I acquired about my own budget.

Your budget can be divided into pre-trip and trip. The proportion each of these is going to claim of your total expenses is highly dependent on two things: what gear you already possess or need to acquire; and your behavior on the route.

Pre-trip, I had spent upwards of US$2500. This may seem like a steep figure, but don't forget, I was not a cyclist before this trip. My entire bike setup needed to be purchased. My bike I bought brand new at just over $1000. That plus the additions/modifications, shoes, clothes, the bags, and all the spare parts accounted for over half of my pre-trip budget.

My camping gear closet was empty at this time as well. My bivy sack came in just under $200 while I also found it was time to replace my down sweater. The new one ran just over $150. Then I bought the backpacking stove and cookware and other odds and ends.

Your pre-trip total can definitely come in substantially under mine depending on what you already own.

I also spent a considerable amount during the trip itself. Some of these expenses were unavoidable like food, bike mechanic fees, and (for me) brand new panniers. Unfortunately, I don't have information on my total expenses. I can say they were much greater than I had anticipated.

Your behavior will determine how much you spend on the route. If you camp and cook your own food, you can get by on a few dollars a day. On the other hand, spending every night in a hotel/motel/hostel and eating all of your meals at restaurants will push your daily expenses way up. Personally, I had envisioned much more camping than actually happened on my own trip.

One other expense to keep in mind is transportation to/from the route termini. I had the good fortune of having a friend drive me to Banff, so the cost was minimal. My return trip to Washington state on the other hand cost a few hundred dollars and took a couple of days by train.

In all, your budget might seem like quite the investment. This route though is quite the experience. Another way to frame your budget is to take your total costs and divide it down to a daily expense. If you feel like you've already spent a lot, then take your time on the route...make the investment count. Instead of dividing $3000 over 4 weeks ($107/day), take your time and enjoy the route over 8 weeks ($53/day). Taking a more leisurely pace will allow you to cook and camp, reducing food and lodging expenses.

There are other money saving methods too. Camping in national forests, stealth camping, or pitching your tent on someone's yard can save on campground fees. Seek out trail angels. The Toaster House in Pie Town was filled with all manner of gear hikers and cyclists had left to cut weight: batteries, stove fuel, bear spray—that's not to mention the refrigerator stocked with pizza and beer. Even performing your own bike repairs or at least taking care of the more routine maintenance can save money on mechanic bills.

If you're still worried about your budget, ask for donations from family, friends, and coworkers. Seek sponsorship from your local shop or club. Let everyone follow your progress with a SPOT tracker or social media updates.

What I'm trying to say is, don't let the cost stop you. My trip down the GDMBR was a great investment, a great experience that I couldn't put a price on. And if all else fails you, just sell your gear when you get back...the first thing I sold was that bivy, and it was oh so satisfying.

Once again, good luck with your planning and with your tour. If you have questions reach out through my website or by email at nathan@nathandoneen.com

Made in the USA
Columbia, SC
28 July 2023